AGAINST RELIGION

H.P. Lovecraft

AGAINST RELIGION

The Atheist Writings of H. P. Lovecraft

Edited by S. T. Joshi

Foreword by Christopher Hitchens

Sporting
Gentlemen
Publishers

Published by Sporting Gentlemen, New York
www.sportinggentlemen.com
Some rights reserved. Contact us for permissions.

ISBN: 978-0-578-05248-9

Cover Design and Illustrations: Mike Force

Contents

On The Varieties of Non-Religious Experience

As the public dispute between believers and non-believers revived and intensified in the first decade of the twenty-first century, an increasingly defensive "faith community" and its apologists came up with a consoling propagandistic absurdity. The atheist movement, it announced, was itself a form of "fundamentalism". I can't be sure quite where this last-ditch tactic originated – my suspicion lights upon a certain Canon Colin Slee of the Church of England – but before long it was babbling merrily off the lips of supposedly "secular" critics like Robert Wright, and appearing in the "talking points" of almost every religious foundation with whom I and others were debating.

In point of fact, one of the many advantages of the unbeliever is that he and she do *not* have to attend regular sessions of incantation and inculcation and "positive reinforcement". Merely to think during the day is far more satisfying than praying five times, as Muslims are enjoined to do, or attending divine service according to a medieval calendar, or memorizing six hundred and thirteen Jewish commandments (most of them prohibitions and repressions). And the same questions and doubts will occur to any serious mind, whether the rituals are performed or not. This is why it is a pleasure to read - and to recommend – the work of H.P. Lovecraft. We all come to atheism in our own way, and many of us hold other opinions on other matters that are highly incompatible with those of our fellow-unbelievers.

This unusual author decided to face squarely the problems that confront all reflective people. How likely is it that human life is the outcome of a design? Even if it is indeed a design, how come some humans claim knowledge of its author: even personal acquaintance with him? Is a belief in the supernatural the cause of superior moral behavior? Are the crime and stupidities of religion just blemishes, or are they the expected outcome of blind faith itself?

Some are born with unbelief, some achieve it, and others have it thrust upon them. Encounters with fellow-skeptics disclose a variety of experience that is just as rich and various as the many "revelations" or "insights" of those who assert a spiritual warrant for their points of view. Lovecraft, in his own work and in debates with religious friends, registered most of the chief questions, anticipated many of the salient objections to unbelief, and exhibited his own idiosyncrasies.

It is fairly safe to say that he first discovered his objection to theism when he contemplated his favorite subject, which was the cosmic. It takes a certain arrogance for man, once he has discovered the real place of our global speck in this galaxy, let alone the pace of this galaxy in the universe, to assume that all is intended with himself as the finished object. (And they dare to call this humility!) Bear in mind that Lovecraft himself did not live to see the vast current and ongoing expansion of our knowledge, about everything from the "macro" elements in quantum physics to the relatively "micro" contents of our own genome. But he knew enough to possess that most important moral and aesthetic property – a sense of proportion – and was able to write with agreeable Stoicism in 1931 that "pretty soon the solar system will play out, and nobody in the cosmos will ever know that there has ever been any earth or human race or Brahmins or Moslems or Christians or Shintoists or such....dust to dust...and the ironic laughter of any entity which may happen to be watching the cosmos from outside...ho, hum!"

I should like to call attention to an aspect of that sentence. Atheists do not presume to know for certain that there is no such unquantifiable "entity". They merely – merely! – deny the claim of any human to be able to "know" it, and to claim authority over other humans as a consequence. Indeed, Lovecraft spent some commendable time considering the differences between an agnostic and an atheist world-view. He understood the dangers of nihilism and insisted only that "virtue and honor" can be practiced without faith: conceivably even practiced with more integrity. He most certainly did not believe that the removal of religion would in itself be an improvement, and reproved the "idealistic" sort of atheist – he didn't give any names – who thought that unbelief itself would redeem the world. But he declined to dodge the main challenge, which is whether the absence of evidence does indeed suggest an evidence of absence, and he wouldn't anchor his bark in T.H. Huxley's ostensibly safe harbor:

> In theory I am an *agnostic*, but pending the appearance of radical evidence I must be classed, practically and provisionally, as an *atheist*. The chances of theism's truth being to my mind so microscopically small, I would be a pedant and a hypocrite to call myself anything else. (66)

These days, the apologists for religion have divided ever-more sharply between textual literalists who do not believe in evolution or the "Big Bang" and those who, giving up this antique stupidity as a bad job, have decided to claim that molecular biology and astro-physics are valid tributes to the workings of the same divine will that once appeared to forbid discussion of such topics. But it isn't really progress to teach a parrot a new word, and in my favorite of these letters – *Religion and Relativity* – Lovecraft went out of his way to show how the god delusion was infinitely adaptable to new findings, and how it was precisely in that way that it showed its fatal weakness. A system of belief that does not require evidence in the first place makes a huge confession of failure when it abruptly asserts that all subsequent evidence is in its favor. Have the faithful no more need of the sheer faith that supposedly once sustained them? Sad for them if so, because their later attempts to conscript the evidence of the natural and material world are somewhat pathetic. All "ontological" efforts are vulnerable to this fatal criticism.

Like so many of us, Lovecraft was by no means indifferent to the discrepant appeals of the traditional, the aesthetic, and the artistic. He returned again and again to the noble steeples of his beloved Rhode Island, and expressed respect for the aspirations that they expressed. But he could never allow himself to forget that these, too, were products of time and place and even of old sectarian rivalries – in other words that they were *man-made*. As of course are all gods and all cults and religions, and in the recognition of this fact is the beginning of all wisdom. What comes *after* such wisdom is of course an open question, and Lovecraft was much too modest – except in his capacity as a fiction-writer – to attempt to compose the music of the future.

A useful book to keep in company with the work of this author would be Keith Thomas's magisterial *Religion And The Decline of Magic*. Enlightened modern people have dismissed the entire possibility of witchcraft and thus scoffed at any "hunting" of non-existent entities. But Lovecraft's rootedness in New England may have helped him understand that there was, at least, such a thing as Satanism. In his extraordinary letter on "The Psychology of Puritanism" he gave his reasons for believing in the reality of ancient and wicked cults – other forms of faith, after all – and in the mad spiritual warfare to which they gave rise. It is after all not necessary to believe in The Devil to recognize Charles Manson and his capacity for evil: a word (like those other important words "virtue and honor") from which many lofty and refined secularists and atheists are inclined to flinch. Not so Lovecraft.

His well-honed New England allegiance may also have led him into what many would now call a eugenic or even racialist interpretation of the origins of monotheism. In his letter on "Protestants and Catholics" he relies very heavily on the sort of ethnography that was more common in his time than ours, and employs words such as "Aryan" and "Semitick" (*sic*) in what I find to be jarring and even ugly ways. One cannot be a true materialist and still think with one's blood or one's epidermis, or so I would want to maintain. Such biases also make it harder rather than easier to combat the "Chester-Belloc" quasi-nationalist religiosity that Lovecraft so despised. But there it is: some people truly are Protestant atheists. I would myself hold out for everyone to be a non-sectarian unbeliever even though debates with the faithful have left me with ever-diminishing respect for those who demand or expect the impossible.

Christopher Hitchens
Stanford, California January 2010

Introduction

How does it happen that a man like H. P. Lovecraft (1890–1937)—almost entirely unknown in his time except as the author of seemingly lurid and flamboyant tales of "cosmic" horror, and who contributed almost nothing to the public discussion of the central questions of religion, politics, and society—has become, more than a half-century after his death, a kind of patron saint of atheism? The conundrum might be explained in part by considering his remarkable posthumous reputation, a reputation that has seen not only the publication of his relatively small corpus of fiction in the most prestigious of venues (capped, in 2005, by the Library of America's edition of his *Tales*) but also the issuance of his essays, poetry, and especially his thousands of letters; for it is these letters, clearly not designed for publication and written to friends and colleagues who were themselves little-known, that show him to have been one of the keenest minds of his generation, one who fashioned a comprehensive worldview that saw no place for God in the fabric of the universe and that appealed largely to science as the arbiter of truth, but nonetheless left room for the imaginative stimulus of art. And yet, to explain Lovecraft's eminence, both as a writer and as a thinker, we may also have to look to the nearly mythic figure he has become as the gaunt, lantern-jawed creator of a plethora of "gods" in his stories but who nonetheless heaped scorn on the central religious tenets of the existence of a deity, the immortality of the soul, and the cosmic significance of humankind.

Lovecraft's early life and upbringing laid the foundations for both his impressive intellect and his supernatural fiction. Born on August 20, 1890, in Providence, Rhode Island, to a Baptist mother (Sarah Susan Phillips Lovecraft) and an Anglican father (Winfield Scott Lovecraft), Lovecraft early developed a keen taste for what he would call "the supremely rational 18th century"[1]—the century of David Hume, Edward Gibbon, and the *philosophes*. In his early childhood years, of course, it was not philosophy but literature—especially poetry—that fascinated him; and his enthusiasm for the elegant translations of Greek and Latin poetry by such poets as John Dryden and Alexander Pope led him back to classical antiquity itself. One of his earliest surviving writings is an 88-line verse paraphrase of the *Odyssey,* dating to 1897. In the piquant essay "A Confession of Unfaith" (1922) Lovecraft admits that his absorption of classical myth and literature had much to do with his later atheism. In that same essay, however, he dates his first skeptical utterances to a Sunday school class he attended at the age of five. This would appear to conflict with a 1920 letter in which he dates his Sunday school clashes to a somewhat later period:

> How well I recall my tilts with Sunday-School teachers during my last period of compulsory attendance! I was 12 years old, and the despair of the institution. None of the answers of my pious preceptors would satisfy me, and my demands that they cease taking things for granted quite upset them. Close reasoning was something new in their little world of Semitic mythology. At last I saw that they were hopelessly bound to unfounded dogmata and traditions, and thenceforth ceased to treat them seriously. Sunday-School became to me simply a place wherein to have a little harmless fun spoofing the pious mossbacks. My mother observed this, and no longer sought to enforce my attendance.[2]

Perhaps there is no strict contradiction: Lovecraft's memories, in "A Confession of Unfaith," of attending the "infant class" of the Sunday school at the First Baptist Church in Providence seem authentic, but one suspects he may be exaggerating the degree to which he was able to "tilt" with his teachers at the tender age of five.

Lovecraft's imagination, meanwhile, had been stimulated by his early readings of Grimm's fairy tales (age four), the *Arabian Nights* (age five), and Coleridge's *The Rime of the Ancient Mariner,* in the edition illustrated by Gustave Doré (age six). These and other influences awakened his love of the fantastic, and he was writing short horror tales as early as the age of six. These specimens are very crude, but they laid the groundwork for his later "cosmic" narratives. Equally important, however, was Lovecraft's precocious absorption of science—first chemistry, at the age of eight, and then astronomy, at the age of eleven. Lovecraft speaks truly in "A Confession of Unfaith" that these studies definitively transformed him from agnosticism to full-fledged atheism. The "myriad suns and worlds of infinite space" seemed to reduce all earth life to vanishing insignificance, and Lovecraft admits that he actually entered a period of cosmic pessimism. "The futility of all existence began to impress and oppress me . . ."

Meanwhile, Lovecraft's family life had had its share of instabilities. In 1893, his father, a "commercial traveler," had some kind of seizure while on business in Chicago and was brought back under restraint to Butler Hospital in Providence, where he remained until his death in 1898. It now appears evident that Winfield Lovecraft was in the final stages of syphilis—an ailment probably contracted years before his marriage to Sarah Susan Phillips. The Lovecrafts, then living in the Boston area, returned to the Phillips home in Providence, where Lovecraft grew up a proud Rhode Islander. In the absence of his father, the upbringing of the boy fell to his mother, his two aunts, and especially to his grandfather, Whipple Van Buren Phillips (1833–1904), a successful businessman. In many ways Lovecraft had an idyllic early childhood, full of intellectual adventure and also his share of boyhood friends. But matters turned for the worse upon Whipple Phillips's unexpected death, for the mismanagement of his estate by his executors suddenly depleted the family coffers, and Lovecraft and his mother were compelled to leave their spacious Victorian home at 454 Angell Street and move into smaller quarters a few blocks to the east, at 598 Angell Street. Lovecraft, always sensitive to place, was shattered by the loss of his birthplace; according to a later letter, he even contemplated suicide, as he took long bicycle rides to the Barrington River and thought of enduring a quiet death by drowning. What stopped him— characteristically—was the thirst for knowledge. So many things remained unknown to his young mind:

> Much in the universe baffled me, yet I knew I could pry the answers out of books if I lived & studied longer. Geology, for example. Just *how* did these ancient sediments & stratifications get crystallised & upheaved into granite peaks? Geography—just

what would Scott & Shackleton & Borchgrevink find in the great white antarctic on their next expeditions . . . which I could—if I wished—live to see described? And as to history—as I contemplated an exit without further knowledge I became uncomfortably conscious of what I didn't know. Tantalising gaps existed everywhere. When did people stop speaking Latin & begin to talk Italian & Spanish & French? What on earth ever happened in the black Middle Ages in those parts of the world other than Britain & France (whose story I knew)? What of the vast gulfs of space outside all familiar lands—desert reaches hinted of by Sir John Mandeville & Marco Polo . . . Tartary, Thibet . . . What of unknown Africa?[3]

So Lovecraft decided to stick around for a few more years. His grammar school attendance—at the Slater Avenue School—had been sporadic and augmented by private tutors; but, to his surprise, he found the experience of attending Hope Street High School pleasantly stimulating. It was at this time that he began appearing in print—not with stories, but with astronomy columns in several local newspapers. But in 1908, after having attended only three years of high school (he had sat out one entire year because of some unspecified illness), he suddenly withdrew without a diploma and retreated into a hermitry that lasted a full five years. The precise cause of this abrupt departure remains unclear; Lovecraft refers to it as a "nervous breakdown,"[4] but it is unclear what this means. My own conjecture is that Lovecraft's growing awareness that his difficulties in mathematics would render it nearly impossible to pursue his chosen career as an astronomer was so traumatic that he experienced a crisis of confidence. Unable to attend nearby Brown University and become a professor or scientist, Lovecraft vegetated in an increasingly unhealthy environment, living alone with a mother who (as we shall see) was undergoing emotional traumas of her own.

What saved Lovecraft from remaining the "eccentric recluse" that many have assumed him to have been was a highly curious series of events. Having taken up the habit of reading some of the popular magazines of the day, especially such magazines published by the Frank

A. Munsey Company as the *Argosy* and the *All-Story,* Lovecraft was so offended by the romance writings of one Fred Jackson, featured heavily in the magazines, that he wrote a strong letter attacking them. The letter was published in the *All-Story* and incited a spate of hostile comment by Jackson's supporters. Lovecraft then took to writing *in verse*—producing pungent satires in the manner of Alexander Pope. These too were published, and Lovecraft became a kind of mini-celebrity in the letter columns. This literary controversy was observed by Edward F. Daas, an officer of the United Amateur Press Association (UAPA), one of two nationwide groups of amateur writers, the other being the older National Amateur Press Association (NAPA). Daas invited Lovecraft to join, and Lovecraft did so with alacrity in 1914.

These amateur press groups, each numbering about 250 members, were just the sort of venue to allow a shy and diffident writer like Lovecraft to find his voice. Members would write essays, poetry, editorials, and other matter and either publish them themselves in small-press journals or contribute them to other members' journals. Lovecraft both established his own journal—the *Conservative,* thirteen issues of which appeared between 1915 and 1923, the title reflecting his political and social conservatism—and contributed voluminously to other journals. He quickly became a celebrity in this tiny realm, serving in several official capacities. It was during this period that he developed some of his strongest and most enduring friendships. These friendships were forged largely through correspondence, and Lovecraft began his career as an epistolarian by writing immense letters both to individuals and to round-robin correspondence cycles he helped to establish. It was largely through these letters, written to colleagues of highly differing views and temperaments, that Lovecraft fashioned the outlines of his cosmic, atheistic philosophy.

Lovecraft had abandoned the writing of fiction after 1908, thinking himself a failure in that capacity. But, after he had allowed some of his teenage stories to appear in the amateur press, where they received an enthusiastic response from friends and colleagues, Lovecraft resumed the writing of fiction in 1917. He had no thought of publishing professionally—he had long before adopted the eighteenth-century stance of writing as an elegant amusement, later to be augmented by an "art for art's sake" attitude that vaunted pure "self-expression" and scorned the profit motive in writing—until the establishment of the pulp magazine *Weird Tales* in 1923. This was the first magazine devoted exclusively to supernatural or horror fiction, and several of Lovecraft's colleagues—who now numbered such fellow fantasists as Frank Belknap Long and Clark Ashton Smith—urged Lovecraft to submit his work. Lovecraft grudgingly did so and was pleased that it was readily accepted. Within a few years he was a leading figure in the *Weird Tales* stable of writers, receiving its highest level of payment (the princely sum of one and a half cents per word) and consistent commendation in the letter column.

This entry into the world of professional publishing might have led to stable employment for Lovecraft, but he never produced—or sold—enough writing in the pulps to make a genuine living at it. His fiction writing was always subject to fleeting bouts of inspiration, and on occasion he would write only one or two stories a year—sometimes none. His lack of formal education barred him from clerical jobs that his general self-education would presumably have rendered him suitable for, and the regular occupation that he ultimately fashioned for himself—the freelance revision or ghost-writing of books, articles, poetry, and even textbooks—paid so poorly and was so haphazard that it scarcely brought in any significant income. Lovecraft was forced to live in increasing poverty, reliant upon revision work, sporadic sales of stories, and a dwindling family inheritance.

Matters were not helped by various traumas in his family life. Lovecraft's mother, with whom he had been living alone since 1904, took ill in 1919 and was herself confined to Butler Hospital. She had had a serious nervous breakdown, the result of financial worries and also, perhaps, of her dim horror at the unseemly demise of her husband. She developed a curious love-hate relationship with her son, alternately showering him with smothering affection and referring to him in public as "hideous." Her death in 1921, from a botched gall bladder operation, affected Lovecraft deeply, but in the end it was his savior. He began traveling more widely, first to amateur gatherings in New England and

New York, and then to various antiquarian oases where he could indulge his love of the past.

At one of these amateur gatherings, in Boston in 1921, he met a Russian Jewish woman, Sonia Haft Greene, seven years his elder. As a result of her systematic pursuit of him, they married in 1924 and Lovecraft uprooted himself from his Providence abode to live with her in Brooklyn. It was a catastrophic mistake. Lovecraft, raised as a straitlaced New Englander and disturbed by the masses of "foreigners" on the streets, and also unable to find a remunerative position in writing or publishing, became deeply disturbed and unstable. His wife, meanwhile, had lost her well-paying job in the clothing industry and was forced to pursue employment in the Midwest. Left alone, albeit with numerous friends and colleagues in the city, Lovecraft deteriorated mentally, until at last Frank Belknap Long and his two aunts helped to arrange for his return to Providence. Where Sonia fit into the picture was unclear. Eventually she realized that the marriage was over, and they divorced in 1929.

Lovecraft's return to Providence in 1926 initiated a spurt of creativity such as he had never experienced before. Such landmark works as "The Call of Cthulhu" (1926), "The Colour out of Space" (1927), and *The Case of Charles Dexter Ward* (1927) were produced within a six-month period. The rest of Lovecraft's life can be recounted simply: he spent his time writing—some stories, some poems and essays, but mostly thousands and thousands of letters to hundreds of far-flung correspondents, some of the letters extending to 40, 50, or even 70 pages—and, in the summer time, he would expend his small modicum of cash on antiquarian trips up and down the eastern seaboard, from as far north as Quebec to as far south as St. Augustine and Key West. Lovecraft became the hub of a complex network of literary ties, which included such notables among the pulp magazine world as Robert E. Howard, August Derleth, Donald Wandrei, Henry S. Whitehead, and E. Hoffmann Price. Young writers such as Robert Bloch, Henry Kuttner, C. L. Moore, and Fritz Leiber benefited immensely from the literary tutelage that Lovecraft bestowed upon them, almost exclusively through the venue of correspondence. And, of course, he continued to debate issues of religion, science, and politics in his letters, gradually shedding his political conservatism and becoming a moderate (non-Marxist) socialist who felt that Franklin D. Roosevelt's New Deal reforms were far tamer than they need have been to deal with the crisis of the Great Depression.

And yet, Lovecraft's unworldliness—his pose as a gentleman who wrote only for the amusement of himself and his friends—hindered him from attaining the celebrity that could have been his. His dealings with book publishers—including G. P. Putnam's Sons and Alfred A. Knopf—were in part undermined by his diffidence in marketing his work, and no book of his stories appeared in his lifetime. Only one book bearing his name—a misprinted small-press edition of his novella, *The Shadow over Innsmouth* (1936)—was published, a few months before his death on March 15, 1937. And yet, the firm ties of friendship that Lovecraft had forged largely—and in some cases entirely—through correspondence proved to be his posthumous literary salvation. August Derleth and Donald Wandrei were so determined that Lovecraft's stories not be engulfed in the oblivion of the pulp magazines that they formed a publishing company, Arkham House, initially for the sole purpose of publishing Lovecraft's work in hardcover. In short order, of course, Arkham House published other writers of supernatural fiction, including many of Lovecraft's colleagues, and became the most prestigious small press in the field.

Wandrei, however, was particularly keen on embalming Lovecraft's letters in print, as he was convinced that Lovecraft was one of the great epistolarians in literary history. He spent decades editing what ultimately became the five-volume *Selected Letters* (1965–76), a series of books that definitively established Lovecraft as a leading intellect and a forthright and highly articulate spokesman for atheism. A man who had never published an essay (much less a letter) in a major magazine or newspaper was suddenly inspiring legions of atheists, agnostics, and secularists a half-century after his death. Today articles on Lovecraft frequently appear in the freethought press,[5] and yet the full extent and details of his atheist writings—embodied as they are chiefly in correspondence—have not been made available until the present compilation.

Lovecraft's devotion to the eighteenth century should not deceive us into thinking that he was much influenced by—or, to be frank, even very familiar with—the writings of the leading secular thinkers of that century. Although he charmingly affected eighteenth-century diction in his letters, there is little reason to assume that he was intimately conversant with the writings of (to quote more fully the letter cited earlier) "La Mettrie, Diderot, Helvetius, Hume, and dozens of others . . . in the supremely rational 18th century." Even Voltaire, the most forceful opponent of religious obscurantism and intolerance in the eighteenth century, was probably not one of Lovecraft's favourite reads, although no doubt he would have enjoyed Voltaire's unrestrained flair in attacking the "infamy" of the church.

Lovecraft's atheism was based, as was that of so many others in the early part of the twentieth century, upon a remarkable convergence of scientific advance in the course of the nineteenth century that systematically destroyed many previously unassailable pillars of religious thought. Both the "hard" sciences—astrophysics, chemistry, biology—and the social sciences, such as history and (especially) anthropology, each pursuing their own courses of research, presented naturalistic explanations for phenomena previously thought to be the work of a deity; and anthropological advances were, in a way, the capstone of this process, for it accounted with unfailing accuracy and plausibility for the *origin* of religious belief. Lovecraft is correct, in the "In Defence of Dagon" essays of 1921, in speaking of anthropology as the "trump card" in the downfall of religion. Such works as Edward Burnett Tylor's *Primitive Culture* (1871) and Sir James George Frazer's *The Golden Bough* (1890–1915) added an immense quantity of fieldwork to the highly theoretical accounts found in David Hume's *The Natural History of Religion* (1757) and other works. (Lovecraft himself may not have read Tylor's dense work, but he unquestionably read John Fiske's popularization of contemporary anthropology, *Myths and Myth-Makers* [1872].)

Of course, Lovecraft was well-versed in the hard sciences as well, and his absorption of Darwinian evolution—as well as of the work of Darwin's two most prominent disciples and advocates, Thomas Henry Huxley and Ernst Haeckel—laid strong foundations for his criticism of religion. His refutation of the immortality of the soul rested largely on Darwinian principles; for, as he cleverly notes, "One must ask . . . just how the evolving organism began to acquire 'spirit' after it crossed the boundary betwixt advanced ape and primitive human." His understanding of chemistry and biology led him to speculate (correctly) that life would one day be generated in the laboratory (as was in fact done in the 1950s), thereby confounding the religious conception that life and consciousness could only have been bestowed by a god.

Astrophysics presented the greatest difficulties for Lovecraft, chiefly because his essentially layman's training prevented him from understanding some of the more abstruse theories propounded in the early twentieth century. Lovecraft early announced himself as a "mechanistic materialist"—one who believed the universe was a "mechanism" (i.e, governed by fixed deterministic laws) and was composed wholly of matter (i.e., that "soul" or "spirit" does not and cannot exist). In an early letter he presents a keen understanding of the implications of determinism, distinguishing it from the fallacy of fatalism:

> Determinism—what you call Destiny—rules inexorably; though not exactly in the personal way you seem to fancy. We have no specific destiny against which we can fight—for the fighting would be as much a part of the destiny as the final end. The real fact is simply that every event in the cosmos is caused by the action of antecedent and circumjacent forces, so that whatever we do is unconsciously the inevitable product of Nature rather than of our own volition. If an act corresponds with our wish, it is Nature that made the wish, and ensured its fulfilment. When we see an apparent chain of circumstances leading toward some striking denouement, we say it is "Fate". That is not true in the sense meant, for all of those circumstances might have been deceptive, so that a hidden and

unexpected cause would have turned matters to an utterly opposite conclusion. The chain of appearances are [*sic*] as much a part of fate as the result, whichever the latter may be....[6]

Mechanistic materialism was, of course, challenged on two fronts—by Einstein's theory of relativity (which saw matter and energy as interchangeable) and by Max Planck's quantum theory (which was thought by many to have destroyed causality in its ultimate sense). Lovecraft's initial response to Einstein was little short of traumatic. In 1923, when certain solar observations rendered the theory all but irrefutable, Lovecraft reacted as follows:

> My cynicism and scepticism are increasing, and from an entirely new cause—the Einstein theory. The latest eclipse observations seem to place this system among the facts which cannot be dismissed, and assumedly it removes the last hold which reality or the universe can have on the independent mind. All is chance, accident, and empheral illusion—a fly may be greater than Arcturus, and Durfee Hill may surpass Mount Everest—assuming them to be removed from the present planet and differently emvironed in the continuum of space-time. There are no values in all infinity—the least idea that there are is the supreme mockery of all. All the cosmos is a jest, and fit to be treated only as a jest, and one thing is as true as another. I believe everything and nothing—for all is chaos, always has been, and always will be.[7]

There is no need to examine the multiple fallacies of this statement, especially Lovecraft's rash assumption of moral nihilism. What is remarkable is that, only six years after writing the above, he came to terms with relativity and saw it, not as a threat to materialism (and, hence, to his ongoing attack on religious conceptions of "soul" or "spirit"), but as an ally. His 1929 letter, reprinted here, warns a correspondent not to be tricked by the "Einstein-twisters"—of whom there were many both among scientists and litterateurs, who were using Einstein to bolster previously outmoded views regarding both God and the soul. Lovecraft concludes:

Matter, we learn, is a definite phenomenon instituted by certain modifications of energy; *but does this circumstance make it less distinctive in itself, or permit us to imagine the presence of another kind of modified energy in places where no sign or result of energy can be discovered?* It is to laugh! The truth is, that the discovery of matter's identity with energy—and of its consequent lack of vital intrinsic difference from empty space—is *an absolute coup de grace to the primitive and irresponsible myth of "spirit". For matter, it appears, really is exactly what "spirit" was always supposed to be.* Thus it is proved *that wandering energy always has a detectable form*—that if it doesn't take the form of waves or electron-streams, *it becomes matter itself;* and that the absence of matter or any other detectable energy-form indicates *not the presence of spirit, but the absence of anything whatever.*

Whether an astrophysicist would accept this conclusion or not, it is a clever resolution of the difficulty.

Quantum theory gave Lovecraft more difficulty. He maintained in a 1930 letter: "What most physicists take the quantum theory, at present, to mean, is *not that any cosmic uncertainty exists* as to which of several courses a given reaction will take; but that in certain instances *no conceivable channel of information can ever tell human beings which course will be taken,* or by what exact course a certain observed result came about." Lovecraft wants to believe that the "uncertainty" of quantum theory is not ontological but epistemological. This conclusion is apparently false, for the "uncertainty" really does persist—on a subatomic level. But there is no question that macro-atomic phenomena remain largely materialistic and deterministic, so that Lovecraft's materialism—the word, as he recognized, being used in a purely historical sense—remains largely intact.

Lovecraft was merciless in his skewering of muddle-headed thinkers who were using relativity, quantum theory, and other scientific advances to lobby for the resurrection of religious theories that had already been conclusively shown to be false. He speaks of a

. . . new mysticism or neo-metaphysics bred of the advertised uncertainties of recent science—Einstein, the quantum theory, and the resolution of matter into force. Although these new turns of science don't really mean a thing in relation to the myth of cosmic consciousness and teleology, a new brood of despairing and horrified moderns is seizing on the doubt of all positive knowledge which they imply; and is deducing therefrom that, *since nothing is true,* therefore *anything can be true* . . . whence one may invent or revive any sort of mythology that fancy or nostalgia or desperation may dictate, and defy anyone to prove that it isn't *emotionally* true—whatever that means. This sickly, decadent neo-mysticism—a protest not only against machine materialism but against pure science with its destruction of the mystery and dignity of human emotion and experience—will be the dominant creed of middle twentieth century aesthetes, as the [T. S.] Eliot and [Aldous] Huxley penumbra well prognosticate.[8]

It may be worth noting that Lovecraft did not appear to be much interested in, or very aware of, another important advance that severely called into question the inerrancy of the Bible—the school of biblical criticism called the "higher criticism," emerging in Germany in the late eighteenth century and popularized by many important books such as Ernest Renan's *Life of Jesus* (1864). This school systematically studied the origins and sources of the Bible, establishing conclusively that it was written over a long period of time—spanning perhaps as much as a millennium—and finally assembled in a manner that can only be called haphazard. The work of the "higher criticism" dethroned the conception of the Bible as a work dictated or inspired by God, especially when other commentators pointed out that it contained not a few traces of barbarism that could not possibly be suitable for contemporary society, such as the death penalty for witches (Exodus 22:18), homosexuals (Leviticus 20:13), and sabbath-breakers (Exodus 31:15), the ownership of wives by the husbands (Exodus 20:10), and so forth.

Lovecraft, as I say, did not pay much attention to this work, probably because he couldn't credit how any sane person could believe that the Bible was the product of some kind of stenographic dictation from God. His own (northern) Baptist tradition emphasized the Bible as a guide to moral conduct, and even here Lovecraft saw reason to be skeptical: "Half of what Buddha or Christus or Mahomet said is either simply idiocy or downright destructiveness, as applied to the western world of the twentieth century; whilst virtually *all* of the emotional-imaginative background of assumptions from which they spoke, is now proved to be sheer childish primitiveness."[9] Lovecraft was familiar with the Bible as a literary document, and he was highly taken with the style of the Anglo-Irish writer Lord Dunsany, who (although he himself was also an atheist) consciously used the King James Bible as the basis of his fantastic prose; but beyond that, Lovecraft exhibited little interest in the Bible as a religious text.

Lovecraft, in the final analysis, appealed to *probability* as the ultimate basis for his atheism; and, interestingly, he used probability as a means of distinguishing his atheism from agnosticism. In his mind, the probability of the truth of theism was so vanishingly small that he felt it irresponsible to think of himself as a mere agnostic:

> All I say is that I think it is *damned unlikely* that anything like a central cosmic will, a spirit world, or an eternal survival of personality exist. They are the most preposterous and unjustified of all the guesses which can be made about the universe, and I am not enough of a hair-splitter to pretend that I don't regard them as arrant and negligible moonshine. In theory I am an *agnostic,* but pending the appearance of radical evidence I must be classed, practically and provisionally, as an *atheist.*

One of the most provocative questions pertaining to Lovecraft and religion is the seeming paradox of a vigorously atheistic writer producing stories filled to the brim with "gods" and their worshippers. His so-called Cthulhu Mythos (a term invented by his disciple, August Derleth), a mythology that dominates the stories of the last decade of his life, seems to envision a universe populated by all-powerful gods who can crush the human race—or at least certain venturesome individuals—at will. How can this be squared with the materialistic atheist of his letters? The matter is considerably complex, but some hints can be provided here.

Some commentators have believed that Lovecraft's "evil" gods—Cthulhu, Yog-Sothoth, Nyarlathotep, Azathoth, Shub-Niggurath, and so forth—are themselves representative of the evils of religious belief, since they embody the viciousness that many of the actual gods invented by human beings, not excluding the Christian god, appear to display. I am not entirely convinced of this notion, largely because Lovecraft's "gods" are not "evil" in any meaningful sense. They are inimical to human beings only because they render our position on this earth highly tenuous and fragile, but they are as much "beyond good and evil" (as Lovecraft actually states in "The Call of Cthulhu") as we ourselves would be from an ant's perspective. Lovecraft's "gods" are, in large part, symbols for the inscrutability of the cosmos: scientific materialist that he was, he knew that the universe held an infinite reservoir of mystery, and even scientific advance could do little to minimize it; as he wrote in a late letter, "the more we learn about the cosmos, the more bewildering does it appear."[10]

And, in the end, Lovecraft's "gods" aren't really gods at all. It is true that, in "The Call of Cthulhu" and "The Dunwich Horror," various cults are stated as worshipping Cthulhu and Yog-Sothoth; indeed, in the former story one of these worshippers gives a history of the eon-old cult:

> Then . . . those first men formed the cult around small idols which the Great Ones shewed them; idols brought in dim aeras from dark stars. That cult would never die till the stars came right again, and the secret priests would take great Cthulhu from His tomb to revive His subjects and resume His rule of earth. The time would be easy to know, for then mankind would have become as the Great Old Ones; free and wild and beyond good and evil, with laws and morals thrown aside and all men shouting and killing and revelling in joy. Then the liberated Old Ones would teach them new ways to shout and kill and revel and enjoy themselves, and all the earth would flame with a holocaust of ecstasy and freedom.[11]

The overriding question is: Are we to take this statement at face value? It is true that a virtual library of "forbidden" books invented by Lovecraft and his colleagues—ranging from the *Necronomicon* of the mad Arab, Abdul Alhazred, to the *Unaussprechlichen Kulten* of von Juntz—appear to speak in like terms of the old gods; but what one gradually discovers, as Lovecraft's work progresses, is that these cultists are as pathetically deluded about the nature of the "gods" they worship as most human beings are in their devotion to Yahweh or Allah. The critical passage comes in the short novel *At the Mountains of Madness* (1931), where an immense stone city evidently built by extraterrestrials, coming from the depths of space, is discovered by explorers penetrating a previously unknown corner of Antarctica:

> The things rearing and dwelling in this frightful masonry in the age of dinosaurs were not indeed dinosaurs, but far worse. Mere dinosaurs were new and almost brainless objects—but the builders of the city were wise and old, and had left certain traces in rocks even then laid down well-nigh a thousand million years . . . rocks laid down before the true life of earth had advanced beyond plastic groups of cells . . . rocks laid down before the true life of earth had existed at all. They were the makers and enslavers of that life, and above all doubt the originals of the fiendish elder myths which things like the Pnakotic Manuscripts and the *Necronomicon* affrightedly hint about.[12]

So now the stories about the "gods" as found in the *Necronomicon* have been reduced to "myths"! The "gods" are merely space aliens. This appears to have been Lovecraft's conception right from the beginning, for even in "The Call of Cthulhu," which launched the Cthulhu Mythos, Cthulhu and his "spawn" are merely extraterrestrials who come from some infinitely far galaxy to the earth, where they are unwittingly trapped in the underwater city of R'lyeh beneath the Pacific. Cthulhu and R'lyeh rise up in that story, but not because the "stars are right" or because of any actions taken by his human cult, but merely by accident—an earthquake—and they sink back under the waves by a similar accident.

Lovecraft's signature element in his fiction is its "cosmic" quality—its suggestion of the infinite gulfs of space and time, and the resulting inconsequence of humanity within these gulfs. It is an element that Lovecraft may well have conveyed more powerfully and poignantly than any writer in literature, and it constitutes one of the chief justifications of the canonical status he has attained today. But it should be made clear that that cosmic vision is strictly dependent on Lovecraft's metaphysical—and, specifically, his atheistic—viewpoint. For in Lovecraft's universe, humanity is indeed alone in the cosmos; and whereas the object of most religions is, in John Milton's words, to "justify the ways of God to men," Lovecraft's "anti-mythology," as it has been appropriately called,[13] establishes that human beings can appeal to no higher power when faced with threats to our fleeting sinecure on this earth. A moment ago, in cosmic terms, we did not exist; a moment hence, the universe shall have forgotten that we did exist.

It is, in truth, a bleak vision, but the prose-poetry with which Lovecraft infuses it in his stories lends it a strange and exhilirating beauty. In scarcely less powerful a fashion, the liveliness, vigor, and at times satirical flair of his discussions of religion and atheism in his letters and essays exhibit a mind wrestling with the central questions of existence and hammering out a cogent, forward-looking philosophy shorn of outmoded religious belief and courageously prepared to face a universe in which humanity is indeed alone and friendless. Comforting as Lovecraft knew the myths of religion may be, he was determined to contemplate the universe with the blinkers removed from his eyes and mind.

—S. T. JOSHI

A Note on the Texts

This volume consists of letters and essays by Lovecraft on religion, atheism, and related subjects. I have used manuscript sources where possible. In some cases, the texts of the letters are derived from transcripts made under the aegis of Arkham House during its preparation of the *Selected Letters;* the whereabouts of the manuscripts of these letters are not currently known. In a few passages the text appears to be garbled or mistranscribed. I have sought to transcribe the letters without alteration, except that I have replaced Lovecraft's habitual ampersands (&) with "and."

I have written some explanatory notes, clarifying historical, literary, and other references that may be unfamiliar to contemporary readers. Abbreviations used in the notes are as follows:

AT   *The Ancient Track: Complete Poetical Works* (Night Shade Books, 2001)

F   *H. P. Lovecraft: The Fiction* (Barnes & Noble, 2008)

SL   *Selected Letters* (Arkham House, 1965–76; 5 vols.)

I am grateful to David E. Schultz for assistance in the preparation of this edition.

—S. T. J.

AGAINST RELIGION

I. SOME PERSONAL REFLECTIONS

A Confession of Unfaith

[The following essay was published in the February 1922 issue of the *Liberal,* an amateur periodical edited by Lovecraft's friend Paul J. Campbell. It was evidently part of a series of autobiographical articles in which various writers expressed the development of their philosophical and religious views. Lovecraft copied much of the essay in his autobiographical letter to Edwin Baird (the first editor of *Weird Tales*) of 3 February 1924. It features some of Lovecraft's most poignant comments on his early interest in classical myth and in science, and their influence in the formation of his "cosmic" worldview.]

As a participant in *The Liberal's* Experience Meeting, wherein amateurs are invited to state their theories of the universe, I must preface all remarks by the qualifying admission that they do not necessarily constitute a permanent view. The seeker of truth for its own sake is chained to no conventional system, but always shapes his philosophical opinions upon what seems to him the best evidence at hand. Changes, therefore, are constantly possible; and occur whenever new or revalued evidence makes them logical.

I am by nature a sceptic and analyst, hence settled early into my present general attitude of cynical materialism, subsequently changing in regard to details and degree rather than to basic ideals. The environment into which I was born was that of the average American Protestant of urban, civilised type—in theory quite orthodox, but in practice very liberal. Morals rather than faith formed the real keynote. I was instructed in the legends of the Bible and of Saint Nicholas at the age of about two, and gave to both a passive acceptance not especially distinguished either for its critical keenness or its enthusiastic comprehension. Within the next few years I added to my supernatural lore the fairy tales of Grimm and the Arabian Nights; and by the time I was five had small choice amongst these speculations so far as truth was concerned, though for attractiveness I favoured the Arabian Nights. At one time I formed a juvenile collection of Oriental pottery and *objets d'art,* announcing myself as a devout Mussulman and assuming the pseudonym of "Abdul Alhazred".[1] My first positive utterance of a sceptical nature probably occurred before my fifth birthday, when I was told what I really knew before, that "Santa Claus" is a myth. This admission caused me to ask why "God" is not equally a myth. Not long afterwards I was placed in the "infant class" at the Sunday school of the venerable First Baptist Church, an ecclesiastical landmark dating from 1775; and there resigned all vestiges of Christian belief. The absurdity of the myths I was called upon to accept, and the sombre greyness of the whole faith as compared with the Eastern magnificence of Mahometanism, made me definitely an agnostic; and caused me to become so pestiferous a questioner that I was permitted to discontinue attendance. No statement of the kind-hearted and motherly preceptress had seemed to me to answer in any way the doubts I honestly and explicitly expressed, and I was fast becoming a marked "man" through my searching iconoclasm. No doubt I was regarded as a corrupter of the simple faith of the other "infants".[2]

When I was six my philosophical evolution received its most aesthetically significant impetus—the dawn of Graeco-Roman thought. Always avid for fairy lore, I had chanced on Hawthorne's "Wonder Book" and "Tanglewood Tales",[3] and was enraptured by the Hellenic myths even in their Teutonised form. Then a tiny book in the private library of my elder aunt—the story of the Odyssey in "Harper's Half-Hour Series"—caught my attention. From the opening chapter I was electrified, and by the time I reached the end I was for evermore a Graeco-Roman. My Bagdad name and affiliations disappeared at once, for the magic of silks and colours faded before that of fragrant templed groves, faun-peopled meadows in the twilight, and the blue, beckoning Mediterranean that billowed mysteriously out from Hellas into the reaches of haunting wounder where dwelt Lotophagi and Laestrygonians, where Aeolus kept his winds and Circe her swine, and where in Thrinacian pastures roamed the oxen of the radiant Helios. As soon as possible I procured an illustrated edition of Bulfinch's "Age of Fable",[4] and gave all my time to the reading of the text, in which the true spirit of Hellenism is delightfully preserved, and to the contemplation of the pictures, splendid designs, and half-tones of the standard classical statues and paintings of classical subjects. Before long I was fairly familiar with the principal Grecian myths, and had become a constant visitor at the classical art museums of Providence and Boston. I commenced a collection of small plaster casts of the Greek sculptural masterpieces, and learned the Greek alphabet and the rudiments of the Latin language. I adopted the pseudonym of "Lucius Valerius Messala"[5]—Roman and not Greek, since Rome had a charm all its own for me. My grandfather had travelled observingly through Italy, and delighted me with long first-hand accounts of its beauties and memorials of ancient grandeur. I mention this aesthetic tendency in detail only to lead up to its philosophical result—my last flickering of religious belief. When about seven or eight I was a genuine pagan, so intoxicated with the beauty of Greece that I acquired a half-sincere belief in the old gods and Nature-spirits. I have in literal truth built altars to Pan, Apollo, Diana, and Athena, and have watched for dryads and satyrs in the woods and fields at dusk. Once I firmly thought I beheld some of these sylvan creatures dancing under autumnal oaks; a kind of "religious experience" as true in its way as the subjective ecstasies of any Christian. If a Christian tell me he has *felt* the reality of his Jesus or Jahveh, I can reply that I have *seen* the hoofed Pan and the sisters of the Hesperian Phaëthusa.

But in my ninth year, as I was reading the Grecian myths in their standard poetical translations and thus acquiring unconsciously my taste for Queen-Anne English, the real foundations of my scepticism were laid. Impelled by the fascinating pictures of scientific instruments in the back of Webster's Unabridged, I began to take an interest in natural philosophy and chemistry; and soon had a promising laboratory in my cellar, and a new stock of simple scientific text-books in my budding library. Ere long I was more of a scientific student than pagan dreamer. In 1897 my leading "literary" work was a "poem" entitled "The New Odyssey"; in 1899 it was a compendious treatise on chemistry in several pencil-scribbled "volumes".[6] But mythology was by no means neglected. In this period I read much in Egyptian, Hindoo, and Teutonic mythology, and tried experiments in pretending to believe each one, to see which might contain the greatest truth. I had, it will be noted, immediately adopted the method and manner of science! Naturally, having an open and unemotional mind, I was soon a complete sceptic and materialist. My scientific studies had enlarged to include geographical, geological, biological, and astronomical rudiments, and I had acquired the habit of relentless analysis in all matters. My pompous "book" called "Poemata Minora", written when I was eleven, was dedicated "To the Gods, Heroes, and Ideals of the Ancients", and harped in disillusioned, world-weary tones on the sorrow of the pagan robbed of his antique pantheon. Some of these very juvenile "poemata" were reprinted in *The Tryout* for April, 1919, under new titles and pseudonyms.[7]

Hitherto my philosophy had been distinctly juvenile and empirical. It was a revolt from obvious falsities and ugliness, but involved no particular cosmic or ethical theory. In ethical questions I had no analytical interest because I did not realise that they were questions. I accepted Victorianism, with consciousness of many prevailing hypocrisies aside from Sabbatarian and supernatural matters, without dispute; never having heard of inquiries which reached "beyond good and evil". Though at times interested in reforms, notably prohibition (I have never tasted alcoholic liquor), I was inclined to be bored by ethical casuistry; since I believed conduct to be a matter of taste and breeding, with virtue, delicacy, and truthfulness as symbols of gentility. Of my word and honour I was inordinately proud, and would permit no reflections to be cast upon them. I thought ethics too obvious and commonplace to be scientifically discussed, and considered philosophy solely in its relation to truth and beauty. I was, and still am, pagan to the core. Regarding man's place in Nature, and the structure of the universe, I was as yet unawakened. This awakening was to come in the winter of 1902–3, when astronomy asserted its supremacy amongst my studies.

The most poignant sensations of my existence are those of 1896, when I discovered the Hellenic world, and of 1902, when I discovered the myriad suns and worlds of infinite space. Sometimes I think the latter event the greater, for the grandeur of that growing conception of the universe still excites a thrill hardly to be duplicated. I made of astronomy my principal scientific study, obtaining larger and larger telescopes, collecting astronomical books to the number of 61, and writing copiously on the subject in the form of special and monthly articles in the local daily press. By my thirteenth birthday I was thoroughly impressed with man's impermanence and insignificance, and by my seventeenth, about which time I did some particularly detailed writing on the subject, I had formed in all essential particulars my present pessimistic cosmic views. The futility of all existence began to impress and oppress me; and my references to human progress, formerly hopeful, began to decline in enthusiasm. Always partial to antiquity, I allowed myself to originate a sort of one-man cult of retrospective suspiration. Realistic analysis, favoured by history and by diffusive scientific leanings which now embraced Darwin, Haeckel,[8] Huxley, and various other pioneers, was checked by my aversion for realistic literature. In fiction I was devoted to the phantasy of Poe; in poetry and essays to the elegant formalism and conventionality of the eighteenth century. I was not at all wedded to what illusions I retained. My attitude has always been cosmic, and I looked on man as if from another planet. He was merely an interesting species presented for study and classification. I had strong prejudices and partialities in many fields, but could not help seeing the race in its cosmic futility as well as in its terrestrial importance. By the time I was of age, I had scant faith in the world's betterment; and felt a decreasing interest in its cherished pomps and prides. When I entered amateurdom in my twenty-fourth year, I was well on the road to my present cynicism; a cynicism tempered with immeasurable pity for man's eternal tragedy of aspirations beyond the possibility of fulfilment.

The war confirmed all the views I had begun to hold. The cant of idealists sickened me increasingly, and I employed no more than was necessary for literary embellishment. With me democracy was a minor question, my anger being aroused primarily by the audacity of a challenge to Anglo-Saxon supremacy, and by the needless territorial greed and disgusting ruthlessness of the Huns. I was unvexed by the scruples which beset the average liberal. Blunders I expected; a German defeat was all I asked or hoped for. I am, I hardly need add, a warm partisan of Anglo-American reunion; my opinion being that the division of a single culture into two national units is wasteful and often dangerous. In this case my opinion is doubly strong because I believe that the entire existing civilisation depends on Saxon dominance.

About this time my philosophical thought received its greatest and latest stimulus through discussion with several amateurs; notably Maurice Winter Moe, an orthodox but tolerant Christian and inspiring opponent, and Alfred Galpin, Jr., a youth in approximate agreement with me, but with a mind so far in the lead that comparison is impossible without humility on my part. Correspondence with these thinkers led to a recapitulation and codification of my views, revealing many flaws in my elaborated doctrines, and enabling me to secure greater clearness and consistency. The impetus also enlarged my philosophical reading and research, and broke down many hindering prejudices. I ceased my literal adherence to Epicurus and Lucretius, and reluctantly dismissed free-will forever in favour of determinism.

The Peace Conference, Friedrich Nietzsche, Samuel Butler (the modern), H. L. Mencken, and other influences have perfected my cynicism; a quality which grows more intense as the advent of middle life removes the blind prejudice whereby youth clings to the vapid "all's right with the world" hallucination from sheer force of desire to have it 'so. As I near thirty-two I have no particular wishes, save to perceive facts as they are. My objectivity, always marked, is now paramount and unopposed, so that there is nothing I am not *willing* to believe. I no longer really desire anything but oblivion, and am thus ready to discard any gilded illusion or accept any unpalatable fact with perfect equanimity. I can at last concede willingly that the wishes, hopes, and values of humanity are matters of total indifference to the blind cosmic mechanism. Happiness I recognise as an ethical phantom whose simulacrum comes fully to none and even partially to but few, and whose position as the goal of all human striving is a grotesque mixture of farce and tragedy.

The Insignificance of Man

[The following is an extract from a letter to the Kleicomolo (8
August 1916). The Kleicomolo was a round-robin correspondence
cycle—formed from the first syllable of the last names of the
amateur writers Rheinhart Kleiner, Ira A. Cole, Maurice W. Moe,
and Lovecraft. It constitutes one of Lovecraft's earliest expressions of
his belief that the immensity of space and time renders the human
race cosmically insignificant.]

But after all, what is life and its purpose? What right has man arbitrarily
to assume his own importance in creation? Science can trace our world
to its source; to the moment of its birth from the great solar nebula in
the remote past. More—Science can demonstrate that all the planets of
our system had a similar origin. Extending the principle to the sidereal
heavens, from whose contemplation, indeed, the nebular hypothesis was
originally derived, we find the nebular form is the present condition of
all creation—a condition which precludes the existence of life. Therefore
we are able to comprehend that the human race is but a thing of the
moment; that its existence on this planet is extremely recent, as infinity
is reckoned; and that its possible existence in all the expanse of
illimitable space is but a matter of yesterday. Space and time have always
existed and always will exist. This is the only legitimate axiom in all
philosophy. And we are able to see that not only humanity but all other

forms of organic life as well are mere innovations; unless, perchance, previous and unknown universes have flourished and perished in the irretrievable recesses of the incomprehensibly remote past. Our human race is only a trivial incident in the history of creation. It is of no more importance in the annals of eternity and infinity than is the child's snow-man in the annals of terrestrial tribes and nations. And more: may not all mankind be a mistake—an abnormal growth—a disease in the system of Nature—an excrescence on the body of infinite progression like a wart on the human hand? Might not the total destruction of humanity, as well as of all animate creation, be a positive *boon* to Nature as a whole? How arrogant of us, creatures of the moment, whose very species is but an experiment of the *Deus Naturae,* to arrogate to ourselves an immortal future and considerable status! How do we know that we have a right to live? Our philosophy is all childishly *subjective*— we imagine that the welfare of our race is the paramount consideration, when as a matter of fact the very existence of the race may be an obstacle to the predestined course of the aggregated universes of infinity! How do we know that that form of atomic and molecular motion called "life" is the highest of all forms? Perhaps the dominant creature—the most rational and God-like of all beings—is an invisible gas![1] Or perhaps it is a flaming and effulgent mass of molten star-dust. Who can say that men have souls while rocks have none? Perhaps the best thing a man might do is to annihilate himself! But of this we know nothing. We are here on a grain of dust called the Earth, and endowed with a certain imperfect and unhappy consciousness called "life". It is not for us to destroy what the Gods have given; we might err as sadly in one direction as in the other. It is obviously our right and our duty to heed our own ignorance, and to permit Nature to work out her processes without interference from these puny, shadow-haunted centres of unrest which we call our minds. It is our right and our duty to mould the minor manifestations of human character in such a way that the entire race may derive the least amount of pain and misery from the pitiful satire known as "life". Certain evils are beyond redemption, many are capable of amelioration, whilst a very few might possibly be cured. There is such a thing as pleasure and happiness tho' it is experienced by few, and only to be obtained by a career of such strenuous achievement that the majority are

9

denied more than a sip. False, loose pleasures are not happiness at all, and are invariably compensated for by misery, the certain result of wide deviation from the normal. In short, most of us have no hope of happiness, nor should we waste our energy in striving for it, since it is all but unattainable. As Mr. Campbell[2] well repeats after other moralists, happiness is to be had only incidentally, as a by-product of the pursuit of virtue. But after all, what is the use of happiness? We cannot say we have a right to it, for we do not even know of what it consists. Let us be content with the absence of poignant pain, nor complain should we fail to achieve positive satisfaction. Much has been said of "the sheer joy of living", an ebullient sensation enjoyed by those in close communion with Nature. This feeling undoubtedly exists, but it is in itself a sinister thing, since it is but an atavistic delight in prehistoric things which the intelligent are leaving behind. It is, indeed, a sort of warning against the continued progress of mankind; a finger beckoning us back to the simpler ages we have survived. I have often wondered if mankind would not be happier for a deliberate destruction of learning and civilisation—an absolute and unqualified return to the happy pastoral barbarism of our legendary ancestors! But the magnitude of such a thing is equaled only by its impossibility. We have outlived happiness, and must make the best of our loss. For a few the atoning delights of aesthetic values have arisen; but that mankind as a unit will ever attain to an appreciation of these milder joys is highly improbable. For the majority today, *forgetfulness* is the only road to endurable existence. It is this yearning for relief from the world and its intolerable monotony which undoubtedly gave rise to the spread of drunkenness and its attendant evils. Man has no natural taste for drink, and the solution of the temperance question really lies in providing the race with a substitute means of escaping the realities of existence. In the sodden brawler of the corner saloon we may trace the degraded effigy of the battle-brave Diomedes, who choked the Xanthus with the bodies of his slain.[3] We have lost all the natural outlets of energy and are blindly groping for new ones. Amidst the bewildering chaos of thwarted instinct and imperfect intellect, the one cry of mankind is "Forget!" Let us then seek to adjust contemporary conditions to man, rather than adapt man to arbitrary conditions. Let us strive for adjustments based on the known nature of the human beast. Let us seek to accomodate his known instincts with harmless activities or painless counter-actives. It is the momentary destiny of that evanescent ephemera called "man" to seek as much surcease as he can from the dulness of life; to do what he can to mould his oft-erring race to the manifest course of Nature, and to await the end prepared for him by the mighty elements which mould not only his own transitory tribe, but all the eternal and unfathomed recesses of existence that yawn about him, even beyond the vision of his excited and disordered fancy. Man knows nothing. Man probably is nothing. But let the poor creatures do what they can to avoid open conflict with destiny. Of all the judgments of man enunciated by the various philosophers and poets of this world, I find most sense and satisfaction in the lines of my own beloved Mr. Pope, who hath writ:

"Plac'd on this isthmus of a middle state,

A being darkly wise, and rudely great,

With too much knowledge for the sceptic's side,

With too much weakness for the Stoic's pride,

He hangs between, in doubt to act or rest;

In doubt to deem himself a God, or beast;

In doubt his mind or body to prefer;

Born but to die, and reas'ning but to err;

Alike in ignorance, his reason such,

Whether he thinks too little or too much;

Chaos of thought and passion, all confused;

Still by himself abus'd, or disabus'd;

Created half to rise, and half to fall;

Great lord of all things, yet a prey to all;

Sole judge of truth, in endless error hurl'd:

The glory, jest, and riddle of the world!"[4]

What I Have against Religion

[The following is an extract from a letter to Maurice W. Moe (15 May 1918). Moe, an English teacher in Wisconsin, was fervently religious and maintained that religious belief was necessary to ensure social and moral order. Lovecraft states that this stance ignores the central issue of the truth or falsity of religion, and, assuming (rather than establishing) its falsity, Lovecraft goes on to assert that a social or moral order founded upon a falsehood is inherently flawed and unstable.]

Your wonderment 'what I have against religion' reminds me of your recent *Vagrant* essay—which I had the honour of perusing in manuscript some three years ago. To my mind, that essay *misses one point altogether.* Your "agnostic" has neglected to mention the very crux of all agnosticism—namely that the Judaeo-Christian mythology is NOT TRUE. I can see that in your philosophy *truth per se* has so small a place, that you can scarcely realise what it is that Galpin and I are insisting upon. In your mind, MAN is the centre of everything, and his exact conformation to certain regulations of conduct HOWEVER EFFECTED, the only problem in the universe. Your world (if you will pardon my saying so) is *contracted.* All the mental vigour and erudition of the ages fail to disturb your complacent endorsement of empirical doctrines and purely pragmatical notions, because you voluntarily limit your horizon—*excluding certain facts, and certain undeniable mental tendencies of mankind.* In your eyes, man is torn between *only two* influences; the degrading instincts of the savage, and the temperate impulses of the philanthropist. To you, men are of but two classes—lovers of self and lovers of the race. To you, men have but two types of emotion—self-gratification, to be combatent; and altruism, to be fostered. But you, consciously or unconsciously, are leaving out a vast and potent *tertium quid*—making an omission which cannot but interfere with the validity of your philosophical conceptions. You are forgetting a human impulse which, despite its restriction to a relatively small number of men, has all through history proved itself as real and as vital as hunger—as potent as thirst or greed. I need not say that I refer to that simplest yet most exalted attribute of our species—the acute, persistent, unquenchable craving TO KNOW. Do you realise that to many men it makes a vast and profound difference whether or not the things about them are as they appear? Let me use an analogy, since you love concreteness. You recognise a difference between mere pleasure and true happiness. As a consistent theologian, you must chaw this distinction. You point to two men; one a merely frivolous creature, amusing himself by drowning his cares in wine or gaiety; the other a conscientious worker of good, who takes satisfaction in knowing that he is properly adjusted to society and his fellowmen. Both are equally contented, but you will undoubtedly say that only the second man is truly happy. You will say, and rightly, that the joy of the first man is merely mental apathy; and that if ever he should be forced to think about himself and his relation to others around him, he would be acutely dissatisfied—would seek to find his place in life and thereby satisfy the new misgivings which thought aroused in him. But at this point you and other orthodox thinkers find it expedient to "draw a herring across the trail" and turn to other lines of investigation. For the very distinction you draw between empty pleasure and true happiness would by one more step of ratiocination force you to acknowledge the element of the *absolute* whose existence you are so anxious to deny or conceal. In differentiating between pleasure and happiness, you concede that the reality of the source of contentment is a very important thing.

13

Otherwise the serenity of the sensualist and of the saint stand on a level. If effect is all we are to consider, the drunken loafer or the madman who fancies himself a King may be deemed just as blessed as the person whose happiness is founded on actual things. If there be not some virtue in plain TRUTH; then our fair dreams, delusions, and follies, are as much to be esteemed as our sober waking hours and the comforts they bring. If TRUTH amounts to nothing, then we must regard the phantasma of our slumbers just as seriously as the events of our daily lives. Several nights ago I had a strange dream of a strange city—a city of many palaces and gilded domes, lying in a hollow betwixt ranges of grey, horrible hills.[1] There was not a soul in this vast region of stone-paved streets and marble walls and columns, and the numerous statues in the public places were of strange bearded men in robes the like whereof I have never seen before or since. I was, as I said, aware of this city visually. I was in it and around it. But certainly I had no corporeal existence. I saw, it seemed, everything at once; without the limitations of direction. I did not move, but transferred my perception from point to point at will. I occupied no space and had no form. I was only a consciousness, a perceptive presence. I recall a lively curiosity at the scene, and a tormenting struggle to recall its identity; for I felt that I had once known it well, and that if I could remember, I should be carried back to a very remote period—many thousand years, when something vaguely horrible had happened. Once I was almost on the verge of realisation, and was frantic with fear at the prospect, though I did not know what it was that I should recall. But here I awaked—in a very cramped posture and with too much bedclothing for the steadily increasing temperature. I have related this in detail because it impressed me very vividly. This is not a Co^2 romance of reincarnation—you will see that it has no climax or point—but it was very real. I am now trying to recall if I felt any sensation or had any notion of *heat* in the dream. The excessive covering would account for that, if I did. But as a matter of fact, I cannot remember such an impression.

At this point you will ask me whence these stories! I answer—according to your pragmatism that dream was as real as my presence at this table, pen in hand! If the truth or falsity of our beliefs and

14

impressions be immaterial, then I am, or was, actually and indisputably an unbodied spirit hovering over a very singular, very silent, and very ancient city somewhere between grey, dead hills. I thought I was at the time—so what else matters? Do you think that I was just as truly that spirit as I am now H. P. Lovecraft? I do not. "'And there ye are', as Mr. Dooley says."[3]

I recognise a distinction between dream life and real life, between appearances and actualities. I confess to an over-powering desire to know whether I am asleep or awake—whether the environment and laws which affect me are external and permanent, or the transitory products of my own brain. I admit that I am very much interested in the relation I bear to the things about me—the time relation, the space relation, and the causative relation. I desire to know approximately what my life is in terms of history—human, terrestrial, solar, and cosmical; what my magnitude may be in terms of extension,—terrestrial, solar, and cosmical; and above all, what may be my manner of linkage to the general system—in what way, through what agency, and to what extent, the obvious guiding forces of creation act upon me and govern my existence. And if there be any less obvious forces, I desire to know them and their relation to me as well. Foolish, do I hear you say? Undoubtedly! I had better be a consistent pragmatist: get drunk and confine myself to a happy, swinish, contented little world—the gutter— till some policeman's No. 13 boot intrudes upon my philosophic repose. But I *cannot.* Why? Because some well-defined human impulse prompts me to discard the relative for the absolute. You would encourage me as far as the moral stage. You would agree with me that I had better see the world as it is than to forget my woes in the flowing bowl. But because I have a certain *momentum,* and am carried a step further from the merely relative, you frown upon me and declare me to be a queer, unaccountable creature, "immersed . . . . . in the VICIOUS abstractions of philosophy!"

Here, then, is the beginning of my religious or philosophical thought. I have not begun talking about *morality* yet, because I have not reached that point in the argument. *Entity* precedes morality. It is a prerequisite. What am I? What is the nature of the energy about me, and how does it affect me? So far I have seen nothing which could possibly give me the notion that cosmic force is the manifestation of a mind and will like my own infinitely magnified; a potent and purposeful consciousness which deals individually and directly with the miserable denizens of a wretched little flyspeck on the back door of a microscopic universe, and which singles this putrid excrescence out as the one spot whereto to send an onlie-begotten Son, whose mission is to redeem those accursed flyspeck-inhabiting lice which we call human beings—bah!! Pardon the "bah!" I feel several "bahs!", but out of courtesy I only say one. But it is all so very childish. I cannot help taking exception to a philosophy which would force this rubbish down my throat. 'What have I against religion?' That is what I have against it! (Do not mistake me—I have a great deal *for* it as well. I do *not* 'deny it a place in the life of the world'. I am coming to this about twenty or thirty pages farther on!!)

Now let us view *morality*—which despite your preconceived classification and identification has nothing to do with any particular form of religion. Morality is the adjustment of matter to its environment—the natural arrangement of molecules. More especially it may be considered as dealing with organic molecules. Conventionally it is the science of reconciling the animal *homo* (more or less) *sapiens* to the forces and conditions with which he is surrounded. It is linked with religion only so far as the natural elements it deals with are deified and personified. Morality antedated the Christian religion, and has many times risen superior to co-existent religions. It has powerful support from very non-religious human impulses. Personally, I am intensely moral and intensely irreligious. My morality can be traced to two distinct sources, scientific and aesthetic. My love of truth is outraged by the flagrant disturbance of sociological relations involved in so-called "wrong"; whilst my aesthetic sense is outraged and disgusted with the violations of taste and harmony thereupon attendant. But to me the question presents no ground for connection with the grovelling instinct of religion. However—you may exclude me from the argument, if you will. I *am* unduly secluded though unavoidably so. We will deal only with materials which may presumably lie within my feeble reach. Only one more touch of ego. I am *not* at all passive or indifferent in my zeal for a high morality. But I cannot consider morality the essence of religion as you seem to. In discussing religion, the whole fabric must bear examination before the uses or purposes are considered. We must investigate the cause as well as alleged effects if we are to define the relation between the two, and the reality of the former. And more, granting that the phenomenon of faith is indeed the true cause of the observed moral effects; the absolute basis of that phenomenon remains to be examined. The issue between theists and atheists is certainly not, as you seem to think, the mere question of whether religion is useful or detrimental. In your intensely pragmatical mind, this question stands paramount—to such an extent that you presented no other subject of discussion in your very clever *Vagrant* article. But the "agnostic" of your essay must have been a very utilitarian agnostic (that such "utilitarian Agnostics" do exist, I will not deny. *Vide* any issue of *The Truthseeker!* But are they typical?)! What the honest thinker wishes to know, has nothing to do with complex human conduct. He simply demands a scientific *explanation* of the things he sees. His only animus toward the church concerns its deliberate inculcation of demonstrable untruths in the community. This is human nature. No matter how white a lie may be—no matter how much good it may do—we are always more or less disgusted by its diffusion. The honest agnostic regards the church with respect for what it has done in the direction of virtue. He even supports it if he is magnanimous, and he certainly does nothing to impair whatever public usefulness it may possess. But in private, he would be more than a mere mortal if he were able to suppress a certain abstract resentment, or to curb the feeling of humour and so-called irreverence which inevitably arises from the contemplation of pious fraud, howsoever high-minded and benevolent.

The good effects of Christianity are neither to be denied, nor lightly esteemed, though candidly I will admit that I think them overrated. For example, the insignia of the Red Cross is practically the only religious thing about it. It is purely humanitarian and philanthropic, and has received just as much of its vitality from agnostic—or Jewish—sources, as from Christian sources. I once heard of a foot powder called "White Cross". Was it by divine healing that it relieved (or claimed to relieve) tired feet? Likewise the Y. M. C. A. There is some psalm-singing in this organisation, but I have read from many reliable sources (including *The Outlook*)[5] that its work in France is more social than religious. In its campaign for support it has proclaimed its social purpose, nor has any of my tainted agnostic money, contributed for moral and ethical reasons, been contemptuously returned! These nominally Christian societies usurp the lion's share of social service merely because they are on the ground first. Free and rational thought is relatively new, and rationalists find it just as practicable to support these existing Christian charities as to organise new ones which might create a division of energy and therefore decrease the efficiency of organised charity as a whole. And by the way—was not Belgium relief work largely non-religious? I may be mistaken—but all this is aside from my main argument anyway. I am not protesting against the recognition of Christianity's accomplishments. This has nothing to do with absolute bases of faith.

[. . .]

But lest you think I have wandered far from my previously expressed respect for religion as a lever to move the masses, let me reaffirm that respect. I recognise the power of the primal—which amongst the illiterate, semi-literate, and a few of the literate, is a force capable of much good if skillfully wielded. Conversely, I recognise the dangerous potentialities of an ignorantly atheistical mob—a mob whose atheism comes not from thought, but from copying others. All rationalism tends to minimise the value and importance of life, and to decrease the sum total of human happiness. In many cases the truth may cause suicidal or nearly suicidal depression. Therefore, I concede that the church deserves support as long as it can exist, and that agnosticism ought never to be diffused artificially. Yea, more. I will concede that men of religion are justified in hindering the spread of agnosticism among those whose opinions are not particularly settled, and who might easily be swayed either way. But ordinary sense tells us that faith cannot hang on forever. After the war chaos there will be an inevitable reaction toward hard facts. The time is coming when the old formulae will cease to enchant, for nothing can last eternally which is not founded on demonstrable truth. And for that future we must provide while there is time. Without attacking religion in any way, let us admit that virtue and honour are possible outside its charmed circle. Let us cultivate morality as an independent principle. Let us cultivate philanthropy for its own sake. True, religion has hitherto done marvels for these things—but religion will some day perish, and these things must never perish. If you, as I infer, like artistic Victorian media through which to receive ideas; let me recommend to you the recent verse of Thomas Hardy. Hardy is a Victorian who has survived his age—and in his transition from prose to verse he has burst forth with renewed philosophic splendour. He recognises with regret the passing of Christianity. He loves it as he loves classic mythology, but he cannot believe it. A few years ago he wrote a poem on the *death* or *funeral* of God—a poem which doubtless caused many a pair of devout hands to rise in a gesture of holy horror.[6] But Hardy thinks.

II. General Thoughts on God and Religion

The Nature of God

[The following is a series of extracts from letters to the Kleicomolo (October 1916 and April 1917). Lovecraft argues that the standard Christian conception of God is full of implausibilities and paradoxes, but goes on to say that widespread disbelief would probably be harmful to society. Lovecraft also engages in a vigorous defense of the pursuit of "absolute truth."]

Concerning the ultimates of time and space, I fear no philosopher would be quite satisfied with Mr. Mo's light rejection of considerations beyond our own terrestrial globe. The whole structure of our chieftain's orthodox Christianity is built upon the relation of Deity with the one crawling atom we call man; and no theologian can sustain his religion unless he can prove that this speck in infinity is the central point of all creation. Mr. Mo leaves us in perplexity whether his God is absolutely omnipotent, or whether he is a local deity, presiding over this particular little world or universe as some minor hamadryad presides over some particular tree or grove. The latter conception, of a God who is confined in action to our visible universe, leaves us to speculate as to what God or forces may preside over the rest of creation—or if we adhere to the commandment of Scripture, and believe only in one God, we must assume that the rest of space is godless; that no personal loving father-deity is there to bless his sons and subjects. But then, if this be so, why did the personal all-wise parent select this one particular little universe wherein to exercise his beneficence? I fear that all theism consists mostly of reasoning in circles, and guessing or inventing what we do not know. If God is omnipotent, then why did he pick out this one little period and world for his experiment with mankind? Or if he is local, then why did he select this locality, when he had an infinity of universes and an infinity of eras to choose from? And why should the fundamental tenets of theology hold him to be all-pervasive? These are monstrous uncomfortable questions for a pious man to answer, and yet the orthodox clergy continue to assert a complete understanding of all these things, brushing inquiry aside either by sophistry and mysticism, or by evasion and sanctified horror. Why must men of sense thus delude themselves with notions of personal and "loving" gods, spirits, and demons? All this sort of thing is good enough for the rabble, but why should rational brains be tormented with such gibberish? It is perfectly true that the conception of a personal force is a vast help in managing the millions, and in giving them much hope and happiness that truth does not convey. Viewing the question in that light, I am a friend of the church, and would never seek to disturb or diminish its influence among those who are able to swallow its doctrines. I even wish I could believe them myself—it would be so comfortable to know that some day I shall sprout wings and go up to Heaven for a talk with Alexander Pope and Sir Isaac Newton! But, provided a man cannot believe in orthodoxy, why grate on his sensibilities by demanding that he believe? We cannot do what we cannot—at least this has been the general idea since the abolishment of the Popish Inquisition. It is only the forcible propagation of conventional Christianity that makes the agnostic so bitter toward the church. He knows that all the doctrines cannot possibly be true, but he would view them with toleration if he were asked merely to let them alone for the benefit of the masses whom they can help and succour. The agnostic becomes bitter only when someone presumes to affront his reason by demanding that he believe the impossible, under penalty of censure and ostracism. The word "Christianity" becomes noble when applied to the veneration of a wonderfully good man and moral teacher, but it grows undignified when applied to a system of white magic based on the supernatural. Christ probably believed himself a true Messiah, since the tendencies of the times might well inculcate such a notion in anyone of his qualities. Whether his mind was strictly normal or not is out of the question. Very few minds are strictly normal, and all religious fanatics are marked with abnormalities of various sorts. It is well known that psychologists group religious phenomena with other and less divine disturbances of the brain and nervous system. Whether, as the novel of Mr. Moore implies,[1] Christ was alive after his nominal execution; or whether the whole Resurrection legend is a myth, is immaterial. Very little reliable testimony could come from so remote a province as Judaea at that time. For the sensitive mind to harass itself over ancient and mediaeval conceptions, to strain over such questions as how many angels can stand on the point of a needle, (this was actually debated in the Middle Ages) or to wear itself to fragments trying to accept that which it can never accept, is as cruel and reprehensible as to deprive the masses of their spiritual and orthodox solace. I think that Mr. Mo really has the same basic conception of creation that I have, save that his long grounded orthodoxy forbids him to express or even to think consciously the stark, bald facts. Mr. Mo's great argument for orthodoxy is that it accomplishes vast good; an argument which neither affirms nor denies its foundation in absolute truth. Many false beliefs have wrought incalculable good—the observed effects are the effects of the belief; not of the possible truth or untruth that may lie behind the belief. Because a certain preacher has helped reform a drunkard, we have no grounds for acclaiming him as vice-regent of some other person or conscious spirit for whose existence we have no other evidence. Mr. Mo's summing up of his own case may be adopted without change as the summing up of my case. "In the face of these phenomena, what does the nature of absolute, ultimate truth matter to you and me? Christianity pure and undefiled is the truth to this world, *for it works!*" That is, Christianity is "truth to this world". All men may perfectly agree when they admit the existence of more than one kind of truth. Christianity is not necessarily logical or actual truth, but it is "terrestrial truth", and that is enough for the majority. Let us be thankful if anything can govern such an unruly race as man. My point of issue with Mr. Mo is, can thinking men ever be satisfied with a truth short of the ultimate and absolute? Dangerous and hurtful as may be this particular brand of truth, mankind has a shockingly perverse way of chasing after it! An arch-pessimist like myself would naturally wish to avoid the true kind of truth, yet it has the same fascination for me that it had for Copernicus and Galileo! But this is the fault of the age. Why are philosophical studies permitted if their result is so disastrous? We may say of true truth what Mr. Pope said of Vice:

> But seen too oft, familiar with its face,
>
> We first endure, then pity, then embrace![2]

[. . .]

To conclude this weighty discourse, I shall state my attitude toward orthodox theism and Christianity in my own cold-blooded words. I truly believe that Mr. Mo's opinion, if spoken with equal directness, would be precisely the same:

(1) Orthodox Christianity, by playing upon the emotions of man, is able to accomplish wonders toward keeping him in order and relieving his mind. It can frighten or cajole him away from evil more effectively than could reason. Because of its hypnotic and auto-hypnotic power, this faith should be preserved as long as it can be propped up with arguments or diffused through rhetoric. It is a crime publicly to attack the church, since upon that institution rests more than half of the responsibility for maintaining the existing social order. On this account, it is well to refrain from open utterances concerning religion, and at times even to pretend belief. Truth is of no practical value to mankind save as it affects terrestrial phenomena, hence the discoveries of science should be concealed or glossed over wherever they conflict with orthodoxy. It is wisest to invent an artificial sort of "truth" which conforms to the well-being of man. It will never do us any good to know the dimensions of space or the aeons of time, so let us forget all about the universe and the infinity outside the universe. The notion of personal, affectionate Godhead works best with the masses, so let us

gently adapt what we know, to what we ought to think. Anything is justifiable in the interests of humanity.

(2) As to naked reality—we only know that we are a speck in the engulfing vortices of infinity and eternity. We know that all creation obeys certain laws or principles whose source we know not, but which apparently result from the interaction of material particles, or modes of motion. It is utter quibbling to differentiate betwixt Nature, and a Deity immanent in nature. The distinction is purely one of words. We know that yesterday in time our universe and race did not exist. We have no reason for assuming that it will remain in existence save for another moment of eternity. Of our relation to all creation we can never know anything whatsoever. All is immensity and chaos. But, since all this knowledge of our limitations cannot possibly be of any value to us, it is better to ignore it in our daily conduct of life. It is dangerous, and therefore, should not be spread broadcast. But every man has a right to think what he thinks and to believe what he believes.

I am interested in Mr. Co's researches concerning the occult and the supernatural; particularly so since I have encountered several reviews of poor Oliver Lodge's book "Raymond"[3]—a work which I confess I have not perused at first hand. It may be well to state that Sir Oliver, as well as Sir William Crookes,[4] have received little faith since they turned their attention to [the] fallacy-ridden realm of the supernatural. Their speculations in this direction may well be taken as evidences of freakishness—and in Sir William's case, of senility; since he is now eighty-five years of age. It is Lodge, however, who is under consideration, and he cannot plead old age, since he was born in 1851. Of his reported phenomena, and of other cases of a like nature, it is safest to say that insufficient evidence throws them out of court. Disturbed mentality, auto-suggestion, and deliberate charlatanry will be found at the base of most alleged spiritualistic and telepathic manifestations. They most generally occur amongst the ignorant, or amongst those who ardently *wish* to have them occur. Many of the most plausible cases resolve themselves into the most deliberate imposture upon impartial and authentick investigation. More than one "broad-minded" dupe of spiritualism felt the throes of sheepishness when the exceedingly clever Eusapia Palladino was exposed as a fraud;[5] yet each victim might have known that such magic as she exhibited was impossible according to the recognised principles of Nature. Open-mindedness becomes a fault when it fails to take into account the fundamental probabilities of things. I abhor the sickly attitude of a certain soft-headed class of investigators, who so fear the imputation of bigotry, that they will make fools of themselves by wasting serious thought over obvious cheats and impostors. The very vagueness of human reason, and the very subjectivity of human thought, should warn the student to pay scant attention to the fleeting fancies of the mind. Imagination is a very potent thing, and in the uneducated often usurps the place of genuine experience. I have encountered many instances of children who, without conscious falsification, confuse the real with the unreal, and relate in good faith experiences through which they have not passed. It is reasonable to assume that many apparent instances of supernatural manifestations were devised subconsciously in the brains of the narrators. Atavism hath implanted many dark fancies in man; it needs but a little relaxation of intellectualism to bring up the old ghosts of the past, and revive that intense faith, or tendency to have faith, in the supernatural, which originally grew out of our ancestors' attempts to explain nature. The progress of science will eventually, I believe, enunciate at least two laws, which will forever put an end to spiritualism amongst the educated and even the half-educated. They are:

(1) Life, animal and vegetable, including human life, is a mode of motion which ceases absolutely upon the death of the body containing it.

(2) The future, so far as organic beings are concerned, can never be predicted, since individual and unfathomable caprice has power to direct events into any of the innumerable channels possible under the natural law.

[. . .]

As the Mo-Lo theological controversy narrows down to fewer points of difference, it may be correspondingly given a smaller and smaller space in each successive epistle. I perceive that my erudite opponent challenges my assumption that scientific progress must be "concealed or glossed over" in order to ensure the preservation of religious belief. He declares that the church is willing to admit all the discoveries of science, reconciling them to some increasingly vague theistical plan—that is, to use plainer language, altering religion to suit science, and making of God a plastic character to be remodelled whenever obvious truth disproves one of His original legendary attributes. This I am willing to admit; but I am not equally willing to abandon the basic idea of my statement, that it will be found necessary in the end to minimise science in order to preserve faith. Not every man is as happily incurious as Mr. Mo; and for many persons, a mere knowledge of the approximate dimensions of the visible universe is enough to destroy forever the notion of a personal godhead whose whole care is expended upon puny mankind, and whose only genuine and original Messiah was dispatched to save the insignificant vermin, or men, who inhabit this one relatively microscopic globe. Not that science positively refutes religion—it merely makes religion seem [so] monstrously improbable that a large majority of men can no longer believe in it. And to go a step further—sooner or later the relation betwixt organic and inorganic life will be discovered. It will be clearly demonstrated how carbon, hydrogen, oxygen, nitrogen, and other elements combine to form substances possessing vital energy. Probably the chemist or biologist will be able to create in his laboratory some very primitive sort of animal or vegetable organism. This will be the death knell of superstition and theology alike; and unless it be sacredly concealed, the church will cease to exist save amongst the very ignorant. But of course, since this has not yet come to pass, I am aware that it forms no truly legitimate part of my case against orthodoxy. However—the probability is strong!

When Mr. Mo charges me with inconsistency in asking whether thinking men can ever be satisfied with make-shift terrestrial truth as opposed to stark absolute fact, I fear he misapprehends my meaning. I did not ask, can *a thinking man* be so satisfied; my question relating to thinking men as a class—to the majority of the scientists and philosophers of today and tomorrow. Surely Mr. Mo does not deem me so ignorant as not to know that many men of vast culture and attainments are devoutly orthodox. Indeed, there is much in pure humanitarian culture, as opposed to rigid scientific training, which encourages absorption in the affairs of mankind, and more or less indifference to the unfathomed abysses of star-strown space that yawn interminably about this terrestrial grain of dust. Perhaps I am a barbarian at heart—sometimes I believe I am—to be so anxious to know what *is,* and not what *ought to be.* I cannot attach so much importance to mere mankind as I should—the *"Homo sum"* sort of enthusiasm never appealed greatly to me.[6] I am not very proud of being an human being; in fact, I distinctly dislike the species in many ways. I can readily conceive of beings vastly superior in every respect. But to be orthodox, one should have less imagination!

Mr. Mo's frank admission that he is satisfied with the empirical "truth" which results from an evasion of astronomical facts, is in a way surprising to me; yet after reflection I can understand the mental attitude, the direct opposite of my own, which enables him to make such a statement. He is to some extent, consciously or unconsciously, a disciple of that not unknown Oxford don, Prof. Schiller, concerning whom an article lately appeared in THE INDEPENDENT.[7] This philosopher, like our Appletonian comrade, has a rather elastic notion of Truth, giving that supposedly inflexible abstraction a curiously adaptable nature. In a word, he is a pragmatist of extreme type. Until I read of Prof. Schiller, I was unable to understand how such theories could be held; but I now perceive that there is a not inconsiderable school of pragmatists, who hold to similar ideas. This controversy has taught me many things, foremost among them being my own comparative ignorance of formal philosophy and its subdivisions. I intend to give some attention to this subject in future, in an endeavour to comprehend views which seem to me now too absurd for credence on the part of thinkers. I have a notion that I shall become ardently interested in this subject, for I am a born speculator. (In the academic, not the financial sense!) Mr. Mo's final statement: "All your argument has not shown me why it (absolute truth) interests you," brings to my mind an interesting train of thought. Is there, then, no genuineness in that instinct of truth-seeking which we commonly suppose to reside in the human mind? Does nothing matter which has no direct bearing on our daily life? Were the Papists right in torturing men who believed in the Copernican system? Verily, it matters little to man whether the earth revolve around the sun, or the sun around the earth! No one has really shewn why this matter should interest us! It is sufficient if we eat, sleep, and worship! But with all due respect to Mr. Mo, I must reiterate my belief in the necessity of truth to the human mind. [M]y argument does not need to show why truth interests me [...] The fact remains that it *does* interest me, as it has interested thousands of other men. The pages of history are red with the blood of those who have died for their intellectual convictions. Truth-hunger is a hunger just as real as food-hunger—it is equally strong if less explicable; indeed, who can assign a direct reason for any of the obscurer desires and aspirations of man? It is all according to the plan of Nature. In flouting the absolute truth because of its lack of application of the affairs of mankind, Mr. Mo reminds me of the Florentine astronomer Sizzi, who thus argued against the existence of Jupiter's satellites: "Moreover", quoth this sage in the course of his argument, "the satellites are invisible to the naked eye, and therefore can exert no influence on the earth, and therefore would be useless, *and therefore do not exist!*" 'Twas vastly inconsiderate of Galileo to see these troublesome orbs, after they had been conclusively demonstrated not to exist at all! How complex is the mortal brain!

What Is Religion?

[The following is an extract from a letter to Emil Petaja (6 March 1935). Petaja (1915–2000) was at this time a young science fiction fan apparently inclined toward belief in spiritualism. Petaja went on to become a noted science fiction writer and editor.]

Regarding the matter of religion—while a story is of course no place to air philosophic views, I must say that I myself do not believe in any form of the supernatural. While religion was a perfectly natural thing for mankind in early ages, when nothing definite was known about the constitution of matter and the causes of natural phenomena; there is really no basis for its existence in the light of what we know about the universe, and about our own mental and emotional processes, today. We now realise that the varied happenings of the universe, and the phenomena of life and consciousness, are all parts of a general pattern of force-and-matter mutations whose perpetual flux [has no] conscious direction or purpose. While there is no positive *disproof* of a cosmic consciousness, there is *no reason to assume* that any such thing exists. It is just as if I were to say that a man named Smith lives in a brick house in a city called Nuth on the 3d satellite of Jupiter. There is no way of disproving what I say—but who would believe anything so gratuitous and improbable? And when we come to analyse supernaturalism, we

31

find that it forms an assumption no less gratuitous & improbable. What really disposes of supernatural belief is our modern understanding of *the reason it has existed.* Psychology & anthropology have now shown us how and why the concepts of "spirit", "deity", "immortality", "right and wrong" (as distinguished from the sound values based on aesthetic and utilitarian ethics), "worship", "sin", etc., etc. came into existence among primitive races trying to explain the unknown tangle of the external world and their own emotions, and have made it overwhelmingly clear that the growth of these concepts is an inevitable concomitant of primitive ignorance—in no way implying any truth behind them. The same sciences also make it manifest why these concepts have come to exert so great a sway over the emotions of the majority, and why they have survived so persistently in the face of the increased knowledge which has virtually disproved them. Thus it is no longer possible to argue that the intense *wish* or profound emotional *belief* of the majority in all ages forms any indication of the truth of the "deity" or "immortality" concepts. We know today, through psychology, that *any* belief or emotional bias, no matter how untrue or absurd, can be implanted in the brain and nervous system of a human being with tremendous force and firmness if the victim be inoculated with it in infancy. A person thus subjected to indoctrination with some special idea at an age under seven will always have a deeper instinctive predisposition toward that idea—but this has nothing to do with the truth of the idea. There is no natural leaning toward religion. Originally, it merely attempts to explain the unknown through poetic symbolism and crude personification; today it survives among the less analytical majority merely because they lack scientific information, and because their emotional apparatus has been permanently biassed or crippled by religious propaganda hammered into them in childhood, before their mind and emotions had developed beyond the infantile state of helpless and uncritical receptivity. It is really a crime against a child to attempt to influence his intellectual belief in any way. Anything like bias or indoctrination should be confined to such broad concepts as have been universally found expedient and harmonious through racial experience—concepts like honesty, order, non-encroachment, etc., which relate to practical conduct and not to matters of *opinion.* So far as points of theory and belief are concerned, the only decent and honourable thing to do with a child is to teach him *strict openmindedness* and *intellectual integrity*—urging him to accept nothing through mere hearsay or blind tradition, but *to judge everything honestly himself on the basis of existing evidence.* If religion is true, he will then sooner or later accept it. If it is not true, he will then be free from a degrading mental slavery which cannot honestly be called *belief.* The fact is, a *real* friend of religion would not *wish* anyone to accept it if he did not do so through an honest and open-minded appraisal of the evidence offered by the phenomena around and within him. All attempts to mould belief on emotional, non-rational grounds are to be condemned without qualification as unworthy of any organism as highly evolved as man. This applies to non-religious and antireligious propaganda as much as to religious propaganda. The Russian soviets are just as reprehensible in warping popular emotions in favour of religion. What really ought to be taught people is *how to think.* Nine-tenths of the people in the world *never really think* on any topic of large scope. They *imagine* they have "opinions"—but these "opinions" are so completely the product of irrational emotion, blind heritage, and sheer mental indolence, as to be unworthy of the name. And this applies to most atheists as well as to most religious people. We would be a lot better off if our preceptors would stop trying to teach us *special attitudes,* and buckle down to the vital business of teaching us *accurate thought and strict intellectual honesty.*

In view of what we know today about the universe and ourselves, there is very little likelihood that the old concepts of dualism ("spirit"), immortality, and cosmic consciousness and purpose can have any truth in them. But this need not disturb us in the least. Actually, the supposed longing for such things is merely an artificial emotional condition determined by our past environment. As soon as we put such ideas out of our head, we shall cease to feel any sorrow at their untruth. There are plenty of bases for a fruitful, orderly, and harmonious life without any assumption of the supernatural. Although life and mankind are only trivial accidents or incidents in the universe, they are none the less important to themselves. Man has a well-defined set of instincts and

33

emotions; and the planning of a way of life which shall satisfy these with the least possible conflict and disharmony and encroachment, and with the greatest possible opportunities for the growth and expression of the species' most high-evolved attributes, is a full-time job of which no philosopher or leader or ethical teacher need feel ashamed. This task of ethical leadership, based on sound principles of aesthetics and sociology, is the one now awaiting the sort of man who in earlier ages formed a religious leader. I do not advocate the forcible extirpation of religion, but I think it is wise to transfer energies to something which has a foundation in reality. The conditions of life are growing more and more different from what they were in the ages when the various religions took form; hence one can no longer expect any religion-based ethics to be at all times as useful as an ethics based on reality. What is more, religion is rapidly losing its emotional and ethical hold over all classes— even those who consciously believe it. The wide gap between what it teaches and what we now know to be real is too vast a thing to conceal and gloss over. People realise it subconsciously even when they are blind to it with their conscious minds. Religion *as a practical force in life* is dead—and if we expect to rally the emotions of the people to anything today as those emotions were rallied to religion in the past, we must provide something in which they can *really believe* . . . with their subconscious as well as conscious minds. The Russians have got something of the sort in their new way of life based on social adjustment. If we want anything as powerful, we must also devise some ideal of human adjustment *which has a real chance of working* and of offering the people an actually bearable set of living conditions. Religion always promises, but has no power to perform. It is simply a sort of emotional intoxication—as helpless as whiskey to make real the grandiose visions it holds forth. The race is too disillusioned and realistic at this stage of the game to follow any such phantom. If we want to rally everybody to a single purpose, we must formulate a goal which has a demonstrable chance of giving the whole of mankind *better conditions in the only life it is certain of having.* I don't think the soviet ideology embraces the best possible goal, and would hate to see it established in the western world. But at least it is a *real goal*—something to which men can be intelligently loyal. At the moment, the western world possesses no such thing—even though the Nazi movement thinks it has found one. We live in an era of unmistakable decadence—the last phase of a way of life founded on conditions and beliefs forever vanished so far as this cycle of civilisation is concerned. Shall we ever find a substitute—a practicable social order which may at once solve the economic and political problems of the present, and preserve (as the soviet system fails to do) what is still sound and infinitely valuable in the cultural heritage of the past? I don't know—but if we do, we shall have something around which our children can rally as our fathers rallied around the ideals of the past. The chances are about even whether such a thing can come to pass, or whether there will be a long period of decay under some ruthless fascist system . . . or a plunge into a bolshevism for which the western world is certainly not fitted.

Atheism and Probability

[The following is an extract from a letter to Robert E. Howard (16 August 1932). Howard (1906–1936) became celebrated in his lifetime and afterward for the invention of such heroic figures as Conan the Barbarian, Solomon Kane, and King Kull. He and Lovecraft came into correspondence in 1930 and wrote hundreds of thousands of words of letters to each other over the next six years, but they never met. Howard was largely an agnostic and skeptic, but apparently believed that there was insufficient evidence to decide between the truth-claims of religion and those of atheism. Lovecraft responded forcefully and based his argument on probability and the implications of scientific advance.]

As for Outside encroachments—and the subject of supernaturalism, immortality, etc. in general—I am, in theory, not so far from your own position. Actually, of course, we know absolutely nothing of the cosmos beyond the small fragment reachable by our five senses; hence dogmatism in any one direction is as illogical as dogmatism in any other. However, I am not as reluctant as yourself to piece out matters with a few reflections based on *probabilities*. The absence of *positive* knowledge does not stop certain views of things from being, according to present indications, *a damn sight likelier* than certain other views. And when anthropology teaches us that certain traditions of theology had a definite origin in some special condition leading to delusion, we are completely justified in maintaining that these traditions—with their manifestly false origin—*have not one chance in a million* of being the true explanations of the things they profess to explain. It would be too much of a coincidence if our ignorant and blundering forefathers should have *happened* to hit, without any real data and logical method at their disposal, upon infinitely profound truths in complex matters which even today are unreachable. When we know that the reason people believe in a thing is false, we have a right to guess that the belief itself is exceedingly flimsy. Today all the traditional assumptions regarding "god", "spirit", "immortality", etc. etc. are pretty clearly traced to delusive conditions, fears, and wishes of primitive life. *If such things as gods, immortality, etc. did exist, they could never have been really known by the people who made the myths.* The myths, conclusively, are false—being natural products of known forms of illusion. And it would be damned improbable if there were any real phenomena existing unknown in space and happening to correspond to these error-born myths! Looking at it another way—simply forget that the old myths do exist, since of course in sizing up an intrinsic situation we must judge it on its own merits and refuse to take the word of any biassed persons. Glance over the universe today, *in the light of the knowledge of today,* and see if anything in it or pertaining to it suggests such things as a central consciousness, purpose, ghost-world, or possibility of "life" when life's vehicle is destroyed. No person, thus facing the facts directly and keeping free from the mythical lore of the past, could possibly read into the cosmos the extravagant, irrelevant, clumsy, improbable, and unnecessary things which traditional theologians believe. There is no evidence whatsoever for the existence of the supernatural—*and where no positive evidence exists,* it is mere pedantry to continue to take an extravagant and gratuitous improbability seriously *merely for lack of definite negative evidence.* Theoretically, the improbability *may* be *possible*—but the chances are so overwhelmingly infinitesimal that they can well rank as negligible. Practically speaking, there is no earthly reason for believing in a deity, immortality, etc. In the absence of any official evidence, it is silly to give the *least* probable explanation an equal footing with explanations which are *really* probable. What little we know of physics and biology leads us to regard life as a form of energy—a mode of motion—in a material physiological medium. When the material medium has ceased to exist, there is no sense in assuming that the form of motion or energy determined by its parts can continue to exist. Thus according to everything which we do know, "immortality" is a wild improbability; and I am not so naïve—or so pedantic—as to accept *improbabilities* on equal terms with *probabilities.* What we learn from the study of small sections of force and matter indicates that phenomena are caused by the mutual interaction of forces following fixed patterns inherent in the cosmic order. This holds good for all the phenomena we know—on every conceivable scale. Lacking any contrary evidence, we may *reasonably guess* that this mutual interaction holds good for phenomena on *any* scale—even the largest—so that the entire cosmos may be provisionally considered as a huge field of force without beginning or ending, whose automatic and kaleidoscopic rearrangements of parts constitute the physical and material phenomena of which we can glimpse a fraction. Nobody tries to elevate this *reasonable guess* into a positive dogma, but one is certainly justified in saying that it is *probably* a lot nearer the truth than are the wild myths which were born of primitive ignorance *and which insist on being judged arbitrarily without consultation of the real natural evidence around us.* I certainly can't see any sensible position to assume aside from that of *complete scepticism tempered by a leaning toward that which existing evidence makes most probable.* All I say is that I think it is *damned unlikely* that anything like a central cosmic will, a spirit world, or an eternal survival of personality exist. They are the most preposterous and unjustified of all the guesses which can be made about the universe, and I am not enough of a hair-splitter to pretend that I don't regard them as arrant and negligible moonshine. In theory I am an *agnostic,* but pending the appearance of radical evidence I must be classed, practically and provisionally, as an *atheist.* The chances of theism's truth being to my mind so microscopically small, I would be a pedant and a hypocrite to call myself anything else.

Religious Indoctrination

[The following is an extract from a letter to Maurice W. Moe (3 August 1931), in which Lovecraft condemns the brainwashing of the young into religious belief. He maintains that children can be indoctrinated into any belief, however preposterous, if the indoctrination is begun at an early enough age.]

I doubt if S. A. L.[1] would have objected to your use of the immortality-myth so long as you kept it a personal sentiment and did not imply that *he* harboured such a primitive delusion. This ancient legendry has much poetick value and decorative grace when rationally used in the manner of all such legendry—as historic ornament recalling the moods and convictions of our uninformed ancestors in situations similar to those which evoke the citations. I have no patience with untraditional moderns who resent all primitive survivals in nomenclature and folklore; and am just as glad to tolerate Christian vestiges like Candlemas, Whitsuntide, the A.D. chronology, etc., as I am to tolerate those more authentic Aryan vestiges exemplified by names of the planets, constellations, and days of the week. Immortality is a pretty conception, and was natural enough to believe in when almost nothing was known of the details, relationships, relative nature, and proportions of the various objects and modes of motion in the universe. It still serves as a poetic symbol for those comparatively lasting effects produced by an exceptional individual on his environment, and as such has a permanent place in literature beside Pegasus, the Nine, Apollo, and other bits of obsolete imagination. Incidentally—I suppose it is very liberal in a surviving Protestant believer to accord a wicked infidel a place in Elysium! The papists would admit rascals like me and S. A. L. and Galpinius to purgatory, but to a reactionary hard-shell we are all foreordain'd to aeternal roasting. I think I'll have to go Calvinist, so that I can kid myself into thinking there's a place where I can *always* be warm enough! Seriously, though, this kind of thing is dead as a doornail among normal adults with a sense of humour and even the rudiments of a contemporary education. Even those who still hang on to theistic illusions have let most of the damnation trimmings go by the board. Whitehead—an actual Anglican cleric—is a good example.[2] He realises the silliness of "doctrines", and takes the mummery of churchianity as the mere allegory it properly is. It is amusing how closely Whitehead and I agree on almost all social and political points—splitting up only when a scientific view of the causes and directions of natural action are concern'd. The dull and devastating piety and literalism of the backwoods evangelical are destined to survive only in intellectually retarded areas like Tennessee, Mississippi, Iowa, etc., once the elder generation of childhood-biassed standpatters dies off in the ordinary course of events. That lower class among whom contemporary education is not diffused—and who will therefore continue to hand down a naively theistic tradition—are now overwhelmingly Catholic. To think clearly about the cosmos in the light of contemporary information is to abandon any possibility of believing in the fantastic and capricious orthodoxies of yesterday—be they Buddhistic, Judaic, Christian, Hindoo, Mahometan, or any other brand. More liberal wish-delusions, however, will undoubtedly last for several generations more—or until the race has lost that emotional dependence on mythic values...which the earlier centuries of primitive ignorance and fanciful speculation have bred into it. Some of us—as individuals—have lost this primitive dependence already; but we can more or less understand its survival in others—especially since we are ourselves full of primitive and vestigial feelings in other directions . . . . . feelings which (like worship of pageantry, exaltation of the family, love of hunting and fishing, etc.) are no less poignant because of our understanding of their purely mundane and fortuitous origin, and purely relative and transient significance as environmentally adjustive factors. Thus I know what you *mean* when you speak of the illusion of immortality as something emotionally "satisfying"; though to one of the contemporary milieu the element of emotional satisfyingness or its reverse *has nothing whatever to do with the question of a theory's truth or falsity* . . . . . experience and observation having taught us the complete unreliability of the emotions (which bring different and sometimes opposite conclusions to different persons) as a guide or interpreter of the external world. Moreover—the conventional emotional biasses toward immortality and cosmic purpose are themselves very largely accidental results of traditions rather than basic attitudes, as we may see by comparing the moods of different types and individuals—older and younger, unsophisticated and sophisticated. No level-headed modern either wants to be "immortal" himelf (gawd, what boredom!) or to have his favourite characters immortal. Each appears for a second in the pattern and then disappears . . . . . and what of it? What more could anybody not filled up with infantile myth expect or even dream of? It is overwhelmingly true that no sane adult, confronted with the information of today, could possibly think up anything as grotesque, gratuitous, irrelevant, chimerical, and unmotivated as "immortality" unless bludgeoned into the ancient phantasy by the stultifying crime of childhood orthodox training. Religionists openly give away the fakery of their position when they insist on crippling children's emotions with specialised suggestion anterior to the development of a genuine critical faculty. We all know that *any* emotional bias—irrespective of truth or falsity—can be implanted by suggestion in the emotions of the young, hence the inherited traditions of an orthodox community are absolutely without evidential value regarding the real *is-or-isn'tness* of things. Only the exceptional individual reared in the nineteenth century or before has any chance of holding any genuine opinion of value regarding the universe—except by a slow and painful process of courageous disillusionment. If religion were true, its followers would not try to bludgeon their young into an artificial conformity; but would merely insist on their unbending quest for *truth,* irrespective of artificial backgrounds or practical consequences. With such an honest and inflexible *openness to evidence,* they could not fail to receive any *real truth* which might be manifesting itself around them. The fact that religionists do *not* follow this honourable course, but cheat at their game by invoking juvenile quasi-hypnosis, is enough to destroy their pretensions in my eyes even if their absurdity were not manifest in every other direction. Of course, their policy is the habitual ostrich-act of all primitive thinkers. When they see that honest openness to evidence does not incline their children toward the preferred system of myths, they do not behave like civilised beings and question the validity of the myths, but turn about and try to cripple the mental receiving apparatus of their children until the poor mites duplicate the accidental bias of their misinformed elders and forcibly acquire the same set of meaningless moods and obsolete prejudices. Thus each of the deeply-seated myth-systems carries on—the little Hindoo becoming a Brahma-worshipper like papa, the little Moslem continuing the ancestral whine to Allah, the little Yankee intoning nasal psalms to the god or demigods of the Christians, the little Jap burning more and more incense at Shinto shrines . . . . . and so on . . . . . and so on . . . . . ad infinitum . . . . . ad absurdum . . . . . and pretty soon the solar system will play out, and nobody in the cosmos will know that there has ever been any earth or human race or Brahmins or Moslems or Christians or Shintoists or such . . . . . dust to dust . . . . . and the ironic laughter of any entity which may happen to be watching the cosmos from outside . . . . . ho, hum!

III. RELIGION AND SCIENCE

Idealism and Materialism—A Reflection

[The following essay was first published in the *National Amateur* (July 1919). (The issue did not actually appear until the spring of 1921, so the essay could have been written—and probably was written—in late 1920.) It reflects Lovecraft's absorption of the work of nineteenth-century anthropologists who had convincingly argued that religious belief is the inevitable outgrowth of primitive humanity's encounter with natural forces it does not understand, including the phenomenon of dreams.]

Human thought, with its infinite varieties, intensities, aspects, and collisions, is perhaps the most amusing yet discouraging spectacle on our terraqueous globe. It is amusing because of its contradictions, and because of the pompousness with which its possessors try to analyse dogmatically an utterly unknown and unknowable cosmos in which all mankind forms but a transient, negligible atom; it is discouraging because it can never from its very nature attain that ideal degree of unanimity which would make its tremendous energy available for the improvement of the race. The thoughts of men, moulded by an innumerable diversity of circumstances, will always conflict. Groups may coincide in certain ideas long enough to found a few definite intellectual institutions; but men thinking together in one subject differ

44

in others, so that even the strongest of such institutions carries within itself the seed of its ultimate downfall. Conflict is the one inescapable certainty of life; mental conflict which invariably becomes physical and martial when the intellectual breach attains sufficient width and the opposing minds are divided into factions of suitable proportions. Followers of the "world brotherhood" and "universal peace" delusion would do well to remember this scientific truth, grounded on the basic psychological nature of man, before deciding to continue in their always absurd and often disastrous course.

Most decided and obvious of all the eternal conflicts of human thought is that between the reason and the imagination; between the real and the material, and the ideal or spiritual. In every age each of these principals has had its champions; and so basic and vital are the problems involved, that the conflict has exceeded all others in bitterness and universality. Each side, having its own method of approach, is impervious to the attacks of the other; hence it is unlikely that anything resembling agreement will ever be reached. Only the impartial, objective, dispassionate observer can form a just verdict of the dispute; and so few are these observers, that their influence can never be great.

Man, slowly coming into existence as an efflorescence of some simian stock, originally knew nothing beyond the concrete and the immediate. Formerly guided by reflex action or instinct, his evolving brain was an absolute blank regarding everything beyond those simple matters of defence, shelter, and food-procuring whose exigencies had brought it into being. As this primal brain developed along the path of the original impelling force, its intrinsic strength and activity outstripped the material which it had to feed upon. Since no sources of information were in existence to supply it, its dawning curiosity perforce became inventive; and the phenomena of Nature began to be interpreted in such simple terms as a nascent race could devise and comprehend. The sun was good. Men were comfortable when it was present, uncomfortable when it was absent. Therefore men should act toward the sun as they might act toward a chieftain or pack-leader who was able to confer and withdraw favours. Leaders give favours when people praise them or give them presents. Therefore the sun should be praised and propitiated with presents. And so were born the imaginative conceptions of deity, worship, and sacrifice. A new and wholly illusory system of thought had arisen—the spiritual.

The development of an ideal world of imagination, overlying and trying to explain the real world of Nature, was rapid. Since to the untutored mind the conception of impersonal action is impossible, every natural phenomenon was invested with purpose and personality. If lightning struck the earth, it was wilfully hurled by an unseen being in the sky. If a river flowed toward the sea, it was because some unseen being wilfully propelled it. And since men understood no sources of action but themselves, these unseen creatures of imagination were endowed with human forms, despite their more than human powers. So rose the awesome race of anthropomorphic gods, destined to exert so long a sway over their creators. Parallel illusions were almost innumerable. Observing that his welfare depended on conformity to that fixed course of atomic, molecular, and mass interaction which we now call the laws of Nature, primitive man devised the notion of divine government, with the qualities of spiritual right and wrong. Right and wrong indeed existed as actualities in the shape of conformity and non-conformity to Nature; but our first thinking ancestors could conceive of no law save personal will, so deemed themselves the slaves of some celestial tyrant or tyrants of human shape and unlimited authority. Phases of this idea originated the monotheistic religions. Then came the illusion of justice. Observing that exchange is the natural basis of human relations, and that favours are most frequently granted to those who give favours, man's imagination extended the local principle to the cosmos, and formed the sweeping conclusion that boons are always repaid by equal boons; that every human creature shall be rewarded by the powers of governing gods of Nature in proportion to his good deeds, or deeds of conformity. This conclusion was aided by the natural greed or desire of acquisition inherent in the species. All men want more than they have, and in order to explain the instinct they invoke an imaginary "right" to receive more. The idea of retribution and divine punishment was an inevitable concomitant of the idea of reward and divine favour.

This element of desire played a vast part in the extension of idealistic thought. Man's instincts, made more complex by the added impressions received through the nascent intellect, in many cases developed novel physical and mental reactions; and gave rise to the isolated phenomena of emotion. Emotion, working hand in hand with imagination, created such illusions as that of immortality; which is undoubtedly a compound of man's notions of "another world" as gained in dreams, and of the increasing horror of the idea of utter death as appreciated by a brain now able to comprehend as never before the fact that every man must sooner or later lose forever his accustomed pleasures of hunting, fighting, and lying before his favourite tree or cave in the sun. Man does not want to lose these pleasures, and his mind seeks an escape from the unknown and perhaps frightful abyss of death. It is doubtful if the savage, remembering nothing but life, can conceive of absolute non-existence. He finds false analogies like the vernal resurgence of plant life, and the beautiful world of dreams, and succeeds in persuading his half-formed intellect that his existence in the real world is but part of a larger existence; that he will either be re-born on earth or transplanted to some remote and eternal dream-world. Later on the illusion of justice plays a part in the comedy; and man, failing to find abstract equity in actual life, is glad to invent a future life of repayment and adjustment according to merit.

With such a beginning, we need not marvel at the development of an elaborate and highly cherished system of idealistic philosophy. The advance of the intellect without previous scientific knowledge to guide it had the effect of strengthening emotion and imagination without a corresponding strengthening of ratiocinative processes, and the immense residue of unchanged brute instinct fell in with the scheme. Desire and fancy dwarfed fact and observation altogether; and we find all thought based not on truth, but on what man wishes to be the truth. Lacking the power to conceive of a mighty interaction of cosmical forces without a man-like will and a man-like purpose, humanity forms its persistent conviction that all creation has some definite object; that everything tends upward toward some vast unknown purpose or perfection. Thus arise all manner of extravagant hopes which in time fasten themselves on mankind and enslave his intellect beyond easy redemption. Hope becomes a despot, and man comes at last to use it as a final argument against reason, telling the materialist that the truth cannot be true, *because it destroys hope.*

As the complexity of the mind increases, and reason, emotion, and imagination develop, we behold a great refinement, subtilisation, and systematisation of idealistic thought. In the interim aesthetic and intellectual interests have arisen, demanding improvements and concessions in the dominant religions or superstitions of man. Idealising must now be made to conform to the actual facts which have been unearthed, and to the quickened sense of beauty which has grown up. At this stage the great civilisations are forming, and each fashions one or more highly technical and artistic scheme of philosophy or theology. At first the advances tend to confirm the idealistic notion. Beauty breeds wonder and imagination, whilst partial comprehension of the magnitude and operation of Nature breeds awe. Men do not pause to question whether their gods could in truth create and manage a universe so vast and intricate, but merely marvel the more at gods who are able to perform such cosmic prodigies. Likewise, each thing on earth becomes merely the type of some imaginary better thing, or ideal, which is supposed to exist either in another world or in the future of this world. Out of the pleasantest phases of all objects and experiences imagination finds it easy to build illusory corresponding objects and experiences which are *all pleasant.* Whilst all mankind is more or less involved in this wholesale dreaming, particular nations develop particularly notable idealistic systems, based on their especial mental and aesthetic capacity. Here Greece, foremost of cultural centres, easily leads the rest. With a primitive mythology of unexcelled loveliness, she has likewise the foremost of later idealistic philosophies, that of Plato. It is this Platonic system, sometimes operating through the clumsy covering of an alien Hebraic theology, that forms the animating force in idealism today.

The idealists of today form two classes, theological and rationalistic. The former are frankly primitive, and use the crudest and least advanced methods of argument. The latter adopt an outwardly scientific attitude and honestly believe themselves to be working from facts alone, yet are overwhelmingly influenced by the illusions of human perfectibility and a better world. In clinging to these hoary fancies, they generally seize upon the rather recently discovered and indubitably proven law of evolution to sustain them; forgetting the infinite slowness of the process, and overlooking the fact that when evolution shall have really affected our descendants to any appreciable degree, they will no longer belong to the human race, mentally or physically—any more than we belong to the simian race. Of the two idealistic types, the theological deserves respect for its accomplishments, the rationalistic for its intentions. Religion has undoubtedly been the dominant factor in facilitating human relations and enforcing a moral or ethical code of practical benefit in alleviating the sufferings of mankind. The human reason is weak in comparison to instinct and emotion, and up to the present these latter forces, in the guise of theology, have proved the only effective restraint from the disorders of utter licence and animalism. The percentage of men civilised and governed by reason is still relatively slight. True, certain religious have claimed exclusive credit. Christianity, for example, claims to have civilised Europeans; whereas in cold truth it is Europe which has civilised Christianity. The faith of Christus, adopted for political reasons by the Imperator Constantinus, was forcibly seated in power, whence it naturally assimilated to itself all the characteristics of the Graeco-Roman culture of the later Empire and of the European nations which rose from that Empire's ashes; a culture which would have elevated to supreme dignity any religion similarly linked with it. But despite such excessive claims, it remains fairly clear that some form of religion is at least highly desirable among the uneducated. Without it they are despondent and turbulent; miserable with unsatisfied and unsatisfiable aspirations which may yet lead the civilised world to chaos and destruction. The rationalistic idealist neglects this practical consideration, and denounces religion in terms of unmeasured scorn because he knows it to be untrue. Just as the theist forgets that his faith may be fallacious though its effects be good, so does the idealistic atheist forget that his doctrine may have ill effects though it be true.[1] Both are governed by emotion rather than reason in their campaign of mutual destruction. Both cling to the primitive ideal of the ought-to-be. The rationalist is honest, and therefore to be admired. But when he allows his relentless and idealistic hostility to fallacy to lead him into a destructive course, he is to be censured. He should not pull down what he cannot replace; and since a preponderance of obvious evidence is against the possibility of rational self-government of the masses, he should obey the practical judgment which forbids a gardener to saw off the tree-limb in which he is sitting, even though it be dead and useless save as a support. In his passionately intense and narrowly single-minded crusade against religion, the militant atheist shews himself as unbalanced an idealist as the Christian fanatic. Like the latter, he is following up one idea with febrile ardour and conviction; forgetting general conditions and the relative unimportance of truth to the world. Usually he acts in protest against the many undeniable evils of religion; evils which are outweighed by good effects, and which at worst are no graver than the evils inseparable from an atheistical code. It is this crusade against irremediable evils which stamps the idealist of every kind as childish. To fancy that age-old principles can be improved suddenly, or to fancy that the necessary little hypocrisies and injustices of ordinary life form a pretext for overturning the whole social structure, is in truth puerility of the most pitiful sort. The spectacle of Christians and idealistic atheists in mortal combat is indeed grotesque—one thinks of such things as the battles of the frogs and mice, or of the pygmies and the cranes.

The materialist is the only thinker who makes use of the knowledge and experience which ages have brought to the human race. He is the man who, putting aside the instincts and desires which he knows to be animal and primitive, and the fancies and emotions which he knows to be purely subjective and linked to the recognised delusions of dreams and madness, views the cosmos with a minimum of personal bias, as a detached spectator coming with open mind to a sight about which he claims no previous knowledge. He approaches the universe without prejudices or dogmata; intent not upon planning what should be, or of spreading any particular idea throughout the world, but devoted merely to the perception and as far as possible the analysis of whatever may exist. He sees the infinity, eternity, purposelessness, and automatic action of creation, and the utter, abysmal insignificance of man and the

50

world therein. He sees that the world is but a grain of dust in existence for a moment, and that accordingly all the problems of man are as nothing—mere trifles without relation to the infinite, just as man himself is unrelated to the infinite. He sees through the feeble fallacy of justice, and perceives the absurdity of the doctrine of an immortal personality, when in truth personality and thought come only from highly organised matter. He recognises the impossibility of such things as vague, uncorporeal intelligences—"gaseous vertebrates", as Haeckel wittily called them.[2] But while thus disillusioned, he does not fall into the rationalistic idealist's error of condemning as wicked and abnormal all religious and kindred benevolent fancies. Looking beyond the bald facts of atheism, he reconstructs the dawn of the human mind and perceives that its evolution absolutely necessitates a religious and idealistic period; that theism and idealism are perfectly natural, inevitable, and desirable concomitants of primitive thought, or thought without information. That they are still desirable for the many he accepts as a plain consequence of man's backward and atavistical nature. Actually, it can be shewn that man has made but little progress since the dawn of history save in facilities for physical comfort. What arouses the materialist to conflict is not the existence of idealism, but the extent to which idealists obtrude their illusions upon thinking men in an endeavour to befog the truth. Truth, be it pleasant or unpleasant, is the one object of the materialist's quest—for it is the only object worthy of the quest of an enlightened mind. He seeks it not to spread it and wreck happiness, but to satisfy the craving of his intelligence for it; to establish his right to the position of a rational man. When theists or atheistical idealists try to force their childish doctrines down the throat of realistic thinkers, the trouble begins. With the humble and unobtrusive church or the quiet and undemonstrative Utopian the materialist has no quarrel. But when either of these adopts arrogant tactics and seeks to discredit a philosophy which is honest, quiet, and sincere, the eternal enmity of dissimilar thought once more becomes manifest. No manly reasoner will tamely allow himself to be lulled into mental inactivity by the emotional soothing-syrup of faith, be it faith in a supernatural goodness, or a non-existent perfectibility of humanity.

Perhaps it is in the ethical field that materialists clash most decidedly with idealists; and curiously so, since in most cases the difference is one of approach rather than of actual code. Idealists believe in a right and wrong distinct from Nature, and therefore invent something they call "sin", building up a highly artificial system of mythology around it. They measure man's acts not by the standard of practical value in promoting the comfort and smooth existence of the race, but by imaginary ideals of their own construction. That materialists should not believe in this mythical system of ideals enrages idealists vastly, yet when both come to apply their codes of moral government, a surprising similarity is shewn. The fact is, that on the one hand ideals are largely formed with Nature as a pattern; whilst on the other hand, an efficient, practical code of ethics must always demand a bit more than it expects. An harmonious and workable moral system must satisfy as many aspects of Nature as possible, and accommodate itself to the peculiarities of the age and place. Where an idealistic code is well grounded, the materialist leaves it unaltered as a matter of sound common sense. Where it is not, he consults Nature, history, and good taste, and advocates a system most nearly in accord with these things. A study of history will shew that the basic moral ideals of the white race have been but little affected by its beliefs. Some systems bring out certain virtues more strongly than others, and some conceal vices more cleverly than others; but the general average is about the same. Of course, practical enforcement is another matter; and here the sincere materialist concedes the palm to religion. Superstition is stronger than reason, and a code will best touch the masses if sustained by supposed divine authority. In the case of our own Anglo-Saxon code, no honest materialist would wish to cause any marked alteration. With a little less Sabbatarianism and exaltation of meekness, the existing system would be admirably suited to natural wants, and even these slight defects are now wearing rapidly away. If at the present time we complain at the tendency of the church to assume a position of ostentatious moral guardianship, it is because we perceive the signs of its decay, and wish to preserve its ethical legacy as best we can in a rationalistic manner. We do not wish to see faith and morals so inextricably intertwined that the latter will collapse with the former.

Beyond the sphere of simple conduct lies the question of one's attitude toward life as a whole. That the philosophy of materialism is pessimistic, none can deny; but much may be said in favour of a calm, courageous facing of the infinite by the resigned, disillusioned, unhoping, unemotional atom as contrasted with the feverish, pathological struggle and agony of the Christian mind, coping desperately with the mythical shadows and problems it has invented, and agitated by emotions which idealism has overstimulated instead of repressing as emotions should be repressed. The materialist has nothing to lose; the idealist is eternally suffering the pangs of disillusionment. And even the boasted theological "peace that passeth all understanding"[3] is a weak, hollow thing as compared with the virtuous materialist's pride in an unshackled mind and an unsullied honour. If idealism really lived up to its promises, conditions might be otherwise; but no fallacy can wholly envelop the human mind, and there are terrible moments when even the unprepared intellect of the idealist is brought face to face with the truth about the cosmos and the lack of divine justice, purpose, and destiny.

Idealism as we know it today bases itself on the false premise that emotion forms under certain conditions a perfect substitute for reason in imparting positive knowledge. Mr. Dryden expressed this sentiment with great vividness at the beginning of his "Religio Laici":

> "And as those nightly tapers disappear
>
> When day's bright lord ascends our hemisphere;
>
> So pale grows Reason at Religion's sight,
>
> So dies and so dissolves in supernatural light."[4]

Religious persons will assure you that they *know* their faith to be true by means of sensations and intuitions *too deep to be expressed*. The materialist cannot but smile at this readiness to accept hallucinations as evidence. Those who make these assurances forget that *other* religions have undergone the same emotional experiences, and are equally certain that their respective faiths are the only true faiths; and they forget that many a man in bedlam has the certain belief that he is Alexander, Caesar, or Napoleon. The subjective is always vague, variable, and visionary. It is based on false mental images like those of dreams, and can easily be proved to have no weight whatsoever in imparting facts, or distinguishing truth from error. The writer can cite a subjective childhood fancy of his own which illustrates the false position of the intuitive theist. Though the son of an Anglican father and Baptist mother, and early accustomed to the usual pious tales of an orthodox household and Sunday-school, he was never a believer in the prevailing abstract and barren Christian mythology. Instead, he was a devotee of fairy tales and the Arabian Nights' Entertainments; none of which he believed, but which seemed to him fully as true as the Bible tales, and much more attractive. Then, at an age not much above six, he stumbled on the legends of Greece—and became a sincere and enthusiastic classical pagan. Unlearned in science, and reading all the Graeco-Roman lore at hand, he was until the age of eight a rapt devotee of the old gods; building altars to Pan and Apollo, Athena and Artemis, and benignant Saturnus, who ruled the world in the Golden Age. And at times this belief was very real indeed—there are vivid memories of fields and groves at twilight when the now materialistic mind that dictates these lines *knew absolutely that the ancient gods were true.* Did he not see with his own eyes, beyond the possibility of a doubt, the graceful forms of dryads half mingled with the trunks of antique oaks, or spy with clearness and certainty the elusive little fauns and goat-footed old satyrs who leapt about so slyly from the shadow of one rock or thicket to that of another? He saw these things as plainly as he saw the antique oaks and the rocks and the thickets themselves, and laughed at unbelievers, *for he knew.*[5] Now he realises that he saw these things with the eye of imagination only; that his devotion to the gods was but a passing phase of childish dreaming and emotionalism, to be dissipated with time and knowledge. But he has today every jot of evidence for Graeco-Roman paganism that any Christian has for Christianity, any Jew for Judaism, any Mahometan for Mahometanism, or any Lodge for Spiritualism.[6] What mixture of crude instinct, desire, illusion, fancy, auto-hypnotism, delirium, and aesthetic fervour is the religious belief of the average theist! Much of the zeal he displays is undoubtedly derived from a perversion or modification of rather baser instincts, about which a psychologist of the Freudian type could speak more authoritatively than the writer. This very connexion betwixt religious and other emotion should be significant to the observer. It is the less thoughtful and more passionate man or race that possesses the deepest religious instincts, as we see in the case of the negro. The colder and more highly developed mind of the European is the birthplace of materialism.

Idealism and Materialism! Illusion and Truth! Together they will go down into the darkness when men shall have ceased to be; when beneath the last flickering beams of a dying sun shall perish utterly the last vestige of organic life on our tiny grain of cosmic dust. And upon the black planets that reel devilishly about a black sun shall the name of man be forgotten. Nor shall the stars sing his fame as they pierce the aether with cruel needles of pale light. But who shall be so heedless of analogy as to say that men, or things having faculties like men, do not dwell on uncounted myriads of unseen planets that whirl about the far stars? Greater or lesser than our own their minds may be—probably some worlds hold duller creatures, whilst some hold beings whom we would call gods for their wisdom. But be their inhabitants greater or lesser than we, none can doubt that on every world where thought exists, there exist also the systems of Idealism and Materialism, eternally and unalterably opposed.

Remarks on Materialism

[The following is a series of extracts from three essays—"The
Defence Reopens!" (January 1921), "The Defence Remains Open!"
(April 1921), and "Final Words" (September 1921)—written for an
Anglo-American correspondence group called the Transatlantic
Circulator, whose members exchanged manuscripts of stories, essays,
and poetry and criticized them. Lovecraft sent several of his stories
and poems through the group; but at some point the discussion
turned toward religion and philosophy, and Lovecraft was presented
the opportunity of defending his views on religion, immortality, and
related issues. Late in life he prepared extracts from the three essays
under the title "Remarks on Materialism," but apparently never
made an effort to publish the composite work. The following is my
own set of extracts from the three essays. Although correspondence
by many members of the Transatlantic Circulator survives, none by
the Mr. Wickenden to whom Lovecraft chiefly addresses his
philosophical remarks are extant, so it is sometimes difficult to
follow the precise course of the argument. Nevertheless, it is clear
that Wickenden was maintaining a belief in the immortality of the
soul and denying that science had accumulated enough evidence to
overthrow the central tenets of the Christian religion. Lovecraft
presented strong arguments to the contrary.]

The Defence Reopens!

January 1921

Regarding the Wickenden objections to my philosophical views, I am afraid I cannot be as much impressed as I should be, since most of the points on which I am attacked are really points of language rather than belief.[1]* Mr. Wickenden jeers in a cocksure fashion at my use of the word *"know"*, when of course that word was employed with a full recognition of the metaphysical and epistemological difficulties involved. It is the only adequate word, though any philosophical user of it must concede that it is largely relative. And Mr. Wickenden forgets that the absence of certain knowledge militates as strongly against dogmatic theism as against dogmatic atheism; or rather, while not forgetting it, he uses it as propaganda for a set of opinions much less intrinsically probable than those he dismisses as unproven. One should not take too seriously a belittling of the scientific leaders who disposed of theism in the nineteenth century—but perhaps their overpraise by many justifies or explains an impulsive reaction against them. They were certainly not demigods, or even innovators in the ultimate sense. Materialism has represented man's most thoughtful attitude since the days of Leucippus and Democritus, and was the central phase of the Epicurean school. But Darwin, Huxley, Haeckel, and Spencer did perform a vast service in filling in details, systematising, and expounding. Their results were not necessarily perfect, for inaccuracy enters all speculations; yet to say they are "superseded" or "overthrown" is sheer nonsense. It is impossible to produce any subsequent discoveries which controvert their main tenets. Modern science has probed deeper, but the probing has not disestablished the principles. There is a difference between a developed theory and an overturned theory. The atomic theory of Dalton, for example, is not disturbed by the recent subdivision of the atom. The *etymology* of the word is embarrassed,[1] but

---

1*Mr. Bullen mentions my use of the phrase "vacuous and pompous idealists". This did not occur in the course of an argument, nor was it meant to apply to all idealists. It was designed to characterise a certain especially assertive school, to which Mr. Bayne's poem formed a delightful contrast.

so far as the reality of the "atom" as a chemical unit is concerned, very little has happened. "Atoms" exist and combine as Dalton discovered. It is only in the case of radio-activity that we encounter the results of the development.

In dealing with the relative values of reason and intuition Mr. Wickenden is equally sophistical. Common evidence shews him that intuition is as apt to be false as true—that it is [as] apt to lead to subsequently demonstrable errors as to facts, and that emotion is closely allied to it. He knows that both intuition and emotion are erratic, irregular, and frequently completely contradictory; that they depend upon individual wishes and hopes easily explainable on materialistic grounds, and that they inspire obvious hallucinations as often as they produce sensible convictions. Is a lunatic Caesar or Napoleon because his intuitions tell him so? Contrary to the cleverly introduced insinuation of Mr. Wickenden, emotion and intuition DO "fit into my beautiful symmetrical pattern". It would be impossible to conceive of the development of the intellect from the primitive neural functions of low organisms without the existence of these intermediate stages. They are *not* to be ignored, for they furnish important light on all biological and philosophical problems. The only rash thing is to accept their admittedly variable, contradictory, and nebulous evidence as a determinant of facts in opposition to genuine logic and reason, whose rigid consistency and reliability in every field cannot be disputed. A man may one day *feel* that there is a deity and another day *feel* that there is none. An Arab may *feel* that Mahomet is the only true prophet at the same time that an Englishman *feels* that Christ is. But none of these men can possibly differ as to the existence of land and water, or the sequence of the seasons. Reason has never yet failed. Intuition and emotion are constantly failing. Here is strong circumstantial evidence!

Mr. Wickenden asks how I "know" that oblivion awaits us. Again that needless objection to a word which *has* no *literal* meaning, and which is therefore permissible in this case. In reply, of course, I would have to say that while nothing in existence is certain, there is surely no ground for a notion as utterly extravagant and contrary to probability as that of immortality. We have no reason to think that the phenomena of consciousness and personality can arise from anything save complex organic evolution, or that they can exist apart from complex organic matter. All experience has taught us that consciousness and the organic brain are inseparable. A blow on the head can kill the qualities of consciousness and personality whilst the body and a few simple instincts vegetate on. The *person* is dead. Where is he—in heaven? And where were we before we existed—whence came the "immortal soul"? Likewise, since the notion of "soul" and immortality is so clearly akin to the conceptions of duality and eternity formed through dreams and dread of the unknown, what right have we to invent an artificial and less probable explanation, or to accept uncritically the animistic legends handed down from our savage and barbarian ancestors? In the face of such *probabilities*—all on the side of oblivion—it is rather disingenuous of Mr. Wickenden to call in the academic fact that nothing can be *known*. Still—that is true. We *know* nothing—surely nothing sufficient to justify the creation of a fanciful and elaborate eschatology! When we see a brain die and decay, is it more natural to assume that its functions have ceased, or to weave a story about the survival of the motions when the moving particles themselves are gone? Probability is not kind to Mr. Wickenden! But the question is open!!

As to the origin of a supposed deity—if one *always existed* and *always will exist,* how can he be developing creation from one definite state to another? Nothing but a *cycle* is in any case conceivable—a cycle or an infinite rearrangement, if that be a tenable thought. Nietzsche saw this when he spoke of the *ewigen wiederkunft.*[2] In absolute eternity there is neither starting-point nor destination.

Mr. Wickenden frankly amuses me when he compares my rejection of teleology to a small boy's discarding and condemning a book he cannot understand—amuses me, because that is an excellent comparison for his own acceptance of teleology! He sees a process of evolution in operation at one particular cosmic moment in one particular point in space; and at once assumes gratuitously that *all the cosmos* is evolving steadily *in one direction* toward a fixed goal. Moreover, he *feels* that it all must amount to something—he calls it a thing of "heroism and splendour"! So when it is shewn that life on our world will (relatively) soon be extinct through the cooling of the sun; that space is full of such worlds which have died; that human life and the solar system itself are the merest *novelties* in an eternal cosmos; and that all indications point to a gradual breaking down of both matter and energy which will eventually nullify the results of evolution in any particular corner of space; when these things are shewn Mr. Wickenden recoils, and imitating the small boy of his own metaphor, cries out that it's all nonsense—it just *can't* be so!! But what of the actual probability, apart from man's futile wishes? If we cannot prove that the universe means *nothing,* how can we prove that it means *anything*—what right have we to invent a notion of purpose in the utter absence of evidence? Of course our savage forefathers could not conceive of a cosmos without a purpose any more than they could conceive of one without an anthromorphic deity, but what place have their legends in 1921?

And then that Wickendenian sneer at my liking for Mark Twain's ethical precept—which was materialistic because it truly recognised no motive in man but basic selfishness.[3] Mr. W. says or furnishes evidence that it is Christian. I can furnish evidence that it is rationalistic, pre-Christian, and Confucian. It is merely a truth based on expediency, free for any ethical teacher to seize and use, be he theistic or atheistic.

At the end of his discourse Mr. Wickenden professes himself the complete agnostic and relies on circumstantial evidence. I am content to follow his method, though such evidence as I behold leads me in the opposite direction.

Chesterton is hard to take seriously in the field of science.[4] By manipulating the evidence—playing up trifles and minimising important facts—one may make a very brilliant case; but when a man soberly tries to dismiss the results of Darwin[5] we need not give him too much of our valuable time. The exact details of organic progress as described in "The Origin of Species" and "The Descent of Man" may admit of correction or amplification; but to attack the essential principle, which alone is of universal importance, is pathetic. And so in a lesser degree with Freud. The doctrines which Mr. Chesterton so sweepingly sets aside are indeed radical, and decidedly repellent to the average thinker. Certainly, they reduce man's boasted nobility to a hollowness woeful to contemplate. But it is our business merely to observe impartially the extent to which the new views coincide with known phenomena, as compared with views hitherto held. When we do this we are forced to admit that the Freudians have in most respects excelled their predecessors, and that while many of Freud's most important details may be erroneous—one should not be too hasty in substituting any single or simple instinct for the complex and dominant *wille zur macht*[6] as the explanation of man's motive force—he has nevertheless opened up a new path in psychology, devising a system whose doctrines more nearly approximate the real workings of the mind than any heretofore entertained. We may not like to accept Freud, but I fear we shall have to do so. It was only in the early seventeenth century that a Sizzi could refuse to look through Galileo's telescope for fear he would be convinced against his will of the existence of Jupiter's satellites!

The Defence Remains Open!

April 1921

I perceive that Mr. Bullen and his lieutenants are anxious to carry on the controversy regarding materialism and idealism, which is surely agreeable enough to me, however ill it may conform to the rules of the Circulator. If the practice of drawing on "outside talent" be permitted to both sides, it is possible that I may later introduce the arguments of a very brilliant young materialist—Alfred Galpin, Jr., 536 College Ave., Appleton, Wisconsin, President of the United Amateur Press Association. Mr. Galpin is at present a student at Lawrence College, but in spite of his youth is a person of attainments little short of marvellous—a genuine "boy prodigy". He is now only 19, but I consider him already the most remarkable human being of my acquaintance, and believe he will become in time a critic and philosopher of international reputation. Mr. Galpin is a lineal descendant of Capt. James Cook, the celebrated explorer, who was killed by natives in the Sandwich Islands in 1776. His opinions are for the most part identical with my own.

That idealists should turn from the defensive to the offensive is something which cannot but benefit discussion. The tactics of the two attitudes differ, and a question cannot be displayed in its fulness till each antagonist has assumed both positions. Idealists were formerly on the defensive because, as the heirs of primitive tradition, they were first in the field and held all the territory. In their citadel of hereditary strength they were besieged by the materialists, a school of later growth whose doctrines sprang not from savage conjecture but from scientific observation. Now the citadel is captured, and the thinking world is materialistic. Realising that man possesses no innate knowledge, and that any claim regarding invisible and improbable phenomena must be supported by evidence, the victorious materialists hold the citadel and await the assaults of idealism, which now strikes back to regain the territory it has lost. But the strokes are strangely feeble, for the weapons of idealism melt in the sun of discovery.

Mr. Wickenden continues to attack *me* with more success than he attacks the ideas I utter, which are not of my creating. He points out some apparent ineptitude of rhetoric whereby I seem to arrogate to myself the title of "scientist"—which I certainly did not wish or intend to do—and thereupon fancies he has destroyed those other men's theories which I merely repeated. When he declares it more improbable for carbonates to change to protoplasm than for an organic substance to possess a "soul" and "immortality", he shews such an apparent misunderstanding of the principles involved that I despair of mutual comprehension. Perhaps a repetition of some basic facts might be clarifying—helping to define the conditions in each of the two cases. In the first place, no one assumes any *volition* on the part of a piece of chalk or other inorganic compound to change its mode of internal motion to the organic and vital type. The change, when it first occurred, must have been merely a rearrangement of moving particles incidental to the cooling and contraction of the whole planet; with no "volition" save the blind churning of electrons which constitutes all cosmic existence in the ultimate sense. Let Mr. Wickenden see very clearly that no radical change is involved—that nothing is either created or destroyed. The first appearance of life on any planet need be nothing more than a *change of motion* among certain molecules, atoms, and electrons. There is nothing new or occult. Since 1828 organic compounds have been synthesised, and he is indeed a bold speculator who will deny the possibility of actual abiogenesis as a future achievement of chemistry. Utterly different is the absurd conception of a "soul" or "immortality"—so different that Mr. Wickenden's description of it as "comparatively easy" reads more like jest than like sober discussion. Remember that in theorising on the origin of life we have not had to consider anything more than a shifting of material particles. How, then, may we call it "easier" to assume in one wild guess the existence of a whole world of entity, distinct from any provable substance, giving no evidence of itself, and independent of the known laws of matter? If it was hard to conceive of life as the product of lifeless matter, is it indeed easier to conceive of the existence of an airy nothing which can have no source at all, but which is claimed without proof or probability to hover around certain substances for certain periods, and subsequently to retain the personality of the substance around which it last hovers? Or perhaps Mr. Wickenden thinks that the material body creates the "soul"—in which case it would be interesting to discover how he thinks the emanation can be non-material, or how— if it be energy and not matter—it can retain the personality of the parent matter. I will not accuse Mr. Wickenden of being so naive as to perpetrate the blunder of the "Lieut.-Colonel" of Mr. Bullen's cutting— the assumption that the radiant heat emitted by a flame perpetuates in any way the flame itself. That betraying metaphor is ammunition for the materialist; for just as a candle burns itself out in smoke, vapour, and waves of thermal energy, leaving nothing to perpetuate its own individual qualities, so must a human brain burn itself out at last, after sending out irrecoverable ether-waves which disperse to the uttermost recesses of infinity. The tissues and cells which produced the motions of consciousness and personality—"the soul"—finally break down and dissociate, turning to liquid and gaseous decomposition-products and leaving nothing to mark their former temporary assemblage and motions. Can we imagine a continuance of motion when the moving particles are gone? Can we imagine a "soul" in existence after its parent body is dispersed—a candle-flame still burning after its energy and incandescent particles are dispersed? Nothing in human mythology is more patently unthinkable, and yet Mr. Wickenden would have us compare this crude and impossible bit of animism with the wholly commonplace hypothesis that one kind of material motion may at some period have been changed to another kind of material motion! In considering the matter of material change—either that of a fish to a crocodile or of limestone to protoplasm—Mr. Wickenden is handicapped by his belief that internal volition and "divine" guidance are the only two possible alternatives. With this dogma he can get nowhere. He must recognise not only the element of chance in so-called natural selection, but also the fact that the initial change from inorganic to organic matter is probably accomplished by chemical and physical rather than biological laws. It is, in fact, only sensible to regard it as the transition from pure chemistry and physics to biology. Mr. Wickenden's difficulty in understanding why there should be any internal volition in organic types, such as that of a fish for dry land, would be removed if he would realise that all volition is merely a neural molecular process—a blind material instinct or impulse. The universal craving of the organic cell is for expansion of activity—an increase in those conditions which give it the most pleasurable excitation. This blind life-impulse is so clearly correlated with the general run of cosmic forces both organic and inorganic—gravitation, affinity, cohesion, etc.—that it needs no special explanation. There is no distinguishing feature in any of the various local modifications of the universal churning of matter through the endless cycles of the cosmos. An organic being blindly acts in whatever manner gives him the most satisfaction, and so the fish—vivified by the oxygen dissolved in its native waves—strains for as much oxygen as it can get, and eventually tends toward land and the free air. The previous environment and history of each group engaged in the automatic quest no doubt determines its degree of success. Likewise, to the impulse of the animal should be added the modifications of the environment. Perhaps it is too hasty to attribute all evolutional changes to internal causes, since many may result from the animal's struggle to adapt itself to changing surroundings. The recession or evaporation of a body of water, giving rise to a swamp, may be the cause of changing fishes to amphibia in the course of generations; just as the subsequent drying of the swamp into solid land may transform the amphibia to land animals—first of the lizard kind, then mammals, including man, and no one knows what later on, if the planet lasts long enough. Changes are accomplished by all sorts of selective processes, largely choice of mates, dictated by the environment and blind impulses of countless generations. Definite intelligent volition is out of the question, Mr. Wickenden to the contrary.

When Mr. Wickenden jumps to the conclusion that divine guidance must exist simply because there is no readily visible reason why a fish should spontaneously seek land, he is certainly displaying a vast eagerness to accept the more superficial conclusion before analysing the apparent objections which he finds in the other. It would be possible to cite many reasons which would drive fish to land. Should it be demonstrated that the oxygen of the air is an insufficient bait, much might be said for the *light* of the upper regions, with its increased possibilities of pleasurably affecting the eye. Mr. Wickenden displays his weakness in the assumption that fish are "perfectly comfortable" in water—an absurd statement, in view of the obvious lack of continuous comfort in all beings with complex neural development. There is in every phase of vertebrate organic life a constant chafing and unrest, since adaptation to the environment is never perfect. All life is struggle and combat—itself a disproof of divinity—and in this fray an organism fights both its fellows and its surroundings. When a certain act or change is of benefit in securing an advantage, and increasing the opportunities of pleasurable excitation, it is blindly persisted in through the universal tendency of following the line of least resistance. All organisms tend to do what secures them the most pleasure or best facilitates their continued existence; and in the end their course, determined by circumstance, produces various modifications of type. There is no conscious desire, no intelligent aspiration, no definite foreknowledge. It is all a process of stumbling in the dark—of recoiling from greater to lesser discomforts and dangers, and of groping for an increased amount of pleasures faintly tasted. To ignore this, and rush to the notion of divinity, is so rash that such a step may fairly be counted out of an argument. Mr. Wickenden depends on words rather than on facts and ideas, as witnessed in his really delicious epigram about 'explaining evolution'.

I hardly know whether a reply is needed for the statement regarding the anomalous expansion of water just above the freezing-point. Certainly this is an unusual thing, but no more so than countless others having no possible purposive significance. It is not definitely explained—but neither are dozens of other phenomena of molecular physics. Why are all the anomalies of science? Why do the satellites of Uranus move in a plane nearly perpendicular to that of the planet's orbit, and why does Neptune's satellite move backward? Why does the moon appear larger to the naked eye when near the horizon when micrometric measurement and theory unite in shewing the apparent disc as smaller? But I need not make a catalogue—it is too childish. No one talks of "intelligence" in these cases of phenomena whose causes are at present obscure. Why, then, does Mr. Wickenden make such a vital argument of the anomalous expansion of water? Simply because water happens to contain a few organisms edible by man, which it could not contain if its physical properties were less unusual! On this one chance circumstance Mr. Wickenden founds a system of theology, singles out the case of water from that of all the other anomalies in creation, and assumes that the most stable and important of chemical compounds received its properties solely in order that fishes might inhabit brooks! How inconsiderate of Nature not to fashion water so that man might walk through it and build railways on the floor of the Atlantic! The same "intelligence" that created brooks for fishes neglected to make all parts of the land habitable by man—strange oversight! Why are not the Sahara and the Antarctic Continent habitable, if it is the "divine" purpose to adapt everything to the sustenance of life? Conversely, what calamity would result if fishes did *not* inhabit brooks—or if lakes were permanently semi-glacial?

Mr. Wickenden is right in declaring that "it is easy to scoff at any attempted explanation of life, but tremendously difficult to offer any explanation that other people cannot scoff at". In truth, knowledge has not yet extended very far below the surface, so that continual readjustments of thought are necessary. Beyond a certain limit knowledge may be impossible to acquire with man's present sensory and intellectual equipment, so that in all likelihood the universe will never be explained. Perhaps it were wiser not to try, but merely to take life as it comes, enjoying the pleasure and forgetting the pain as best we can. Since, however, our curiosity does prompt us to make inquiries; it is certainly more sensible to build up our speculations humbly, step by step from the known to the unknown, than to cast aside probability and experience altogether and accept dogmatically and uncritically the primitive legends of early man—legends based on transparent analogies and personifications, and professing to solve offhand those cosmic mysteries which offer the least real evidence and involve the most intricate and gradual kind of investigation. All theories may indeed be open to scoffing; but surely those are weakest which claim most and have least corroboration, while those are strongest which depend most on solid observation and make the fewest claims regarding matters beyond actual knowledge. In the absence of proof, the likeliest theory is that which conflicts least with the small amount of knowledge we already have.

"Lieut.-Colonel's" Open Letter contains one point so comic that I cannot forbear comment. After devoting several paragraphs to a vigorous condemnation of materialists who deny "spirit" because it cannot be seen and measured, he fails utterly to shew that Nature contains any phenomena establishing the existence of such an invisible and immensurable force! I might as easily assert the existence of a new ethereal entity called XYZABC, which makes the comets move; and defy any man to *disprove* it. Surely it could not be detected and measured by "calipers and balances"—therefore it is *above* truth!!!

Coming now to the old *Atlantic Monthly* article, "Whither"[7] (in the General Discussion folio), I find much of genuine pathos. There is no real argument of importance in the harangue of the anonymous author, but the atmosphere of sorrow at the passing of the old illusions makes the whole complaint an absorbing human document. Certainly, there is much in the modern advance of knowledge which must of necessity shock and bewilder the mind accustomed to uncritical tradition. That the old illusions cheered and stimulated the average person to a more or less considerable degree cannot be denied—the dream-world of our grandsires was undoubtedly a sort of artificial paradise for mediocrity.

To supply deficiencies in real life there was an imaginary "soul life" or "inner life" which probably seemed very vivid and actual to the subject of the delusion, and which must have helped to render him insensible to the manifold pains of genuine existence. The phenomenon can be duplicated on a small scale by any imaginative person, and those who have succeeded in thus creating for the nonce an unreal world can fully appreciate the sense of relative security and peace existing among those who accepted deity and immortality as actual facts. It is a general objection to Christianity, that it stifled artistic freedom, trampled on healthy instincts, and set up false and unjust standards. On this assumption a friend of mine, Samuel Loveman, Esq., has written a magnificent ode "To Satan".[8] In truth, however, this stultifying effect injured only the most intelligent classes, who were capable of resisting it ultimately; so that we need not deny the narcotic comfort it brought to the less aspiring majority. The faith was, of course, in its details merely a symbol of that majority's own standards and hopes—for all religious systems are the outgrowths rather than rulers of the races which hold them. Just as paganism is the ideal aristocratic attitude—the cult of true strength and beauty—so was Christianity the bourgeois ideal; the *sklavmoral*[9] code of thrift and prudence. Its ultimate development was reached in the anaemic Massachusetts type of the nineteenth century— the Puritanical and Emersonian product which had so much "soul" that it mattered little. Nowadays these fellows, or their grandchildren, are amusing themselves with theosophy, "new thought", Christian Science, and Persian Bahaism.[10] They cannot tell facts when they meet them! But most of the old Christians were less fanatical, and have developed less fantastically. They held their old faith simply from lack of the recent scientific information which most clearly proves it false, so when the information gradually reached them as a result of the unparalleled discoveries of the past century, they simply modified their views and accepted the inevitable. When they saw that their castles were of air— that there 'really is no Santa Claus'—they did not cry or cover up their eyes and ears, but bore the disillusionment like grown men. There had, indeed, been rare imaginative comfort in the old beliefs—but facts are facts! The withdrawal of the "spiritual" drug acted like the withdrawal of liquor from some topers—occasionally causing them to rise to greater mental heights by frankly facing things as they are. But as some lament prohibition, others lament philosophical disillusionment—in both cases a somewhat agreeable false stimulant has been withdrawn. The change has been very subtle; more often tacit than open, and affecting the all-important subconscious springs of thought and action rather than the outward qualities of apparent belief. Of the modern materialists a good majority probably attend some church and consider themselves Christians. That is because most persons never think accurately and searchingly. Their beliefs mean little—what matters is the deep inward disillusionment whereby they feel the change and dare not trust what they trusted before. Regrets are absolutely futile. The change is inevitable, because the last century brought to light facts never suspected before; which not only upset all the old notions, but explain with considerable clearness the psychological and anthropological reasons those notions were held in the past. The suddenness of the change is not surprising—its seeds were sown in the splendour of the Renaissance, when thought was emancipated and scientific progress begun. New instruments, exciting new zeal and opening up new vistas, have appeared in logical succession; and minds formerly applied to other arts have joined in the quest for truth. The nineteenth and twentieth centuries mark the logical culmination of the advance of 500 years—the growth of philosophies on the new data—so that he who would order us back to superstition is like Canute commanding the waves. Unfortunately or not, the illusion of spirituality is dead among the thinking classes. A phase of primitive allegory has retreated into the past, and we must make the best of what we cannot help. If we tried to believe now we should feel the sham, and despise ourselves for it—we simply know better, like the small boy deprived of "Santa Claus". At the same time, we must not ignore the pathetic, sobbing intensity of the reaction among a certain emotionally delicate class. The wrench of disillusion is terrible for them, and according to their temperament they are driven either into blind occultism or passionate Christian apologetics. The author of "Whither" is of the latter type—seeking to stem the tide with sophistry, imperfect data, and weak logic. He weeps vainly for departed values, and pleads weakly for *continuity* in what he calls "spiritual evolution". Alas! he does not see that the "spiritual" is exploded, and that *continuity* is never possible in matters of *discovery*. Before America was discovered it was unknown—then suddenly it *was* known! And so with the facts overturning religion. Searching "Whither" for a real argument, the reader finds only one amidst the manifold question-beggings, sophistries, regrets, and gratuitous assumptions of values. And tragically enough that argument is so easily and fully answerable by natural science that it is no sooner uttered than nullified. "Why," asks the author, "may we not say, 'Here are certain persistent hopes, inner needs, longings, which we can explain only on the assumption that the universe is a universe of spirit?'" Because, the realist replies, all those hopes, longings, and alleged "needs" are natural attributes of a certain stage of primitive development, early implanted in man, and wholly explainable as products of his unfolding mind as it reacted to his surroundings and limited information. This matter of the explanation of "spiritual" feelings is really the most important of all materialistic arguments; since the explanations are not only overwhelmingly forcible, but so adequate as to shew that man could not possibly have developed without acquiring just such false impressions. The idea of deity is a logical and inevitable result of ignorance, since the savage can conceive of no action save by a volition and personality like his own. Animism could not be avoided by any ignorant mind familiar with dreams, and immortality is an easy step once a dual existence is admitted. The savage has always, so far as he can recall, lived—and he cannot picture a state of not living. In this matter of eternal life he is also guided by his dread of extinction—he has seen dead bodies, and cannot think that such will be the end of his consciousness. Desire becomes accomplished fact in his simple opinions. Then, seething through his crudely animal and emotional nature, are a thousand blind organic forces such as made his fish ancestors seek air and his amphibian ancestors seek the dry hills. His mind is not nearly so powerful as the primal, vestigial urges and currents that rack him, and when these are not drained by combative or other uses, they turn on the nervous system and produce the frenzies and wild hallucinations known as "religious experience". Freud has much to say of the share these primal urges play in forming thoughts when partly suppressed. As the savage progresses, he acquires experience and formulates codes of "right" and "wrong" from his memories of those

70

courses which have helped or hurt him. His imagination becomes able to create pictures artificially, and as he dwells on the things he likes best he gradually comes to believe in a possible state of things where everything is homogeneously delightful. He usually places these ideal conditions in the past and future, where disproof is impossible—thus we have the "Golden Age" and "Elysium". The "Garden of Eden" and "Heaven". Then out of the principle of barter comes the illusion of "justice"—and so on, till at length we behold a whole system of theistic and idealistic legendry, developed gradually during man's susceptible childhood, and fastened on him as a second nature by countless generations of inherited belief. There is nothing to wonder at in the long survival and hard death of such a system. Its overthrow comes only as a result of the most conclusive and gigantic array of contrary evidence. The wonderful thing is that it should have been extensively challenged by an important section of Greek philosophers as far back as Democritus. However—perhaps one should not wonder at *anything* Greek; the race was a super-race. In one way religion probably helped to defeat itself. By dividing and subdividing, and developing subtle and scholastic systems of dogmata, it acquired a tinge of rationality fatal to belief. The Papists with their blind faith are the exception. Then man's whole trend has tended to refine him and tone down the brute impulses whose excesses gave rise to extreme religious ecstasy. There is less primal vitality in modern civilised man—we fight less, seldom "run amok", and are generally more human and delicate. Greater delicacy means the subordination of simple protoplasmic cell-impulses to the more complex motions of cerebral tissue—the ascendancy of taste and reason over animal feeling—and as we thus grow away from the primitive, our chief urges toward religious grovelling are removed. All religious demonstrativeness and ceremony is basically orgiastic, as one may gather from the veiled or open symbolism of nearly every typical rite of every race.

But the survivors of Christianity take the whole question of modern change too seriously. Just how much of the possible decadence of this age may be traced to materialism it is impossible to say; at any rate, it cannot be helped. As a matter of fact, the connexion is probably other than causal. Progress and sophistication, arch-enemies of all illusion, have destroyed traditions of behaviour as well as of thought; and acting upon a sensitive and heterogeneous world have culminated in an inevitable bewilderment and realisation of futility. One cause may underlie decadence and materialism, but these two are sisters—not child and parent. No civilisation has lasted for ever, and perhaps our own is perishing of natural old age. If so, the end cannot well be deferred. On the other hand, we may be merely passing from youth to maturity—a period of more realistic and sophisticated life may lie ahead of us, filled with cynical resignation and dreams of languorous beauty rather than with the fire and faith of early life. We can neither predict nor determine, for we are but the creatures of blind destiny.

Materialism is not the tragedy—at least, not the utter tragedy—that idealists picture. It is grey rather than black, for even in the most idealistic ages a goodly share of the prevailing serenity came from physical and subconscious rather than conscious causes. No change of faith can dull the colours and magic of spring, or dampen the native exuberance of perfect health; and the consolations of taste and intellect are infinite. It is easy to remove the mind from harping on the lost illusion of immortality. The disciplined intellect fears nothing and craves no sugar-plum at the day's end, but is content to accept life and serve society as best it may. Personally I should not care for immortality in the least. There is nothing better than oblivion, since in oblivion there is no wish unfulfilled. We had it before we were born, yet did not complain. Shall we then whine because we know it will return? It is Elysium enough for me, at any rate. Altogether, we have depended less than we think on Christian mythology. The French have done without it for a long time, yet their realistic culture maintains its brilliancy, and the national temperament has sunk to no perceptible degree. Our race is younger, but it is fast growing up—and I am confident that the Saxon can face maturity as bravely as the Gaul. If history teaches aright, he should do even better; for who were the victors at Agincourt, Crécy, Poictiers, and Trafalgar[11]? Then, too, we overrate the religious influences we are losing. Stripping the past of its cloak of romantic rationalising and euphemism, we find that most human affairs have *always* been decided on wholly materialistic lines. Even the leading religious movements have their secret history—generally of a materialistic nature. The only human motive since the species has existed has been selfishness. If we are now less pious, we are also less hypocritical. One honest Nietzsche is worth a dozen mock-saints. And Greece, whose culture was the greatest of all, antedated Christianity and originated materialism.

Modern civilisation is the direct heir of Hellenic culture—all that we have is Greek. Since the transient Semitic importation of ascetic idealism has run its course, can we not recapture a trace of the old pagan lightheartedness that once sparkled by the Ægean? Surely we can think of life as having something of beauty, and only a glutton wants eternity.

Final Words

September 1921

Mr. Wickenden's latest controversial assault is very interesting, and I accept with contrition the correction regarding "sneers". As to the "know" controversy—I will let the objectionable polysyllables rest, and merely state that in my opinion (an opinion shared by increasing multitudes) there is no evidence whatever concerning an object or meaning in life and the universe. And in the absence of evidence, all assumptions are totally baseless; the idea of an object or meaning becoming absurd.

Mr. Wickenden tries to demolish this important argument by denying the obvious absurdity and incredibility of the common myths of soul, immortality, and teleology. In support of his contention he cites the many persons who, drawing their ideas from their empirical racial heritage rather than from abstract scientific truths, find the conception of materialism, annihilation, and purposelessness "utterly extravagant and contrary to probability". This move is very clever, but its force dissolves upon analysis. Mr. Wickenden's appeals are all to impression and metaphor—he rejects the obvious *because it is obvious,* and actually presents the spectacle of one defending the grotesque idea that the more improbable and indirect of two theories is to be preferred! He goes back to the age of the disputatious church fathers with their "credo quia impossibile est".[12] The phonograph metaphor is rhetorically brilliant— but that is all. Doubtless it could be "proved" in this way that Caruso himself was only a phonograph, and that we might still enjoy new songs from him if we could find the real singer behind his mortal form. But all this is futile. Metaphor and allegory are the smoke screen wherewith all mystics, theists, and obscurantists have shielded themselves from truth since the dawn of speculative thought. Materialism seems improbable only to those who think in terms of antique myths conceived in imperfect knowledge and utterly contrary to all the basic facts of science as subsequently discovered.

As to the matter of death and resuscitation—I had hardly expected this from Mr. Wickenden, who surely knows that many persons *have* been revived after a momentary cessation of heart-beats, and that true death is due either to a failure of the propelling energy or to a derangement of the organic mechanism. There IS, most decidedly, something missing from a body dead half an hour or even much less. Decomposition always begins at once, and it takes very little to ruin hopelessly the complex and delicate machinery of vital action. When a man dies by accident, as in drowning, there is always a question (a) as to whether the vital momentum suddenly lost can be successfully restored by the crude processes of artificial respiration, and (b) as to whether there be any loss due to the chemical and physical deterioration of the bodily machine. The loss is one either of matter or of energy. If there were a question of another loss—the loss of "soul", as Mr. Wickenden hints—one might with equal ease ask where the "soul" originally came from—a matter which Haeckel treats very cleverly and amusingly.[13]

To express incredulity that a chemical reaction could produce a Beethoven symphony proves absolutely nothing. In the first place, the reaction is probably more physical than chemical in its ultimate manifestation; but even assuming that it may all be chemical, we have before us merely a case of *complexity*. It seems to indicate a lack of constructive imagination when one cannot conceive of a material order involving all degrees of fineness in organisation, and rising eventually to the peak of what we know as psychic, intellectual, and aesthetic accomplishment. The steps between sounds and tears are more physical than chemical, and of course depend on the *working* of the vital cells. Why does not a dead man cry at sad music? . . . . Why does not a still dynamo give current? To argue that one may prove the existence of the human "soul" from the fact that corpses do not weep when the orchestra plays "Hearts and Flowers", is something hardly calculated to disturb the assurance of the mechanistic materialist! Mr. Wickenden avoids the ticklish question of the lower animal world. Here we have organisms for which not even the boldest theist tries to claim "souls"—yet among them we find psychic phenomena of a very advanced order. Even a Beethoven symphony affects many animals strongly—a case where Mr. W. would find difficulty in tracing the physico-chemical action connecting the sounds and the manifestations. One might ask, to the confounding of those who aver that men have "souls" whilst beasts have not, just what the difference may be betwixt the effect of music on man and on beast; and also just how the evolving organism began to acquire "spirit" after it crossed the boundary betwixt advanced ape and primitive human? It is rather hard to believe in "soul" when one has not a jot of evidence for its existence; when all the psychic life of man is demonstrated to be precisely analogous to that of other animals— presumably "soulless". But all this is too childish. When we investigate both ontogeny and phylogeny we find that man has both individually and racially evolved from the unicellular condition. Every man living was at the beginning of his life a single protoplasmic cell, whose simple reflex sensitiveness is the source of all the neural and psychic activity which later develops through increasing complexity of organisation. We can easily trace the whole process of development from the irritability of the simple cell-wall through various intermediate stages of spinal and ganglial activity to the formation of a true brain and finally to the manifestation of those complex functions which we know as intellect and emotion. This development occurs both pre-natally and post-natally in the individual, and can be followed with much exactitude. In the species, we can follow it hardly less exactly by means of comparative anatomy and biology. Haeckel's "Evolution of Man", in its final edition, leaves very little to be said.[14]

When Mr. Wickenden objects to my assumption that he dislikes to face the possibility of a mechanistic cosmos, he is of course not to be disputed; and I ask his pardon for having misrepresented his former utterances. But he is exceeding fact when he calls materialists "strange people" for asserting that most theists are afraid of the truth. This matter of "aletheiophobia"[15] (if I may coin an Hellenism) is something about which the theists themselves leave no doubt—it is they who loudly complain that the materialist is tearing away all the precious values and safeguards of life!

The Materialist Today

[The following essay was published in the October 1926 issue of *Driftwind,* a Vermont magazine edited by Lovecraft's friend Walter J. Coates. It was also issued separately as a 15-copy pamphlet, constituting one of the rarest of Lovecraft's publications. Lovecraft notes in a letter that the work was in reality a letter to Coates, and that Coates later asked Lovecraft if he could publish it as an essay. It is a compact exposition of Lovecraft's materialist philosophy.]

Today a fresh wave of interest in philosophical speculation has arisen. The dissolution of old doctrines under the influence of science in the nineteenth century gave rise for a time to a rational materialism of which Huxley and Haeckel were conspicuous exemplars; but the later crumbling of moral standards, amidst the dizziness of mental liberation, has brought about a sense of restlessness and cerebral panic, and for the moment we witness the amusing spectacle of a reactionary scrambling for shelter beneath the wing of a supernatural belief either blindly conceived without intelligent reflection, or tenuously modified to accommodate as many angles of scientific truth as can be accommodated by a system of extra-rational origin.

Hence spring Fundamentalism and Modernism:[1] both defensive emotional reactions against the ethical chaos of the present; and, as such, entitled to the sincere respect of all who realise that the sole beauty of life resides in its traditional patterns. It would not be the wish of any responsible materialist to destroy or combat the major social conditions at which these fervid believers are aiming; and the utmost attack of logic on faith serves only to replace an irrational with a rational reason for orderly life and thought.

The materialist denies that any standard is divine or absolute, and would free our conceptions of conduct from those supernatural fetters which impart a false perspective and cause the former believer to lose his moral sense as soon as he loses his faith. Conduct, of course, is only a side issue in the search for truth. But, so far as the modern materialist is interested in it at all, he merely recommends with gentle cynicism the adherence of each person to the ethical system in which he was reared, as constituting the only authentic source, in a purposeless cosmos without absolute standards, of those relative standards necessary to the orderly life and mental comfort of mankind.

Many specious arguments continue to be advanced by those labouring for a survival of religion. Fundamentalists, of course, do not argue; but the Modernists are very ingenious in adapting the language and conceptions of their ancient enemy, science, to their own uses, thus hoping to effect a reconciliation with that powerful adversary. Foremost among their contentions is that which affirms the existence of a "soul" and the truth of immortality by proclaiming mind a *thing* and thereupon invoking the scientific principle of the conservation of matter and energy to prove that it can never be destroyed—an argument, of course, which not only confuses the general mental principle with individual personality, but forgets that the law of conservation denies the fresh creation as well as the destruction of matter and energy, a point which would not allow for the birth of new souls! To the materialist, *mind* seems very clearly not a *thing*, but a *mode of motion* or *form of energy*.

Now, although the sum of energy in the universe is (speaking without reference to the very recent discoveries in intra-atomic physics and chemistry) virtually indestructible, we see very clearly that it is most eminently subject to transformations from one form to another.

Mechanical energy becomes electricity under the appropriate conditions, and, under other conditions, that electricity becomes light and heat. Nothing is *lost*, but all is *changed*.

Now I regard the vital principle as just such a form of energy—and *mind* is only one of the many complex manifestations of that principle. It is a product and attribute of certain forms and processes of matter; and when that matter is disintegrated, it ceases to exist—just as molecular heat ceases to exist upon the dispersal or disintegration of the material molecules which make it possible. Nothing is *lost,* any more than when electrical energy is transformed to luminous energy; but a complete metamorphosis occurs, and the identity of mind and life becomes effaced as the units of energy pass away in other forms—mostly radiant heat and other waves in the ether. Mind is no more immortal than a candle flame. The flame is just as *immortal,* if we wish to take a poetic view and reflect that the units of energy therein are never lost to the universe, but merely dissipated and incorporated into other forms and phenomena.

> "Imperious Caesar, dead and turn'd to clay,
> Might stop a hole to keep the wind away."[2]

One might add, as noted above, that ultra-modern discovery, as based upon the phenomena of radio-activity, has opened wide and strange vistas, and perhaps defeated *in the last analysis* the idea of the indestructibility of matter and energy. Whilst matter and energy are clearly indestructible so far as any hitherto understood principles are concerned, it seems increasingly clear that cosmic force and substance have other and deeper relations and limitations—whose kinship to the phenomena we know is like that of an hour-hand to a minute- or second-hand on a clock.

It seems, in the light of recent discoveries, that all matter is in a state of balance betwixt formation and disintegration—evolution and de-volution—and that the infinite cosmos is like a vast patch of summer sky out of which little cirrus clouds gather here and there, presently to be dissolved into blankness again. The universes we know correspond to the little cirrus clouds of that summer sky, being merely transient aggregations of electrons condensed from that field of ungrouped electrons which we call space, and soon to be dissolved into that space again. This process of formation and destruction is the fundamental attribute of all entity—it is infinite Nature, and it always has been and always will be. The world, life, and universe we know, are only a passing cloud—yesterday in eternity it did not exist, and tomorrow its existence will be forgotten. Nothing matters—all that happens happens through the automatic and inflexible interacting of the electrons, atoms, and molecules of infinity according to patterns which are co-existent with basic entity itself. The general idea is that of a kaleidoscope with its endless rearrangements—there is no object or purpose in ultimate creation, since all is a ceaseless repetitive cycle of transitions from nothing back to nothing again.

However, all this need give worry to none. The aspirations of the human spirit, so movingly cited by theists, are pretty enough in themselves; and one need neither go to the trouble of breaking them up and finding their physiological components (although that is relatively easy to do) nor impute to them a cosmic significance which, though poetic to imagine, is certainly not logically deducible from their existence and characteristics. It is most sensible just to accept the universe as it is, and be done with it. All is illusion, hollowness, and nothingness—but what does that matter? Illusions are all we have, so let us pretend to cling to them; they lend dramatic values and comforting sensations of purpose to things which are really valueless and purposeless. All one can logically do is to jog placidly and cynically on, according to the artificial standards and traditions with which heredity and environment have endowed him. He will get the most satisfaction in the end by keeping faithful to these things.

Religion and Relativity

[The following is an extract from a letter to Frank Belknap Long (20 February 1929). Long (1901–1994), a writer of fantastic fiction and poet living in New York, was one of Lovecraft's closest friends; they had come into correspondence in 1920 and had met on many occasions, especially when Lovecraft was living in New York (1924–26). Long, although generally an unbeliever, was at times inclined toward mysticism, and his deficiencies in scientific education occasionally betrayed him into making errors in both his philosophy and in his science fiction tales. Lovecraft's letter warns Long of being taken in by "Einstein-twisters" who are using contemporary advances in astrophysics to resurrect outmoded religious views. He then expounds a multiplicity of reasons for continued religious belief in spite of overwhelming evidence to the contrary.]

The actual cosmos of pattern'd energy, including what we know as matter, is of a contour and nature absolutely impossible of realisation by the human brain; and the more we learn of it the more we perceive this circumstance. All we can say of it, is that it contains no visible central principle so like the physical brains of terrestrial mammals that we may reasonably attribute to it the purely terrestrial and biological phaenomenon call'd *conscious purpose;* and that we form, even allowing

81

for the most radical conceptions of the relativist, so insignificant and temporary a part of it (whether all space be infinite or curved, and trans-galactic distances constant or variable, we know that within the bounds of our stellar universe no relativistic circumstance can banish the approximate dimensions we recognise. The relative place of our solar system among the stars is as much a proximate reality as the relative positions of Providence, N.Y., and Chicago) that all notions of special relationships and names and destinies expressed in human conduct must necessarily be vestigial myths. Moreover, we know that a cosmos which is eternal (and any other kind would be a paradoxical impossibility) can have no such thing as a permanent direction or goal; since such would imply a beginning and ending, thus postulating a larger creating and managing cosmos outside this one—and so on ad infinitum like a nest of Chinese boxes. This point remains the same whether we consider eternity as a measure of regular pattern-movements (time) or as a fourth dimension. The latter merely makes all these intimations of a cosmos which our senses and calculations present to us. We must admit at the outset that the spectacle gives us no indications of a central consciousness or purpose, and suggests no reason why a cosmos should possess such; that it renders the notion of special human standards and destinies absurd; and that it makes the idea of a permanent direction or goal improbable to the point of impossibility. *Theoretically* it *can* be almost anything—but when we have not the faintest shadow of reason for believing certain specific things exactly contrary to all the principles of probability and experience in our limited part of space, it becomes a piece of hallucination or affectation to try to believe such things. Here are we—and yonder yawns the universe. If there be indeed any central governor, any set of standards, or any final goal, we can never hope to get even the faintest inkling of any of these things; since the ultimate reality of space is clearly a complex churning of energy of which the human mind can never form any even approximate picture, and which can touch us only through the veil of local apparent manifestations which we call the visible and material universe. So far as analogy and probability go, there is strong presumptive evidence on the negative side—evidence based on the observation of small material systems like the electrons of an atom or the planets circling the sun. This evidence tells us that all small units of mass-energy are (that is, all humanly visible and conceivable presentations of such units are) rotating systems organised in a certain way and preserving a balance and dovetailing of functions, absolute regularity and the exclusion of chance, (and hence of volition or conscious action) and the infinite uniformity of this system of interlocking rotations and forms of regularity, seem to confront us wherever we delve beneath the surface; so that these circumstances actually form the sum total of all our knowledge of the composition and administration of infinity. To say that such an array of evidence suggests a central will, a one-way direction, and a special concern for any one of the infinitesimal temporary force-combinations which form incidents of the eternal cycles within cycles of constant rearrangement, is to utter simple and unadulterated damn foolishness. It is like saying that the descent of the thermometer on the 7th of January suggests a hot summer day on the morrow. It is simply self-hallucination to which no sane adult need feel obliged to listen without laughing. And there is scarcely less idiocy in the pitiful whine of the modern supernatural-dupe, that the discovery of the identity of matter and energy breaks down 18th century materialism and reopens the way for mystical myth-making. Nothing could be more contrary to fact. The collapse of cosmic dimensions supplies no iota of evidence or suggestion either for or against materialistic reason, whilst the elimination of matter as a separate entity is simply a step *toward the unification of all being and the consequent destruction of the myth of worker separate from work or goal separate from present position.* What these feeble-minded theists are howling about as a sudden victory for themselves is *really the materialist's trump card.* The poor fools think they have beaten him because they have seen the disappearance of that for which his *name* stood. It is characteristic of a tribe who have always dealt in words and myths alone to fancy their opponent is bound to the externals of an empty *word.* *Matter* indeed has been shewn to be a passing phase of *energy*—or the raw stuff of sheer entity as envisaged from our terrestrial and physical observation-point—*but what is this save a perfect confirmation of the basic essentials of Haeckelian monism?* Thus the *materialist,* now using that title in an historical sense only, emerges strengthened in his position as *an atheistical (or agnostic) monist.* He has sounded space a little deeper and found what he always finds on further penetration—simply *a profounder disintegration, and a profounder mechanistic impersonality.* Hitherto he has felt forced to *describe* entity somewhat; now he feels more and more able to swear to the absence of any purposeful *riddle* in creation, and to sum up all there is of cosmic existence and apparent purpose in one final sentence—*entity is, always has been, and always will be.* Of its detailed design and minute operative secrets he will never know. Of his relation to it he may guess very shrewdly *because his extreme insignificance makes him so small a part even of the infinitesimal fraction of infinity he can envisage.* He knows he is minute and temporary, because the local laws of his immediate milieu and mode of entity can be *tested conclusively for their small positive radius;* and in consonance with their unfailing applicability to time and space units which *even for human perception are small,* (that is, the earth's seasons, effect of heat and cold on organic life, etc.) can be extended over a slightly larger area in which the same conditions hold good (that is, the galactic universe, and time-reaches involving the birth and death of suns) and in which they shew with *absolute* accuracy the very brief span capable of being occupied by the history of terrestrial life past and present. Here is where the atheist makes an ass of himself trying to catch the theist by using the jargon of relativity. He tries to erase all our physical knowledge by pointing to the subjective nature of our relation to infinite time and space—forgetting that *the history of terrestrial life is not being reckoned against the background of infinity.* He is knocking over, for the purpose of crowing over a fake victory, a man of straw which he himself has set up. Nobody is trying to envisage infinity, for it very clearly can't be done. The atheist is merely shewing that man cannot reasonably occupy any considerable place in the scheme of things—relative or otherwise—and he is doing it *by working outward from the physically known.* He doesn't have to get mixed up in the impossible problem of what relation the apparent universe has to infinite reality, because his business is all within a small fraction of the apparent universe. *He aims to show that, no matter what the visible universe is or what mankind is, mankind is only a transient incident in any one part of the the visible universe.* Note that he is not risking any confusion of terms. He is working with *like quantities.* He doesn't seek to learn the relation of either man or the visible universe to infinity, but simply to learn the relation of the apparent entity man to the apparent entity called the visible universe. Only indirectly does this give him a hint of anything larger—the hint being that if man can be proved temporary and insignificant *in his universe,* he cannot very well be otherwise in infinity! As for the mode of proof—it is simply to apply the local laws whose infallible working *on earth* prove them *absolutely correct for that part of space immediately around us.* We *know* these laws work *here,* because we have applied them in countless ways and have *never* found them to fail. Birth and death, heat and cold, weight and pulley, acid and alkali. Our whole life and civilisation and engineering are a proof of the *perfect certainty and dependability* of these laws. Now the line between earth and sky is only an arbitrary one—which aeroplanes are indeed pushing outward every day—and the application of suitable optical devices to the sky proves that for many trillion and quadrillion miles outward from us the conditions of space are sufficiently like our own to be comparatively unaffected by relativity. This is, these surrounding stellar regions may be taken as part of our illusion-island in infinity, since the laws that work on earth work scarcely less well some distance beyond it. Despite *minor* illusions caused by unknown factors in light transmission, it can be checked up, tested, and *proved* by the parallel application of *different* mensurational methods that the region of nearer stars is, practically speaking, *as much what it seems to us as the surface of the earth is.*

Don't let the Einstein-twisters catch you here! It may be illusion all right, but it's the same batch of illusion which makes you think New York exists and that you move when you walk. Distances among the planets and nearer stars are, allowing for all possible variations, constant enough to make our picture of them as roughly true as our picture of the distances among the various cities of America. You can no more conceive of a vastly varied distance between Sirius and the sun as a result of place and motion, than you can conceive of a practically varied distance between your house and honest old Mac's joint[1] as a result of the direction and speed of the Interborough train you're riding in. The given area *isn't big enough* to let relativity get in its major effects—*hence we can rely on the never-failing laws of earth to give absolutely reliable results in the nearer heavens.* There's no getting around this. If we can study the relation of a race of ants to a coral atoll or a volcanic islet which has risen and will sink again—and nobody dares deny that we can—then it will be *equally possible* for us, if we have suitable instruments and methods, to study the relation of man and the earth to the solar system and the nearer stars. The result will, when obtained, be just as conclusive as that of a study in terrestrial zoölogy or geology. The radius is too small to give relativity or mysticism a chance. The universe may be a dream, but it cannot be considered a *human* dream if we can shew that it must antedate and outlast all human dreamers just as surely as an ocean must antedate and outlast the denizens of one of its alternately rising and submerging volcanic islands. The laws that work on earth work in the nearer sky; and if we can trace man's beginning and finish, we can say *absolutely* (a) that what corresponds to our universe is *not humanly subjective in essence,* (although our sensory picture of it is wholly so) and (b) that man and organic life, or at least man and organic life on this globe (or any like it, if we find the law of temporary worlds common to the visible universe), cannot be a central concern of infinity. This positively obtainable knowledge will knock the bottom out of any ideas of cosmic human destiny save those based on the self-evident insanity of immortality and spiritualism. Now what *do* we find? Well—read what Harlow Shapley, A. S. Eddington, J. H. Jeans,[2] or any contemporary astrophysicist has to say. We find a cycle of constantly shifting energy, marked by the birth of nebulae from stars, the condensation of nebulae into stars, the loss of energy as radiant heat and the radio-active breakdown of matter into energy, and the possible (cf. Millikan's "cosmic ray")[3] building up of matter from free energy. Outstanding are the facts that *all stars are temporary in the long run,* that the birth of planets from them is comparatively rare, (induced by tidal action of other stars that pass by them under rare conditions) and that life on a planet can hardly survive the death of the star whose radiations made it possible in the first place. All this belongs to *positive physical knowledge*—as positive as the knowledge that an inkstand will fall if you drop it from the window to the ground, or that a rat will die if you keep it under water fifteen minutes.

It took a long time to work up to this simple statement—just as the mountain in labour took a long time to bring forth a mouse—but the primer stuff was necessary as a counteractive to the popular theological misuse of relativity. The point is, that we *know* organic life to be a rare, short, and negligible phenomenon. *Know* it beyond the reach of any trick metaphysics. If the cosmos be a momentary illusion, *then mankind is a still briefer one!*

One word on the silly attempt of spiritualists to argue that the non-solid and non-separate nature of matter, as newly proved, indicates the reality of their mythical "soul matter" or "ectoplasm", and makes immortality any less absurd a notion than it was before. Here, as in the case of their comment on the word materialist, they are merely evading facts in a cheap game of verbalism. Matter, we learn, is a definite phenomenon instituted by certain modifications of energy; *but does this circumstance make it less distinctive in itself, or permit us to imagine the presence of another kind of modified energy in places where no sign or result of energy can be discovered?* It is to laugh! The truth is, that the discovery of matter's identity with energy—and of its consequent lack of vital intrinsic difference from empty space—is *an absolute coup de grace to the primitive and irresponsible myth of "spirit". For matter, it appears, really is exactly what "spirit" was always supposed to be.* Thus it is proved *that wandering energy always has a detectable form*—that if it doesn't take the form of waves or electron-streams, *it becomes matter itself;* and that the absence of matter or any other detectable energy-form indicates *not the presence of spirit, but the absence of anything whatever.* The new discovery *doesn't abolish matter,* or make it any closer to the occult world than it's ever been. If any mystic thinks that matter has lost its known properties because it's been found made of invisible energy, just let him read Einstein and try to apply his new conception by butting his head into a stone wall. He will quickly discover that matter is still the same old stuff, and that knowing more about it doesn't have much effect on its disconcerting solidity. It may be made up of something which is itself non-solid and non-material, just as heavy, harmless water is made up of airy, intoxicating oxygen and ethereal, explosive, and inflammable hydrogen—but it's pretty damn definite on its own hook, and there's no more use comparing it to thin mythical ectoplasm than there is in trying to breathe water for oxygen or burn water for hydrogen. The hard fact of the whole business is—and this is what the mystics close their eyes to—that *matter is a definite condition involving fixed and certain laws; the laws being known and invariable, applicable to no other phenomenon, and having nothing so do with any other hypothetical relationship between an invisible entity and actual effects.* We've known the laws of matter for a long time—does a new explanation of them enlarge their field of application? Because we have found that the body of a human being is composed of certain energy-streams which gradually undergo transformations (though retaining the form of matter in various decomposition-products) after the withdrawal of the chemical and physical process called life, are we any more justified in believing that these demonstrable streams are during life accompanied by another set which gives no evidence of its presence, and which at the cessation of the life-reactions retains its specialised grouping, contrary to all laws of energy, and at a time when even the solid streams of matter-energy— whose existence is really capable of proof—are unable to retain a similar grouping? Passing over for the moment the utterly puerile unjustifiedness of such a supposition in the first place, let us consider the only sane analogy the mystic could possibly draw—that is, the analogy of the bony shell or skeleton, which remains undestroyed and undissociated after the death of the organism. This ought not to stand up a moment when we consider *what it is* that spiritualists claim as surviving. That surviving element, they say, is *the personality*—a particularly unfortunate choice in view of the fact that we happen to know just what bodily parts involve the personality; modifying and guiding it in health, and unerringly impairing their respective sections of it when they are themselves injured. If we were really anxious for tangible suggestions that the dead still live, we would believe that they survive in the indestructible parts of their bodies, and would pray to and converse with their dried bones—as indeed many primitive peoples do. Or we would mummify their whole corpses—as indeed do many somewhat less primitive peoples. Either of these courses would be less flagrantly ridiculous than inventing out of whole cloth the notion of an airy near-matter which hovers around the real matter and acquires and retains complex configurations which we know are produced only through long aeons of evolution in the one specific substance known as the protoplasmic form of energy-acting-as-matter. Personality, we know, is a mode of motion in the neural tissue of highly evolved vertebrate animals; centreing in the brain and spine, and governed largely by glandular hormones conveyed by the blood. It suffers when its material medium suffers, and visibly changes as that medium alters with age. It has no demonstrable existence—and there is every reason why it couldn't have—after the cessation of the life-reactions in the matter on which it depends; nor could we conceive of it rationally as anything apart from the complex and slowly evolved biological mechanism which typifies so well its own rarity, delicacy, and subtlety, and complexity. And yet there are adults at large who associate this involvedly physiological-mechanical peak of bodily development with the thin air of a loosely unorganised ghost-substance which never gave any evidence of existence—and who perversely fancy that the existence of such a mythical spook-gas is less absurdly unlikely because matter itself—with all its certain evidences of existence—has been found to have a basis in phenomena not themselves solid or ponderable. Surely a triumph of fallacy and inverse reasoning! It is no more sensible to assume that personality exists and survives as a shadow beside the material human body, than to assume that every manifestation of matter has a parallel shadow of more tenuous substance to accompany and survive it. The frank animism of the savage fetish-worshipper is much more consistent and less anachronistic than the smug, fact-shy soul-belief of educated quibblers like the bland and pious William Herbert Perry Faunce, D.D., LL.D., Retiring President of Brown University.[4]

But what, after all, really is behind the persistent myth-hugging of the incurable theist and mystic—a phenomenon too numerous to be set down as isolated freakishness, ignorance, or disease? We know that his beliefs could not possibly arise from a close and impartial survey of nature and the cosmos today, because there's nothing in reality as now understood to suggest such notions. The answer must obviously be historic, psychological, and pedagogical. [. . .]

Primarily, of course, men began to be religious and mystical because at intellect's dawn they knew no other way to explain the phenomena they saw around them, or to work off such residues of excess emotional energy as war and eroticism did not take care of. They could not understand any phenomenon without a cause as personal and purposeful as that which made the axe and club move in their own hands, or account for their vague emotions and dual life in dreams on any basis except that of a spirit-world parallelling theirs. That they attributed to nature a set of human personalities with definite sentiments for or against themselves was only to be expected; and this formed of course an imperative reason for the gesture of worship—hortatory, propitiatory, laudatory, grateful, ecstatic, symbolic, or simply orgiastic. Believing themselves in the absolute sway of their nature-gods, primitive men of course quickly connected them with the systems of tribal polity which their stumbling experience had evolved—thus bringing into being the myth of morals and the legend of good and evil. Confusing wishes with hopes, and hopes with realities, [they] coined the idea of an immortality for the dream-bodies of themselves, their dogs and cattle, their spears and clubs, their wives, and their food, clothing, and armaments. All the foundations of religion were laid, and in a perfectly natural and inevitable way. At that stage of existence, no other result of the contact of the human mind with nature was possible. And it is equally plain why, in the absence of the analytical and scientific spirit, the system hung on even after the advancing race began to find out things for itself, and to understand the natural and impersonal character of many phenomena once thought personal. The system was still the only explanation for many things; and it was all the while working itself closer and closer into the affections and traditions of every struggling race-stock, taking a different form in each separate case as it became the mirror and outward expression of that race's individual perspective and emotions as determined by its particular experience. Just as it grew from every race, so every race grew into it, reciprocally. It permeated all dawning art and thought and feeling, and became a rallying-point for all the vague sentiments and instinctive loyalties of the race. As national life developed, it became synonymous with the state, so that the tribal chief always had the threefold function of King, Priest, and War-Leader. By historic times it was so imbedded in tradition as to be a permanent part of the emotional heritage of all mankind—a crutch on which the race had leaned too long to be able to walk alone save through a pure intellectualism never attainable by the masses. The very processes of thought had become so chained to the traditional myths and formulae that only generations of a scientific knowledge never dreamed of then could ever hope to liberate man's mind, in the mass, for the calm pursuit of impersonal information and the unbiased investigation of the earth's place in the cosmos of time and space. The myths were fixed in every child's mind at the most impressionable age, and those emotions which bolstered up the physical and ecstatic side of religious feeling were cultivated and whipped into activity. The cosmic connections of good conduct and good taste were dinned into everyone's ears till everyone believed in them—and to all this positive stimulus was added the negative circumstance that science, advancing much more slowly than general culture, consistently failed to advance explanations of the universe capable of competing with the made-to-order myths. Only the superlative mind of philosophic Greece was capable, in the absence of scientific instruments and methods, of breaking through the mists a trifle and producing the line of atomic philosophers of whom Leucippus, Democritus, Epicurus, and (in Rome) Lucretius are the chief examples. After Rome, darkness—and after the Renaissance, slow growth. Then the dawn of science and the awakening of speculation— and the imperfect, half-diffident, half-belligerent rationalism of the 18th century—the age of French Encyclopaedists and English Deists—of Gibhon, Hume, Swift, Lord Bolingbroke, Thomas Jefferson, and Thomas Paine.

The 19th century—as mighty in sheer scientific intellect as it was ridiculous in decoration and social philosophy—nearly finished the business. After Darwin and *my* friend Huxley[5] the residue of unexplained things in nature had begun to shrink so much that, in conjunction with the astronomical discoveries of Herschel[6] in the previous century, the current scientific field was making a new view of religious myths inevitable. Schopenhauer and Nietzsche said their say, and Ernst Haeckel was not mute. Scholarship was shewing the Judaeo-

Christian Bible to be just another Oriental melange of myth, history, poetry, and ethics, and psychology was commencing to explain the pathological character of religious zealots, and the physical-emotional basis of most ordinary worship. By 1900 there was not much intellectual reason to believe in the supernatural; for though the precise mechanism of the cosmos was not then, is not now, and never will be understood, enough facts were known to prove the absolute gratuitousness of all celestial personificaion, and the primitive mythological nature of the attitude, acts, and rites of extra-human and superphysical worship. More powerfully disillusioning than the actual discovery of the hollowness of the myths was the perfect psychological, anthropological, and historical *accounting for* the religious attitude and temperament on a basis of observant materialism. The synonymity of faith and folklore, and the similarity of Jehovah and Santa Claus, became clearly apparent to the cooly discerning. But of course the majority kept on believing naturally enough. Why shouldn't they, with an overwhelming pressure of tradition and inherited and acquired feeling behind them, and with no especial urge to follow up and correlate all the separate scientific threads whose combined grasping could alone present the stern and unwelcome facts of the case with full force?

Now another generation has passed—and how are we? Oddly muddled! About half the new generation of thinkers has thrown the supernatural overboard, whilst the other half clings on in varying degrees of incompleteness, doubt, and insincerity. One very cultivated element stands pat and refuses to think at all in purely scientific fields— but this is represented less and less in each new college class. A large group retains the myth of absolute ethics whilst professing to repudiate the non-physical; turning to abstract illusions like "justice", "equality", and "democracy" instead of to the ancient gods or saints. The herd, of course, is as densely superstitious as ever, from Dago and Canuck papists to Tennessee Baptists, and from Georgia Methodists to Pennsylvania witch-fearers. But even this herd has felt an emotional letdown—*more* of an *emotional* letdown than the most open of *intellectual* atheists, so that they are increasingly vulgar, swinish, and unmanageable. They don't figure in an intellectual-emotional problem (nor do *consciously insincere* persons of any grade)—but how about the residual believers of taste, information, and cultivation?

I think the causes of their belief are about as follows:

(a) Habit of tradition rather than thought. Oversensitiveness to abstract principle of authority.

(b) Wish-thinking—dread of emotional-intellectual consequences of truth.

(c) Lack of specific information, causing apprehensive belief that good morals and civilisation depend on religion.

(d) Emotional bias—intense devotion to past cuts off mental processes of investigation.

(e) Literal rather than inclusively imaginative mind which accepts religious statistics and casuistry before investigating other side, and thus has mind-closing first impression.

(f) Emotional overdevelopment requiring ritually orgiastic outlet.

(g) Aesthetic bias—conception of life in terms of art rather than thought. This is the great Catholic-breeder.

(h) Metaphysical temperament—constitutional addiction to formal scholasticism which induces insensitiveness to facts presented in the spirit of experiment and inductive science. Overemphasis of the possible import of modern discoveries like relativity and quantum theory.

(i) Subconscious fear of loss of social position through departure from tradition.

(j) Idiosyncrasies of temperament, largely hereditary, which help out one's natural wish for order and conservatism by subtly responding to all arguments based on the past and the usual, and subtly remaining insensitive to the opposite side.

(k) Passionate group-feeling—altruism, brother-saving, justice-enforcing, liquor-banishing, etc. etc., which exaggerate ethics to a point where poetic personification automatically takes place and reason goes by the board.

(l) Overdeveloped *reverence*—conscious or subconscious—for once potent symbols or for the massed opinions of the believing generations of yesterday and the eminent surviving believers of today. Also—excessive sense of *awe* at magnitude and complexity of the cosmos.

(m) Extreme introversion, with its solemnly proportionless exaltation of intuition and subjective experience at the expense of realistic observation, comparison, and experiment. Naive belief in realities apart from those sensorily apprehended.

(n) *And most potent of all*—an out-and-out infantile fixation developed by early childhood influences and absolutely shutting off the current of brain-power from areas of religious and philosophical speculation.

But I won't attempt any more cataloguing. These points also serve to explain the messianic altruist or Aldine semi-introvert in many ways. I'm not yet quite sure, though, just what the exact *intellectual* position of the typical introvert is. Does he realise as a scientific fact that nothing exists except in objective reality and as a more or less disguised derivative of something therein, or does he try to give his subjective illusions a grounding in alleged philosophy? If the latter, I can never understand him—that is, unless he partakes more or less of the religious mind. All reason unites to prove that we can apprehend the cosmos only through our five senses as guided by our intellect and intellectually tinged *imagination,* (not *fancy*) and that there is nothing in any living being's head which he did not get through those channels, either directly, unifiedly, and consciously, or indirectly, subconsciously, and fragmentarily. The inner mind can rearrange, select, combine, dissociate and recombine, re-proportion, re-stress, and so on, till the "subjective" idea loses all resemblance to its unconscious sources; but it cannot create anything wholly new because the human mind is a blank apart from what sensory intake gives it. Extroverts imagine realistically—the pictures they conjure up are life-size scenes with the aspect of real life, and in which they might walk if the scenes were objective. Fantastic forms, if present, will tend to follow natural laws; and the proportions of visible objects will adhere to the normal laws of perspective. Introverts, I think, must tend to imagine more or less distortedly—in the William Blake or semi-cubist manner. It must be from extreme and exaggerated introversion that the bulk of affected ultra-modern aestheticism comes—the brass foundry-slag of "sculptors" like Brancusi, the woodcut hash of Masereel and Rockwell Kent, and the ramshackle shantihs of T. S. Eliot and his ilk. Extroversion means sanity at its best and prosaic commonplaceness at its worst. Introversion means originality at its best and affectation or madness at its worst. I have much admiration for the best type of introvert if he is only emotionally such, and does not try to read non-existent meanings into the meaningless sensations and images which form the whole of life, and produce the whole of thought and illusion by punching at the various emotional nerve-centres with the bland and mischievous impersonality of a small boy punching strangers' doorbells at random. The only introverts I can't stand are those who "feel a deep meaning in it all", and take their emotions as seriously as a man of sense takes his Gothick windows and Shelleyan odes and Constable landscapes. Not that a man of sense lacks emotions—indeed, I can't abide a man who isn't a patriot for England or art or facts or morals or something of the sort—but that he preserves a sense of proportion regarding them, and recognises their place in a futile and meaningless cosmos. I would doubtless admire much in Grandson Aldous—especially his refusal to succumb to the "democracy" pandemic—though there is doubtless much which would alienate me. He is probably right about popery—it is undoubtedly the most superior religion today, though I fancy I would prefer the actual Graeco-Roman rites and mysteries on which it is based . . . . that is, such of them as may not have conflicted with the aesthetick decorum-sense of a New England gentleman. I think, though, that popery conflicts with one thing besides liberty, and that is scientific truth. I don't care for liberty, but truth does occasionally interest me—as a gratification of cosmick curiosity.

Religion and Indeterminacy

[The following is an extract from a letter to Frank Belknap Long (22 November 1930). In part a follow-up to the preceding letter, this document asserts that the truth or falsity of religious belief must be based upon a wide survey of contemporary knowledge, taking no need of the adventitious circumstance that religious belief has persisted for centuries or millennia.]

I perus'd the Jeans article,[1] and your comment thereon, with very great interest; and agree with you that only train'd mathematicians are able to conduct original research into the question of "what is anything". Nay, more—these mathematicians are, in themselves, *just as powerless as the rankest layman* to make any definitive pronouncement; insomuch as they have no means of testing the operations of their own mental processes in the steps whereby they reach their tentative conclusions. For this latter testing, the aid of the train'd psychologist, anthropologist, and biologist is absolutely essential; so that in truth the significant probing of the unknown must necessarily consist of "team-work", with both mathematicians and psychologists working in concert upon the concrete data which physicists, chemists, biologists, astronomers, and the like unearth. The only thing the layman can do amidst this complex situation is to check one expert's statements and conclusions against those of another—correlating all the current data with a mind kept free of preconceived myths, traditions, and other biasses, and subjecting his own tentative conclusions to a round of searching criticisms from experts in the various intellectual fields involved. In these criticisms many points of view will be disclosed, and the comments of one expert critick upon the differing views of another critick in the same field will often prove extremely illuminating. In the end, whilst it cannot be promis'd that any *certainty* is attainable, it wou'd be the sheerest pedantry and affectation to claim that no *probabilities* are indicated. They may not be as strong probabilities as the experts themselves could obtain if freed of emotion, but they are at least tangible provisional foundations for a temporary working hypothesis. Something of the kind is accessible to every layman who carefully reads all sides of a general argument among experts. It would be absurd to declare that, despite his technical ignorance, he is not *somewhat* further advanc'd along the route of fallacy-elimination than one who never gave any attention to the matter.

Thus with the conclusions of Jeans—which we must correlate with Millikan, Compton, Eddington, Shapley, Freud, Watson, Russell, Frazer, Einstein, Eddington, Santayana, Keith, and dozens of others before they can have even the least definitive evidential value. Some of the issues at stake—such as the nature of the cosmic rays—must be held as wholly unsettled. Other assertions can, after a fashion, be appraised in the light of parallel authorities. In passing, we must remark that virtually all *reviews* of experts' books, as printed in popular conventional newspapers and magazines, contain a bias toward the traditional myths and delusions of the race. We must see beyond this whenever we are unable to get at an authority first-handedly.

Now as for Jeans—in the beginning a conventional product of his traditional milieu, with perspective and emotions crippled in infancy by orthodox training—what have we to say to his conclusions? Well, for one thing, we must asseverate that the spectre of "19th century mechanistic materialism" which he professes to dethrone is very largely a man of straw. The system of thought based on the laws of the conservation of matter and energy was, like other provisional hypotheses, a working basis of thought for a considerable time; but it would be naive to suppose that it ignored the disparity between appearance and reality, or that it founded its larger speculations upon precise quantitative formulae involving the absolute integrity and indivisibility of the atom. It was a step in a series of advances from illusion toward exactitude; and its assumptions were based more on the general direction of the progress than on any particular stage of it. Of course some individual speculators spoke in a mathematically positive way which emotionally biassed obscurantists are now very quick to seize as ammunition against all rational thinkers; but to imagine that the responsible majority transcended cautious *probabilities* is to misapprehend the whole nature of recent philosophy. Only the extravagant ever began with a positive cosmic assumption and worked inward from it. The real thinkers of all ages have adhered to the sound reverse process—of testing phenomena near at hand and working *outward* from these solid foundations. Early 20th century opinion concerning man's relation to the cosmos represented a certain degree of outward-pushed observation. Today observation has been pushed much farther outward—in some cases overwhelmingly farther outward—hence it is inevitable that we ask how greatly the added territory has affected our tentative picture of conditions; whether it has weakened, strengthen'd, confirm'd, modify'd, or altogether superseded the conception of 1900. Obviously we must re-draw our basic guess at what is and what isn't—refusing to be influenced by our view of 1900 just as resolutely as we refuse to be influenced by our views of 1880 or 1850 or 1800 or 1650 or 1300 or 500 or B.C. 450. But we must be no more eager and predisposed to find a *difference,* than we are eager and predisposed to find a *similarity.* We must not seek to cater to any *wish* or *loyalty* or other emotional consideration apart from the instinct of *pure curiosity.* Our only watchword must be a resolve to seek nothing but the impartial probabilities in the matter of *what is* versus *what isn't.*

Well—what do we find? First of all, a radical increase in that element of unknowability *which we always admitted.* We are bidden to accept, as the one paradoxical *certainty* of experience, the fact that we can never have any other ultimate certainty. All conclusions for an infinite time to come, barring wholly unexpected data, must be regarded as no more than *competitive probabilities*. So far as *actual knowledge* is concerned, the theistic myths of tradition are as *absolutely and finally dethroned from all pretension to authority* as are any of the earlier conclusions of science. Ancient tradition and earlier science must alike resign all *former* claims to truth which they may ever have put forward. They, together with every other possible attempt to explain the cosmos, now stand on a basis of *complete and fundamental equality* so far as their original claims are concerned. The old game is over, and the cards are shuffled again. Nothing whatever can *now* be done toward reaching probabilities in the matter of cosmic organisation, *except by assembling all the tentative data of 1930 and forming a fresh chain of partial indications based exclusively on that data and on no conceptions derived from earlier arrays of data;* meanwhile testing, by the psychological knowledge of 1930, the workings and inclinations of our minds in accepting, correlating, and making deductions from data, *and most particularly weeding out all tendencies to give more than equal consideration to conceptions which would never have occurred to us had we not formerly harboured ideas of the universe now conclusively known to be false.* Let this last point be supremely plain, for it is through *a deliberate and dishonest ignoring of it* that every contemporary claim of traditional theism is advanced. Nothing but shoddy emotionalism and irresponsible irrationality can account for the pathetick and contemptible asininity with which the Chestertons and Eliots, and even the Fosdicks and Eddingtons and Osborns,[2] try to brush it aside or cover it up in their attempts to capitalise the new uncertainty of everything in the interest of historical mythology. What this means—and it means it just as plainly, for all the jaunty flippancy of touch-and-go epigrammatists who dare not put their fallacies to the test of honest reason and original cerebration—is simply this: that although each of the conflicting orthodoxies of the past, founded on known fallacies among primitive and ignorant races, certainly has an *equal theoretical chance* with any other orthodoxy or with any theory of science of being true, *it most positively has no greater chance* than has ANY RANDOM SYSTEM OF FICTION, DEVISED CAPRICIOUSLY BY IGNORANCE, DISEASE, WHIM, ACCIDENT, EMOTION, GREED, OR ANY

OTHER AGENCY INCLUDING CONSCIOUS MENDACITY, HALLUCINATION, POLITICAL OR SOCIAL INTEREST, AND ULTERIOR CONSIDERATIONS IN GENERAL. If we could shave off the moustachelets of our Chestertons and rub their noses in this plain truth, we would have fewer spectacles of neo-obscurantism. It is this one crucial circumstance which renders utterly valueless all half-baked attempts to utilise the admitted uncertainty of knowledge in bolstering up obsolete lies whose natural origin and total emptiness are obvious to all psychologists, biologists, and anthropologists. Let us grant that *in theory* the doctrine of Buddha, or of Mohammed, or of Lao-Tse, or of Christus, or of Zoroaster, or of some Congo witch-doctor, or of T. S. Eliot, or of Mary Baker Eddy, or of Dionysus, or of Plato, or of Ralph Waldo Emerson, *has just as much or as little positive evidence for it as has any other attempted explanation of the cosmos.* So far, so good. *But this concession cannot possibly be made without extending equal theoretical authority to Chambers's Yellow Sign, Dunsany's Pegāna, your Tindalos, Klarkash-Ton's Tsathoggua, my Cthulhu, or any other fantastic concoction anybody may choose to invent.*[3] *Who can disprove any such concoction,* or say that it is not "esoterically true" even if its creator did think he invented it in jest or fiction? What shall be our guide in deciding which, out of an infinity of possible speculations, is the most likely to be a correct explanation of surrounding entity? How shall we establish a test of comparative validity or authority for the various conflicting claims which present themselves? If the theism of Christus is "true" because our ancestors believed it, why is not the devil-worship of the Yezidis equally "true" because they and their ancestors have believed it?[4] What is anything? Can any one explanation be deemed more acceptable than any other? If so, on what principle? At this point the moustacheletted fat neo-papists begin to crack brilliant and irrelevant jokes and spout emotional generalities designed to get the mind of the seeker off the facts and confuse him into the acceptance of ready-made traditional hokum. But men of sense pause a bit and try to see what *really can be done* toward a tentative elimination leading in the direction of general probabilities. The result, inevitably, is that conclusion stated a few paragraphs back—*that probabilities can now be reached only by assembling all the data of 1930, and forming a fresh chain of partial indications based exclusively on that data and on no conceptions derived from earlier arrays of data;* meanwhile testing, by the psychological knowledge of 1930, the workings and inclinations of our minds in accepting, correlating, and making deductions from data, AND MOST PARTICULARLY WEEDING OUT ALL TENDENCIES TO GIVE MORE THAN EQUAL CONSIDERATION TO CONCEPTIONS WHICH WOULD NEVER HAVE OCCURRED TO US HAD WE NOT FORMERLY HARBOURED IDEAS OF THE UNIVERSE NOW CONCLUSIVELY KNOWN TO BE FALSE.

Specifically (for no sane human being disputes the *general* proposition just stated) our job is to test (a) the intrinsic probability, as judged by our contemporary observations of what we see of the universe, of any system which enters a claim; and more particularly (b) to investigate the sources of such a system, *and the probable reason why anybody believes or ever has believed in it;* the latter point to be worked at by the most thorough psychological analyses we can devise.

Get this straight—*for there is no other road to probability.*

First, what is the likelihood of a theory as judged by the general action of nature manifest in regular and predictable phenomena? (Day and night, heat and cold, seasons, laws of mechanics, etc. etc.)

Second, if it squares less readily with observed reality than does some other theory, then why was it proposed in the first place?

Third, if in answer to (2) it be said that certain persons at a certain time found this theory more in accord with nature than any other, then what relationship has the conception of nature at that time to our conception of it today?

Fourth, on what mental principles are all these conceptions of nature, and of the relation of this theory to any observed set of phenomena or parallel theory based on such phenomena, formed? How does contemporary psychology interpret the processes causing the formation of these conceptions?

Going back to the general proposition—what does the natural evidence of 1930 suggest, anyhow? Well, *uncertainty* in the first place. A definite limitation of our knowledge of what lies behind the visible aspects of the cosmos as seen by human beings from this planet. But how far can we extend this uncertainty? Certainly, it has no place in our immediate environment. Grandpa Theobald[5] will never dodge a hateful northern winter because time and space are relative in infinity, nor will the planet Pluto ever revolve around the sun as swiftly as Mercury from the point of view of this part of space. No person in Providence, without circumnavigating the globe, will ever get to Charleston by starting for Quebec; nor will any projectile in the solar system ever hit Saturn by being aimed at the opposite part of its orbit. We live in a cosmos in which a certain amount of regularity is an essential part; and in which time and space, far from being illusions, have definite and recognisable functions so far as the relationship of any small unit to its immediate environment is concerned. Whatever be the relationship of our galactic universe to any larger unit—whether or not the totality of entity and extension—the relationship of our star-group to the galaxy, of our solar system to its star group, of our earth to the solar system, and of organic life to the earth, may and must still be regarded as *roughly* what it seems; or rather, as something with so limited a relativity-latitude that the underlying "reality" rhythms cannot be out of all *quantitative* correspondence with the phenomena we observe. We see a certain interplay of patterned forces not discernibly dissimilar *in kind* from the formation of the smallest crystal to the shaping and kinetic balance of the whole immediate galaxy. The evidence on hand points to a sort of general rhythmic seething of force-streams along channels automatically predetermined in ultimate ends, though conceivably subject to slight variations in route (quantum theory) and with certain developments definitely unpredictable *although not, in the opinion of conservative physicists, forming actual violations of the basic principle of causation.* What most physicists take the quantum theory, at present, to mean, is *not that any cosmic uncertainty exists* as to which of several courses a given reaction will take; but that in certain instances *no conceivable channel of information can ever tell human beings which course will be taken,* or by what exact course a certain observed result came about. There is room for much discussion on this point, and I can cite some very pertinent articles on the subject if necessary. Organic life, of which consciousness is an incidental process, and which rises and falls through varying degrees of complexity, (mankind being at present its most intricate example within our scope of vision) is a phenomenon of apparent rarity, though of so well-defined a type that it would be rash to deem it confined to this solar system alone in all the history of the cosmos. We know, roughly, the relationship it bears to our solar system, and realise that it must be a very transient phase in the history of such planets as contain it. We can look back geologically, on this earth, to a relatively recent time when it did not exist; (a time which is *not* an illusion *in the history of this system*) and forward to a comparatively early moment when it shall have ceased to be. In other words, we know it to be a matter of supreme indifference and impermanence so far as the immediate universe is concerned. In several trillion years it will be a matter of absolute indifference whether or not this phenomenon has ever existed on the planets in this part of space. If the laws governing this phenomenon are basically different from those governing other immediate and observed phenomena, we have yet to be shewn evidence based on anything but assumptions and conceptions without sources in ascertainable reality as recognised today. Proof—and even probability— is likewise required to justify the assumption that organic life, either as a whole or in that department known as consciousness, has any special or significant relationship to the pattern and motions of the cosmos as a whole; *even allowing for a radical and causation-disturbing interpretation of the quantum theory* (even proof of a cosmic "purpose" and "consciousness" would indicate nothing as to man's place therein. All life might well be a trifling pimple or disease.). While it is perfectly true, in theory, that we require a mathematician's knowledge in order to test a mathematician's statement of a special resemblance between cosmic law and the cerebral processes of terrestrial organisms; it is equally true that common sense, after hearing the mathematician explain the basis of his claim, and after comparing this claim with the views of other and equally noted mathematicians, has a certain unofficial right to formulate concepts of probability or the reverse. And when we learn that the sole ground for the mind-and-cosmos-comparison is merely the possibility (certainly not the probability) that occasional chance tempers the dominant determinism of infinity, we are certainly justified in demanding confirmatory data before so palpably strained and artificial (and so obviously myth-and-tradition-suggested) an analogy is accepted.

Is anyone so naive as to believe that the mind-cosmos comparison would have been made solely from the present evidence of 1930, if unsuggested by ancient mythology? Let us analyse the comparison in the exclusive light of contemporary evidence and see how great a part of it consists of mere words and artificially forced parallels. Let us not forget that Einstein and others do not attempt such merely poetic analogies. Einstein has much to say of "religion"—which to him means a human emotion of ecstasy excited by the individual's correlation of himself with the cosmos—but he does not use the language of Jeans. And it would be superfluous to point out—except to purblind neo-obscurantists amongst whom all distinctions are dead—that none of these modern cosmic views has anything in common with any interpretation of the cosmos, and man's relation to it, which has traditionally gone under the name of religion. These cosmic philosophers are using ancient names to describe a cloudy pantheism utterly unlike anything those ancient names ever stood for in their heyday. It is folly and hypocrisy to use the hack terms "God" and "religion" to describe things having no relationship to the original concepts back of those terms. Whilst certain of the valuecentric and teleological implications of these fellows may be said to form a pale echo of the obsolete theism, especially in some of its more mystical Hindoo phases, it is ridiculous to consider them as a prolongation of the highly dogmatic and childishly specific set of delusions constituting the nominal Christianity of the Western World. According to any person following the Christian religion in its basic essence, be he a Papist or Protestant, both Jeans and Einstein are definite atheists. Thus we see the element of puerile fashion and irrational mob-psychology in any popular trend inclusive enough to favour at once, and allegedly on the same grounds, the crazy archaism of a Chesterton and the indecisive word-juggling of a Jeans or an Einstein.

Having now seen that the actual visual and mathematical evidence of 1930 *does not suggest anything very strikingly different in its general probabilities* (probabilities, that is, regarding the absence of conscious purpose and governance, and the absence of any significant special relationship betwixt man and the infinite. All this not at all affected by our changed conceptions of space-time-matter-energy relationships.)

104

from the automatick and impersonal cosmos envisaged at an earlier period, which was as a negligible, purposeless, accidental, and ephemeral atom fortuitously occurring amidst the kaleidoscopic pattern-seething, let us try to see why such a frantic series of attempts is being made to exhume the old myths so definitely exploded since 1850. What is there in current experience which makes certain people choose wholly gratuitous and irrelevant myths and improbabilities as cosmic explanations; proclaiming them more probable than the really probable, and nominating them for consideration under the plea that any old cock and bull story is technically possible in a demonstrably uncertain universe? Well—in general, we may say that the causes are manifold. Chief of all is the fact that the generation of men now in the saddle is old enough to have been mentally crippled by early pro-mythological bias in conventional homes. Their emotions are permanently distorted— trained to think the unreal real, and eager to grasp at any excuse for belief. They resent the cold probabilities of the cosmos because they have been taught to expect fairy-tale values and adjustments—hence as soon as any uncertainty appears in positive knowledge, they catch avidly at the loophole as an excuse to revive their comfortingly familiar superstitions. Second—many persons attribute the present bewildering changes in the social and cultural order to the decline of theistic belief, hence snatch at any chance to bolster up a placid and stabilising mythology—whether or not they inwardly believe it. Third—some persons think habitually in terms of vague, grandiose, and superficial emotions, hence find it difficult to envisage the impersonal cosmos as it is. Any system seems actually improbable to them which does not satisfy their false sense of importance, their artificial set of purpose-values, and their pseudo-wonder springing from an arbitrary and unreal standard of norms and causations. This class is sincere, and often intelligent except where habitual bias is concerned. Fourth—there is an element of witty and insincere posers who become bored with plain fact and instinctively resent the non-sensational; reacting against every-day probability at the least excuse, and revelling in any mythological extravagance, [. . .?] which certain persons, hesitant in analysing reputed "occult" phenomena and assigning the probable psychological and anthropological causes, consider the pretentiously published accounts of such things as a body of evidence solid and irrefutable enough to establish the supernatural despite the overwhelming contrary probabilities. To these five causes of myth-revival may be added the mental inertia and fashion-following instinct of the thoughtless majority. All small minds belong wholly to their age and think only in terms of "periods" determined by noisy transient spokesmen. Original and independent minds are timeless, and pay no attention to ages or fashions, but simply face the universe with all the evidence in hand on an 'is-or-isn't' basis. Today the superficial herd, who merely absorb second-hand opinions and never think for themselves, are naturally coloured by the voluble emanations of biassed thinkers reflecting the five listed causes. They get this way simply because they are femininely receptive rather than creative—sensitive to mass-feelings rather than vigorously independent and masculine. They readopt theism as they readopt ping-pong and backgammon—because "everybody", as represented by the most emotionally animated and flashy talkers, is doing it. But of course this herd does not really count; for in twenty more years, after the theistic reaction has passed, it will follow the mental bell-wethers into rationalism once more. The present partial reaction of the timid and sentimental and bewildered is in truth a very natural phenomenon, and might even have occurred without the excuse of an extended scientific perspective. It was clear, once the impersonal nature of the cosmos became manifest, that a certain group of the tender-minded would inevitably start a frightened, traditional retreat from reality as soon as their rather hazy comprehensions began to grasp the fuller implications of the actual facts. These things usually move in cycles—after 18th century reason, the frantic artificial piety of the 1830's and early-Victorianism; after this, the rationality of the later 19th century; after late-Victorian reason the pathetic farce of Eliot-Chesterton-Millikan-Eddington obscurantism, after present obscurantism, the future rationality of 1960 or 1970; after this rationality, the fatigued and meaningless relapse into superstition of the year 2000 . . . . and so on . . . . . . and so on . . . . . . We do not, then, need to wonder at the existing conditions; but only to ascertain upon what pretext, or scheme of self-deception, the present obscurantists put forward the obsolete myths as probabilities to be appraised on equal terms with the actual contrary probabilities of Nature.

To begin with—why did each of these self-cocksure but often conflicting theistic theories or explanations of the cosmos arise in the first place, far back in mankind's days of ignorance? Here history, anthropology, and psychology step in and supply an answer so complete, natural, instinctively satisfying to the reason, and supported by evidence on every hand, that only warped emotion or imperfect perspective can possibly prick flaws and look for other and more "mystical" sources. We know today that the sources of religion are fear, wonder at the unknown, erotic perversion, and the inability to conceive of cosmic governance and causation except in terms of human governance and causation. It was an utterly natural and inevitable phenomenon among any race of dawning intelligence confronted by the varied phenomena of Nature; and could not help occurring, whether or not any "spiritual" or "supernatural" world existed to justify it. If there were any real "gods", the primitive men who invented gods of their own could not have known anything about them. Thus *the existence of religion as an objective fact has not the slightest bearing upon the validity of the beliefs included in religion.* As a matter of fact, psychology and anthropology are constantly supplying explanations for more and more of the curious details of religious belief. The origin of such delusional types as "spirit", "soul", "immortality", "good", "evil", and so on is now so obvious, and so universally recognised by psychologists as natural, that discussion of them as supernatural indications has become frivolous, irrelevant, and meaningless. Your friend Randall[6] hit squarely on this point in the essay you sent me. And again I must remind you that despite the transient crop of praying physicists and Mariolatrous mathematicians, there are *no psychologists or anthropologists* of any standing (poor Osborn!) who have any belief in the supernatural.

But here is the important question. All these facts being known, upon what grounds do the obscurantists base their act when they rake up these exploded concoctions of primitive ages and offer them as competitive probabilities under the theoretical rule that anything is possible in an uncertain cosmos? What justification do they advance for championing a set of arbitrary extravagances now known to be the chance products of ancient misconceptions, and diametrically contradictory to all the probabilities of normal experience and scientific observation? How, in the light of 1930, can they (even allowing for the emotional crippling of a conventionally theistic infancy) seriously claim for these wholly undermined museum curiosities any greater probability than can be claimed by Carcosa, Yian, Tindalos, Chaugnar, and the Aklo and Voorish mysteries?[7] What is the whole principle of unreal judgment upon which the mental and emotional attitude of the modern theist hinges?

Well—people differ. Some, as I have said, give tremendous weight to the cunningly doctored reports of "occult" phenomena popularised by men like Lodge, Doyle, Chevreuil, and Flammarion.[8] Others refuse to *think* about such things at all; but merely read and quote copiously, and take refuge in diverting but irrelevant witticisms and vague sentimental and aesthetic claims which mean nothing and are really understood by no one, least of all their authors. But the most considerable faction rely on metaphysics, and gloss over the facts of psychology in an effort to prove that mankind has informative powers independent of the normal sensory and cerebral apparatus. With this attitude (which it is unlikely they could form today, or hold at all except through the crippling influence of obsolete tradition) they pretend to be informed, by their emotions or imagination, of the "truth" of this or that ancient extravagance—blandly ignoring the fact that different types of emotion and hallucination dictate different kinds of "truth", each in conflict with the others, *and that in every department where testing is at all possible, the emotions have been found absolutely without value as informants concerning reality.* The least openly ridiculous form of this attitude is the generalised and non-dogmatic one represented by honest thinkers like Millikan and the Rev. Harry Emerson Fosdick. These men do not attempt, as do the utterly negligible and buffoon-like neo-papists, to claim that their 'inward emotional news-agencies' confirm any specific set of ancient myths. Rather do they content themselves by thinking that their strong infancy-implanted bias toward certain general conventions—social considerateness, belief in a purposeful cosmic consciousness vaguely linked with mankind, etc. etc.—must have some shadow of reality and justification because it is so strong and persistent and universal. They do not realise that other and opposite emotions are equally strong and often much stronger, and that the persistence and universality are simply natural results of the continuous hereditary tradition which, established partly by social expediency and partly by accident, has persisted everywhere through habit and inertia. Repudiating these realisations, they continue to attach an informative significance to meaningless nerve-reactions caused by the discharge of hormones into the blood from ductless glands. Were any child to be reared in isolation, and surrounded from infancy with the religious precepts of Tsathoggua, YOG-SOTHOTH, or the Doels,[9] his inner emotions would all through life inform him positively of the truth of Tsathogguanism, Yog-Sothothery, or Doelolatry, as the case might be. Iä! Shub-Niggurath! The Goat With a Thousand Young! God! I wonder if there *isn't* some truth in some of this? What is this my emotions are telling me about Great Cthulhu? Ya-R'lyeh! Ya-R'lyeh—Cthulhu fhgthagn . . . . . n'ggah . . . ggll . . . . . Iä! Iä! And so it goes. What more is there to say? We know nothing, of course, about anything, and all possible speculations are technically equal in the theoretical arena of uncertain cosmos's competitive probabilities. But what does ordinary reason, as measured by the daily phenomena about us and by the larger relationships reported by physicists, mathematicians, astronomers, and psychologists, seem to suggest in the matter of choosing a provisional working hypothesis? We see that one group of old-school metaphysicians and sentimentalists, bred up in traditional artificial emotions, prefers to find an "inner" justification for choosing certain hereditary myth-forms and conventions from among the numberless theoretical possibilities which caprice and imagination might devise, and investing these arbitrary choices with the dignity of sacred dogma. But do we honestly believe that they would choose such arbitrary and contradictory improbabilities upon the evidence of 1930 alone, if not stuffed full of ancestral myths and prejudices and predispositions? And can we honestly pretend to follow these vestigial superstitions which the evidence of 1930, while of course not technically contradicting, certainly leaves wholly without foundation, probability, or *raison d'etre?* All honour to men like George Santayana, Bertrand Russell, Sir Arthur Keith, Joseph Wood Krutch, Hugh Elliot,[10] and others with courage and acumen enough to face the facts without flinching or without raising a smoke-screen of sentimentality, mysticism, and aesthetic hokum! And that is all. In a couple of decades the present reaction will have blown over, and our little "mystics" of today (always eager to follow the fashion, from Scotch-terrier mutts to moustachelets) will be among the most assertive of atheists; reading and reading and quoting and quoting, and smiling superiorly at the quaint, out-of-date mysticism of the bygone Jeans and Einstein period—a left-over attitude unthinkable except among persons of atrophied middle age. Grandpa will be dead and gone then, but maybe flaming youth (then growth to paunchy middle age, and perhaps—for hope springs eternal—redeem'd by a real haircut and shave) will look back and remember what the Old Gentleman told him so long ago! But the amusing thing is that even today the faddist reaction is purely on the surface. Among the people at large, despite their professed conscious beliefs, religious feelings are rapidly losing their hold on subconscious motivation and conduct. One has only to compare the psychology of 1830 with that of 1930 to appreciate the point. Paradoxically, this is really a far *less religious* age than rational 1900; since at that time the newly-disillusioned thinkers still acted from the subconscious impulses of an earlier time, whereas now the external pietists have no groundwork of really profound conviction capable of swaying their *acts.* This is an important distinction. The childhood emotional crippling, imposed by frantically conventional parents who themselves were reluctantly half-sceptical, has complete power to obscure clear and independent *thinking* in the present generation of victims; yet has not quite enough extra power to motivate their instinctive *conduct,* since they overhear enough whispers of doubt and cosmic uncertainty to rob them of the naive 100% faith held among the masses prior to 1890 and among thinkers prior to 1850 or 1860. *That* degree of belief could partly motivate conduct as well as shape mental ideas, but there will never be any belief like that again— not even among the most sodden popish rabble. Religion as a vital moving force has been a corpse and a joke since the mid-Victorian period. We can observe the universality of a subconscious irreligion by

110

studying the manners, standards, aspirations, instinctive vocabulary, perspectives, amusements, etc. etc. of this commercial and mechanical aera. To my mind there are few farces and mockeries more pitiful—more disgusting—than the hypocritical attempt of religious exteriors to carry on with face-lifts and goat-glands after all their legitimate justification, both as to foundation in Nature and as to effect on mankind, has been annihilated in the course of social and intellectual development.

As to the views of Bertrand Russell, Esq., upon human happiness, you are right in maintaining that they coincide quite exactly with my own. I have before mention'd, that I do not think positive felicity an universal phaenomenon, or even typical of more than a scant fourth of all mankind; yet I have added, that full half of mankind can get along very endurably thro' the exercise of good sense, so that only a quarter of the race are so permanently vext with emotional conflicts and frustrations that they are radically better off dead than alive. Actually, a certain amount of unhappiness is absolutely inevitable for nearly everyone, since no human personality is wholly free from contrary and clashing emotions, the reasonable satisfaction of one of which sharply pains the other. Some, however, have inner conflicts much more numerous and irreconcilably violent than those of others; these persons being necessarily miserable a considerable part of the time. Allied in effect to the conflict is the permanent frustration caused by emotional needs attuned to imaginary conditions which do not exist. Whatever melancholy I myself possess is of this order—a sense of oppression beneath the limitations of time, space, and natural law, and a curious homesickness for former times, earlier periods in my own existence, and mythical lands of half-familiar wonder beyond the sunset, my pseudo-mnemonic conceptions of which are a jumbled synthesis of various past impressions gleaned from books, pictures, or landscape and architectural experience. I am no advocate of hypocritical grinning, and do not by any means harbour the illusion that everyone can be cheerful at will. My policy is merely not to dwell needlessly on unavoidable dicomforts, or to exaggerate them by maudlin exploitation and the pose of tragedy. Many troubles cannot be removed, but at least they seem less formidable when one recognises their impersonality and exercises a sense of humour, proportion, and objectivity in considering them. The silly, meaningless, and irrelevant thing is to add the artificial and inapplicable quality of *bitterness* or *resentment* to unhappiness not due to the conscious malice or negligence of others. Bitterness and resentment are legitimate sentiments when any other person or persons has deliberately inflicted pain upon one through hostility, cruelty, or a conscious non-performance of aesthetically justify'd obligations; but these things have no meaning in cases where one suffers impersonally and inevitably—that is, through spontaneous inner conflicts determined by one's natural temperament, or through frustrations caused by inability to control environment or by the natural centreing of emotions in non-existent conditions. In these cases one's adversary is the impersonal cosmos alone—against which it is infantile to hold personal sentiments. No human being is to blame for the trouble—so why apply the irrelevant quality of *bitterness* or *resentment,* which has significance only in connexion with other human beings? One needn't be cheerful, but at least it is still more absurd to be violent or sullen. Who's the object of all this turmoil—at whom is the fist of rebellion shaken? The thing becomes farcical upon reflection. The secret of the theatrical brooding of you long-hair'd little poets is that you get a secret kick out of it. You think you're bearing the burdens of the ages, but you're really having a damn good time dramatising yourselves—your egoes are dressing up in costume and strutting before the mirror in an emotionally satisfying pageant of high and grandiose tragedy. Too bad you can't take your pleasures less sadly—as you will, undoubtedly, when you acquire years of good sense, proportion, and reflectiveness. As for the acute, positive, or Stendhal-like unhappiness—that is very scarce; being experienced only at rare intervals by some, but not continuously by anyone. The wisest thing is to jog along on a middle ground—shedding the artificial drama as one grows up, and never taking oneself too seriously.

IV. RELIGION AND SOCIETY

Religion, Art, and Emotion

[The following is an extract from a letter to Woodburn Harris (25 February–1 March 1929). Little is known about Harris (1888–1988), aside from the fact that he lived in Vermont and was a friend of Walter J. Coates. Only a few letters by Lovecraft to Harris survive, but one of them is the longest surviving letter he ever wrote (70 pages—35 sheets written on both sides). In this letter, Lovecraft begins by maintaining that his system of ethics is based, not upon religion, but upon aesthetics. He goes on to declare that his atheism is a product of his intellect, whereas his love of antiquity and devotion to fantasy are the product of his aesthetic sensibility.]

Now returning to our controversy—I don't quite see where you have me cornered regarding the matter of ethics. You deny an undue enthusiasm for this subject, averring that your feelings are akin to those with which you survey the fact of 2 and 2's constituting 4. Well—I shall be convinced when you shew as much *indignation* over a challenge to this belief—which future developments in relativity may conceivably provide—as you do over the idea of disenfranchising all the Protestants in the United States! Personally, I feel more irritated by a challenge to an accepted scientific theory than I do by an act of so-called "evil" or "injustice" amongst mankind; although I never allow my irritation to hamper my acceptance of the new theory as soon as positive evidence warrants it. Thus I have reluctantly exchanged the old nebular for the planetesimal hypothesis, and am beginning to accept the main points of relativity despite a profound intellectual distaste. What is, is—and our emotions regarding the cosmos and its phenomena are of no significance whatever, being wholly subjective matters dependent on individual accidents of neural and glandular physiology and of experience and environment. About my own attitude toward ethics—I thought I made it plain that I object only to (a) grotesquely disproportionate indignations and enthusiasms, (b) illogical extremes involving a reductio ad absurdum, and (c) the nonsensical notion that "right" and "wrong" involve any principles more mystical and universal than those of immediate expediency (with the individual's comfort as a criterion) on the one hand, and those of aesthetic harmony and symmetry (with the individual's emotional-imaginative pleasure as a criterion) on the other hand. I believe I was careful to specify that I do not advocate vice and crime, but that on the other hand I have a marked distaste for immoral and unlawful acts which contravene the harmonious traditions and standards of beautiful living developed by a culture during its long history. This, however, is not *ethics but aesthetics*—a distinction which you are almost alone in considering negligible. The mental and emotional forces behind this attitude, and behind the attitude of the religionist or abstract moralist, are leagues apart; as is clearly recognised by virtually all arguers on both sides. Before I get through I shall quote a very good description of my type of person, from the pen of a man very much on the other side. You can't gauge differences like this by one's daily personal conduct, because personal conduct is largely a matter of response to instinctive stimuli wholly dissociated from intellectual belief. We do what we do automatically, and then try either to rationalise it according to some theory, or to conceal it if it clashes too much with the particular theory which happens to be fastened upon us. We are mostly puppets—automata—though of course the theories we happen to hold may sometimes turn the scales one way or the other in determining a course of action, when all the other factors are evenly divided between two alternatives. So far as I am concerned—I am an aesthete devoted to harmony, and to the extraction of the maximum possible pleasure from life. I find by experience that my chief pleasure is in symbolic identification with the landscape and tradition-stream to which I belong—hence I follow the ancient, simple New England ways of living, and observe the principles of honour expected of a descendant of English gentlemen. It is pride and beauty-sense, plus the automatic instincts of generations trained in certain conduct-patterns, which determine my conduct from day to day. But this is *not ethics,* because the same compulsions and preferences apply, with me, to things wholly outside the ethical zone. For example, I never cheat or steal. Also, I never wear a top-hat with a sack coat or munch bananas in public on the streets, because a gentleman does not do those things either. I would as soon do the one as the other sort of thing—it is all a matter of harmony and good taste—whereas the ethical or "righteous" man would be horrified by dishonesty yet tolerant of coarse personal ways. If I were farming in your district I certainly would assist my neighbours—both as a means of promoting my standing in the community, and because it is good taste to be generous and accomodating. Likewise with the matter of treating the pupils in a school class. But this would not be through any sense of inner compulsion based on principles dissociated from my personal welfare and from the principle of beauty. It would be for the same reason that I would not dress eccentrically or use vulgar language. *Pure aesthetics,* aside from the personal-benefit element; and concerned with emotions of *pleasure versus disgust* rather than of *approval versus indignation.* This is a highly important distinction. Advancing to the question of *collective* conduct as involved in problems of government, social organisation, etc.—I fully see your side of the matter, and would be the last person in the world to advocate any course of civic or economic policy which might tend toward the destruction of the existing culture. In accordance with this attitude, I am distinctly opposed to visibly arrogant and arbitrary extremes of government—but this is simply because I wish the safety of an artistic and intellectual civilisation to be secure, not because I have any sympathy with the coarse-grained herd who would menace the civilisation if not placated by sops. Surely you can see the profound and abysmal difference between this emotional attitude and the emotional attitude of the democratic reformer who becomes wildly excited over the "wrongs of the masses". This reformer has uppermost in his mind the welfare of those masses themselves—he feels with them, takes up a mental-emotional point of view as one of them, regards their advancement as his prime objective independently of anything else, and would willingly sacrifice the finest fruits of the civilisation for the sake of stuffing their bellies and giving them two cinema shows instead of one per day. I, on the other hand, don't give a hang about the masses except so far as I think deliberate cruelty is coarse and unaesthetic—be it toward horses, oxen, undeveloped men, dogs, niggers, or poultry. All that I care about is *the civilisation*—the state of development and organisation which is capable of gratifying the complex mental-emotional-aesthetic needs of highly evolved and acutely sensitive men. Any *indignation* I may feel in the whole matter is not for the woes of the down-trodden, but for the threat of social unrest to the traditional institutions of the civilisation. The reformer cares only for the masses, but may make concessions to the civilisation. I care only for the civilisation, but may make concessions to the masses. Do you not see the antipodal difference between the two positions? Both the reformer and I may unite in opposing an unworkably arrogant piece of legislation, but the motivating reasons will be absolutely antithetical. He wants to give the crowd as *much* as can be given them without wrecking all semblance of civilisation, whereas I want to give them only as much as can be given them without even slightly impairing the level of the national culture. When it's an actual question of masses versus culture, I'm for giving the masses as little as can be given without bringing on a danger of collapse. Thus you see that the reformer and I are very different after all. He has a *spontaneous enthusiasm* for reform and democracy, thinking it imperative to *urge* these things. I, on the other hand, have no enthusiasm at all in this direction; thinking it the best policy not to urge concessions, but merely to grant such things when the safety of the civilisation demands it. He is a democrat at all times, and because he *wants* to be. I am one only occasionally, and when I *have* to be. Still—if you want to be so concrete and pragmatical as to ignore all emotions and motives, and judge persons by acts alone, I suppose you can say that the moderate reformer and I have *something* in common. We are both generally for a safe middle course, although each strains toward opposite boundaries of that course. In terms of the late campaign—all moderates were either for Smith[1] or Hoover, though the reformer often wished the policies of Norman Thomas and the Socialists would work, whilst I would frankly prefer a landholding aristocracy with a cultivated leisure class and a return to the historic authority of the British crown, of which I shall always be spiritually a subject. But as men of more or less rudimentary sense, both the reformer and I know that we can neither of us get what we respectively want—hence last autumn he compromised on Smith whilst I compromised on Hoover. And that's the way of it. We want different things, but have enough sense of reality to take what we can get. He works for as democratic a government *as possible;* I for as aristocratic a one *as possible.* But both recognise the limitations of possibility. Incidentally, the developments of the machine age may conceivably make inevitable a third and altogether different sort of organisation equally dissatisfying to democrat and oligarch! As for the relative value or authority of the democratic and aristocratic ideals— there is not, cosmically speaking, a bit of preference to be given either side. It is all a matter of personal emotion. I happen to favour the system which permits the free exercise of the most complex and evolved vital forces, but I freely concede that there is just as much logic in advocating a system which keeps everything down to the animal level. I would, indeed, freely concede an equal cosmic standing to any design of the insect race to extirpate the mammalian world and bring to dominance the ideals and institutions of the disciplined and efficiently organised articulata. But I couldn't get exactly enthusiastic about it!

All this will shew you that I am not insensible of the various concessions which have to be made now and then to certain elements in order to ensure practical safety—so that in reality one phase of your argument was unnecessary. In the matter of disfranchising certain classes—I simply said *that it would do no harm if it would work.* The country was governed just as well as it is now when certain classes were disfranchised—women everywhere, Catholics and Jews here and there, and men below a certain property level in places. All that has happened is that such cases of disfranchisement *have not been found possible* as matters of direct legislation. There is nothing to crow about—nothing to get excited or complacent about. The change hasn't done anybody any good, and we are no better because we *do* grant universal franchise, than were our ancestors because they *didn't*. Each of us—ancestors and contemporaries—has really done exactly the same thing: 'gotten away with' as much as possible. If anything, our ancestors deserve the more credit, because they 'got away with' more. Certainly, we could make government a neater and more effective thing, and more of a preservative of our best culture, if we could apply the same restrictions that our forefathers did. Apparently we can't—but that's nothing to brag about. No need of spilling slush and sentimentality because we have to retrench. Our modes of life and feeling are very distinctly a product of the English Protestant culture—taken as a culture apart from matters of actual belief. It would be of infinite benefit to the tone of our national life and the growth of our legitimately hereditary arts and letters if none but the English-descended Protestant element were given a share in the government—and only the best and best-chosen part of that element. That we can't establish such a restriction at this date, after our abysmal folly in admitting all sorts of immigrant elements, I am willing to concede as a practical fact; but I am *not* willing to pretend that this condition is a *benefit* to the nation. I'm damned sorry that it's so, and would do almost anything to get rid of the non-English hordes whose heritages and deepest instincts clash so disastrously with ours, and do so much to frustrate the fruition of our 300-year-old cultural stream. Therefore I'm for *any workable policy* which will throw power toward the old-American stock and take power away from the immigrant stock. The longer we can keep the strangers from tangibly tampering with our culture, the better our chance of finally assimilating those which are here (provided we have the sanity to keep others out) and of making them conform to our standards of civilisation. I don't say I'm for any more circuitous measure which will accomplish something of the same thing. My reason is plain and concrete—that it's oppressively unpleasant to live in a country where the customs, folk-ways, literary and artistic tone, and governmental forms are markedly unlike those natural to one's own race and civilisation. English civilisation was here first, and established itself by virtue of its strength. If we beat off Indian influences, we ought to be able to beat off other alien influences. Constant strength and resolution are the price of racial-cultural integrity. Do I make myself plain? You say that the idea of Catholic-Jew-atheist disfranchisement is "monstrous". I say that it is merely *impracticable at this date.* The parallel of red-haired and cross-eyed massacres is not quite valid, because red hair and cross eyes have no symbolic significance in the composition of the civilisation—but so far as abstract principles go, I had as lief as not see carrot-topped and strabismic folk quietly put out of the way. I'd merely think it was *more impracticable* than Papist-Jew-infidel disfranchisement, and would languidly question the aesthetic status of such a violent measure—inquiring whether or not the incident had an artistically adequate object. Another thing—in the past, men *have* been disfranchised because of blood, heritage or belief, whereas adults have never been slaughtered en masse because of individual physical peculiarities. This would argue that the instinctive make-up of mankind does not necessarily protest against blood-culture-creed distinctions, whereas it does seem to discourage less clear-cut discriminations in matters of selection for survival. And so it goes. Nothing is "monstrous"—but some things will work while some things won't, and some things are aesthetic according to our cultural canon while some things aren't. There's really nothing to get excited about. Grant outsiders as little influence and privilege as we safely can, and let it go at that. If we *can't* make disfranchisement work, all right; but don't let's pretend to be glad about it, or egg the foreigners on toward still further demands.

[. . .]

As for religion—of course there is a great deal in what you say about its "dog-in-the-manger" attitude, and I have often dwelt upon the same point in arguing with those who insist on the attempted fostering of faith amongst the intelligent. The only point on which we differ, is that you try to carry the same principle down to cover the unintelligent as well. My contention is that religion is still useful amongst the herd— that it helps their orderly conduct as nothing else could, and that it gives them an emotional satisfaction they could not get elsewhere. I don't say that it does either of these things as well as it used to do, but I do say that I believe nothing else could do them so well even now. The crude

120

human animal is ineradicably superstitious, and there is every biological and historical reason why he should be. An irreligious barbarian is a scientific impossibility. Rationalistic conceptions of the universe involve a type of mental victory over hereditary emotion quite impossible to the undeveloped and uneducated intellect. Agnosticism and atheism mean nothing to a peasant or workman. Mystic and teleological personification of natural forces is in his bone and blood—he cannot envisage the cosmos (i.e., the earth, the only cosmos he grasps) apart from them. Take away his Christian god and saints, and he will worship something else. Many a crude man has been talked into thinking himself an atheist, so that he loudly denies Jehovah and the Virgin and carries a load of Haldeman-Julius blue books in one pocket—yet in his other pocket he is likely to have a rabbit's foot, and the chances are 9 out of 10 that he wouldn't walk under a ladder or stop in an hotel room numbered 13! Where the Father, Son and Holy Ghost don't flourish, voodoo and witch-whispers stand ready to engross primitive emotions. Spiritualism, magic, luck-charms—all this stuff shews how irrevocably the crude human mind is chained to its hereditary illusions. "Life as an end in itself" doesn't form much of a substitute for supernatural illusion, because it isn't what the primitive mind is reaching after when it turns to prayer and mumbo-jumbo. Not but what primitives want all the life they can get; but after they have drained the cup, as they understand it, they are still looking for more. What that "more" is, as I have intimated in an earlier part of this encyclopaedic document, is undoubtedly *an approach to the mystic substance of reality itself*—the hidden reality which our senses only imperfectly apprehend. Naturally the herd do not understand what it is they are looking for. Indeed, they have not the faintest notion of any difference between phenomena and noumena. But the troublesome feeling that the senses are imperfect informers continues to lie at the back of their brains, and without knowing it they are just as restless in their search for ultimate reality as in the highly evolved theologian, philosopher, artist, or scientist. This emotion *must* be satisfied in some way—either by the crude illusion of religion, by the highly refined illusions of philosophy and art, or by the hard certainty of science that the question is absolutely settled by being absolutely unanswerable. Now it is plain to see that the satisfactions of philosophy, art, and science are hopelessly and abysmally beyond the capacity of the herd mind. Only supernaturalism is left. And since the gnawing urge of the primitive personality absolutely demands supernaturalism of some sort, it is better to let that sort be the traditional Christianity than to shift the avid emotions to snake-worship or spirit seances. As for the more intelligent classes—they *are indeed* adopting your recommended attitude of "life as an end in itself." When they cling to the outward forms of religion it is merely as a refined and traditional decoration or social custom. They don't waste much of their serious thought and emotion on the graceful rituals they chant through, and it will be found that their hereditary observances don't constitute much of a motivating force in their lives. Religion doesn't do much harm today, although one must admit that there are cases where it becomes a trifle ridiculous and annoying. What really satisfies the reality-seeking impulse in modern civilised folk is either philosophy, science, or art. Incidentally, though, one can't truthfully say that these diverse media of satisfaction are all antagonistic. Art and religion, in particular, are certainly the very reverse of enemies—so much so that there are whole schools and movements in art which depend altogether upon religious fervour for their inspiration. Religion would be gloriously justified if it had never done more than evoke the Gothic cathedral and the painting of Renaissance Italy. It is only Protestant Puritanism which tries to choke off art and absorb the feelings that ought to go into an appreciation of beauty, but even Puritanism hasn't held that pose very vigorously since the 17th century. The most beautiful thing in Providence is the steeple of the 1st Baptist Church, put up in 1775; and if you saw the half-finished Baptist Church on Riverside Drive, New York, you would have a new revelation of what soaring, pinnacled Gothic loveliness can be. I will, however, concede that the sterner sects, especially in the less populous districts, hold more to the 17th century ideal; hence am ready to sympathise with you regarding the absorption of your youthful appreciative faculties by devotional illusions. I would add, though, that a mind as exceptionally vigorous and presumably resilient as yours ought not to feel that its future is irrevocably settled by the past. Your reaction to nature and to the Albany buildings proves that your aesthetic sense is by no means atrophied; and I have no doubt but that, once you become intellectually convinced of the importance of enlarged sensitivenesses toward life and beauty, you will soon find yourself in the midst of an emotional and imaginative unfolding which will leave you marvellously enriched and more satisfyingly adjusted to the human scene. About *relativity*—I see your point regarding the "immortality" implied in the conception of the cosmos as a fixed unit in which time is merely a dimension. The idea had, indeed, occurred to me before—so that I had even thought of basing a weird tale on it. I do not, however, believe it will have much emotional or philosophical effect; since it is so purely theoretical in its relation to life and the stream of cosmic history as visible to us. Time and sequence are, for us, phenomena so inseparable from our situation in the universe, that they cannot help becoming actual noumena in all but the remotest objective academic sense. All that we can ever subjectively understand as entity, in its opposite to absolute nullity, is coincidence with certain time-sections of space; it being utterly beyond our mental and emotional capacity to envisage the relationship of an attribute of one time-section to a corresponding place in another time-section. "Beginning" and "ending" are as inalienably real to us as if we had never heard of Einstein; and without question the only conception of *immortality* which can have any meaning for us is that of a limitless diffusion through *all* the time-sections of space. That is, our minds work only with what they really experience; and we have found time and sequence to be too vivid a proximate reality in the history of our planet to allow us to consider life, entity and duration independently of them. Unless a given thing can coincide in all its dimensions with every time-section of space which from our standpoint lies in the future, our subjective intellects refuse to grasp it as immortal; for to us existence is measured only by participation in the visible stream of time-space glimpses which our sense-equipment and point of observation lead us to recognise as proximate reality. In other words, the sight of a world on which our forefathers cannot be found, and the realisation that there will some day be a world on which we cannot be found, prohibits us from conceiving perpetual existence on an Einsteinian basis. Possibly astute theologians will devise some subtle interpretation which the masses will swallow—using the idea of relativity to rehabilitate the doctrine of supernaturalism. Indeed, they have already started to do this, as well as to accept the newer ideas of intra-atomic physics as evidence of a spiritual world. But whatever new emotion the world may derive in this way will be due to the cleverness of the theologians rather than to the convincingness of the material. In bald truth, the notion of a relativity-immortality is just as remotely abstract in one direction, as the principle of cosmic futility in another direction!

I read with interest your explanation of your attitude toward my atheism and its clear-cut negations, and can well understand how you feel. Aesthetically I feel the same way; indeed, it is my chief delight to weave verbal images of unreality, in which I can flout, rearrange, and triumph over the impersonal cosmic pattern at will. I am no less impressed than you by the magnitude, complexity, and essential beauty of the cosmos; nor am I less sensible to the veil which separates us from the grasping of ultimate reality. The great difference between us in these matters is that you like to colour your philosophic-scientific speculations with your aesthetic feeling; whilst I feel a great cleavage betwixt emotion and perceptive analysis, and never try to mix the two. *Emotionally* I stand breathless at the awe and loveliness and mystery of space with its ordered suns and worlds. In that mood I endorse religion, and people the fields and streams and groves with the Grecian deities and local spirits of old—for at heart I am a pantheistic pagan of the old tradition which Christianity has never reached. But when I start *thinking* I throw off emotion as excess baggage, and settle down to the prosaic and exact task of seeing simply what is, or probably is, and what isn't, or probably isn't. I love to dream, but I never try to dream and think at the same time. Like the boy in your argument, I would pause a moment in awe and admiration before great whirring wheels—but I fancy neither the boy nor I would stand there gaping for ever. Sooner or later we'd "snap out of it" and try to understand the impressive spectacle before us. The same goes for natural beauty. The morning frost scene which you describe takes hold of my imagination tremendously, (with the room temperature at $+76°$) and creates a genuine thrill of aesthetic mysticism. I can grasp the wonder and perfection of those complex and delicate crystals; for I have seen many, and seen pictures of many more. If confronted by such a sense, I would (in my dying fancy, as the $10°$

below drew me up toward the gates of heaven)[2] surely harbour no thought of scientific laws or philosophic deductions; but would instead feel poignantly the mystic beauty, and would commence to weave dreams of faery workmanship or interplanetary magic around the exquisite objects before me. Not until I got back to the library or the laboratory (assuming that the temperature let me get back at all) would I employ the things I had seen as data in intellectual research or speculation. It is the same with the sky. I am, as I may have told you, rather an astronomical devotee; yet these evenings when I tread the narrow ancient streets on the brow of the hill and look westward over the outspread roofs and spires and domes of the lower town to where the distant hills of the countryside stand out against the fading sky, I do not scan that sky as a measurer or an analyst. Resplendent Venus and Jupiter shine close together, hanging over the great beacon-tower of the terraced Industrial Trust Building as they used to hang 2000 years ago over the towering Pharos in Alexandria's crowded harbour; and as I watch them and compare them with the great red beacon and the mystic twinkling lights of the dusk-shadowed city below, I surely hold no thoughts of their objective nature and position. I do not say to myself that Jupiter is a cloudy belted sphere 1300 times larger than the earth and situated some 480,000,000 miles from the sun, or that Venus is a globe slightly smaller than the earth, perpetually veiled by a cloudy atmosphere, and about 66,000,000 miles from the sun. I do not reflect that Jupiter's orbit is outside the earth's while Venus's is inside, and that this circumstance determines the vastly different apparent motions they display in the terrestrial sky. The fact is, I do not say or reflect anything—I merely watch and dream. I dream of the evenings when these orbs did indeed hang over cryptic and seething Alexandria—and over Carthage before it, and over Thebes and Memphis and Biibylon and Ur of the Chaldees before that. I dream of the hidden messages they bring down the aeons from those distant and half-forgotten places, and from those darker, obscurer, places in the still older world, whereof only whispered rumour dares to speak. As I watch them, I feel that they watch me, and that the beauty they cast upon the thickening night and the candle-pierced, crepuscular town is a symbol of primal glories older than man, older than earth, older than Nature, older even than the gods, and designed for my mystic soul alone. This, indeed, is *feeling*—but when I approach the same objects as an astronomical student I do so very differently. Then I leave my dreams behind and take along my telescope; and instead of glancing at the lighted town below, I curse it for the smoke and heat-vapours it sends up to obscure telescopic definition. I note the phase of Venus and the curve of the terminator, and reflect how far past greatest elongation it is; and when I turn the glass on Jupiter I regret its long distance past opposition. I don't couple the two planets at all now—the pattern vanishes with the aesthetic mood—and would much rather have Jupiter over in the east, where it is on the evenings when it is nearest the earth. As for my story—the idea was not that a world of dream and beauty is meaningless, but that a world of thought is meaningless. I was merely advising people to be poets instead of astronomers. It didn't especially occur to me to stress the liberating side of cosmic meaninglessness, because I think that side has been somewhat overrated. Only a minority, I think, felt really chafed by the mythical demands of theism; whilst vast numbers acquire a very uncomfortable sense of anchorless drifting as a result of modernity's removal of fixed, objective values and points of reference. "Life as an end in itself", as I have opined before, seems to me a trifle beyond the development of the average citizen. Physical and aesthetic sensation are not enough to give him the comfortable illusion of significance.

Religion and Ethics

[The following is an extract from a letter to Natalie H. Wooley (2 May 1936). In it, Lovecraft maintains that religion is unnecessary in establishing a moral code, and that a realistic morality will survive the downfall of religious belief.]

As for religious belief in general—I see no reason for entertaining any. All notions of cosmic consciousness and purpose, and of the importance of man in the limitless pattern of the universe, are plainly myths born of the imperfect information of man's early days. Today we know more about the background of the phenomena around us; and our present knowledge includes nothing which could reasonably lead us to assume the existence of a vast manlike intelligence (the idea is childish, since today we know that the very essence of thought, consciousness, and purpose is the organic brain of highly-developed mammals—a thing utterly inconsistent with vague, unparticled force) in space as a whole. Read the late Ernst Haeckel's "Riddle of the Universe"—translations of which any good library ought to have. Religious superstition is fastened on the race only because of the blind, thoughtless handing down of obsolete myths concocted in ages of total ignorance. Today we not only know the natural forces behind all phenomena once thought supernatural, but realise also the psychological and anthropological

127

forces which caused early man to invent the various myths of gods, cosmic purpose, etc. Modern psychologists know that *any* sort of belief, true or false, can be fastened on the inexperienced emotions of a small child through inculcation—hence realise that religions keep alive only through seizing on each new generation before it can reason for itself, and deliberately hypnotising or crippling its infant judgment in favour of the dominant faith. The very fact that religions are not content to stand on their own feet, but insist on crippling or warping the flexible minds of children in their favour, forms a sufficient proof that there is no truth in them. If there were any truth in religion, it would be even more acceptable to a mature mind than to an infant mind—yet no mature mind ever accepts religion unless it has been crippled in infancy. I believe there should be a law prohibiting religious instruction of any sort for persons under 21. The young mind should be taught only *one* thing—the honest and open search for *truth* irrespective of consequences. Nobody's belief in a given thing means anything unless it is entered into with an open and freely reasoning mind. But religion shrinks from the test of *truth*. It is unwilling to present its case without loaded dice—hence continues to insist that infant minds be crippled in its favour. The fact is, of course, that no active and uncrippled mind could possibly accept any sort of religion in the light of today's scientific knowledge. The whole basis of religion is a symbolic emotionalism which modern knowledge has rendered meaningless and even unhealthy. Today we know that the cosmos is simply a flux of purposeless rearrangement amidst which man is a wholly negligible incident or accident. There is no reason why it should be otherwise, or why we should wish it otherwise. All the florid romancing about man's "dignity", "immortality", etc. etc. is simply egotistical delusion plus primitive ignorance. So, too, are the infantile concepts of "sin" or *cosmic* "right" and "wrong". Actually, organic life on our planet is simply a momentary spark of no importance or meaning whatever. Man matters to nobody except himself. Nor are his "noble" imaginative concepts any proof of the objective reality of the things they visualise. Psychologists understand how these concepts are built up out of fragments of experience, instinct, and misapprehension. Man is essentially a machine of a very complex sort, as La Mettrie recognised nearly two centuries ago.[1] He arises through certain typical chemical and physical reactions, and his members gradually break down into their constituent parts & vanish from existence. The idea of personal "immortality" is merely the dream of a child or of a savage.

However, there is nothing anti-ethical or anti-social in such a realistic view of things. Although meaning nothing *in the cosmos as a whole,* mankind obviously means a good deal *to itself.* Therefore it must be regulated by customs which shall ensure, *for its own benefit,* the full development of its various accidental potentialities. It has a fortuitous jumble of reactions, some of which it instinctively seeks to heighten and prolong, and some of which it instinctively seeks to avoid or shorten or lessen. Also, we see that certain courses of action tend to increase its radius of comprehension and degree of specialised organisation (things usually promoting the wished-for reactions, and in general removing the species from a clod-like, unorganised state), while other courses of action tend to exert an opposite effect. Now since man means nothing in the cosmos, it is plain that his only logical goal (a goal whose sole reference is to *himself*) is simply the achievement of a reasonable equilibrium which shall enhance his likelihood of experiencing the sort of reactions he wishes, and which shall help along his natural impulse to increase his differentiation from unorganised force and matter. This goal can be reached only through teaching individual men how best to keep out of each other's way, and how best to reconcile the various conflicting instincts which a haphazard cosmic drift has placed within the breast of the same person. Here, then, is a practical and imperative system of ethics, resting on the firmest possible foundation & being essentially that taught by Epicurus and Lucretius. It has no need of supernaturalism, and indeed has nothing to do with it. However, an ethical system is always hard to enforce, so that moralists are constantly looking for powerful agents of compulsion. Some favour armed force (and armies and policemen will always be needed), while others look to pride or fear or reason or aesthetic taste. Primitive man used force as a matter of course, but he also realised the powerful compelling nature of superstition. If he could hook up ethical precept with the myth (in which he then believed) of cosmic purpose and will, he would have the most potent of influences working with him to make people accept his preferred code of conduct. It was easy for him to persuade himself and others that the gods liked the various instincts and types of conduct and rational compromises (kindness, honesty, non-encroachment, coöperation, etc.) which make for general harmony among men, and that they disliked the various lawless instincts and types of conduct (egotism, treachery, cruelty, encroachment, lack of social coöperation, etc.) which act in an opposite direction. Hence arose the illusory concepts of "right", "wrong", and "sin" as cosmic matters—and the general popular tendency to identify religion and ethics. Really, of course, there is no essential connexion between religion and ethics. Ethics can stand on its own feet without religion, and the time has come in which it must do so to an increasing degree. Its enforcing agencies— aside from physical power—should be reason and taste and pride; as indeed they are now among the enlightened. It is interesting to observe that many of the world's religions tacitly recognise the lack of connexion between faith and ethics by loftily ignoring the latter. Hellenic religion tended to leave ethics more or less to the philosophers, while even Protestant Christianity had its Antinomian sect (in Massachusetts Bay Colony in 1638 et seq) which proclaimed that "salvation" was a matter of sheer faith irrespective of conduct. Religion has served its purpose, and is meaningless in the light of today's understanding of the universe. We now perceive *that there is no "why" of things*—that, indeed, the whole concept of a "why" is based upon an obsolete perspective. Things simply are—forming momentary phases of ceaseless rearrangement of forces which always have existed and always will exist. Why should they be otherwise? The existing patterns are merely basic conditions of entity—which have nothing to do with the transient ideas and wishes of the negligible organisms of our planet. We now understand the origins of those ideas and wishes, and realise that they are simply automatic nervous phenomena having nothing to do with reality. If it amuses any childish mind to juggle words and apply the name "god" or "the gods" to the automatic principle of regularity in the cosmos, no one need object. Words are pretty things to play with. But we must remember that this pattern principle has not the slightest resemblance to the various deities of traditional religions. It is not a "mind". It has no

130

consciousness or purpose. It doesn't know we exist or care what we do. It has nothing to do with the aesthetic or utilitarian human concepts of "right" and "justice". It is simply a *condition*—like the existence of an atmosphere around the earth. Epicurus vaguely realised all this when he said that although the gods may exist, they never concern themselves with the affairs of mankind.

Today time spent in considering religion is simply wasted. What is needed is *scientific social vision* and *coöperation,* with the rational happiness and balanced development of men, individually and collectively, as its sole object. That is, we need to cultivate a practical morality based on common sense, good taste, & modern sociology . . . doing which, we may well leave supernatural belief and the grovelling worship of unconscious force-patterns to the ignorant and the hyper-emotional. Read H. L. Mencken's "Treatise on the Gods"—and also Nietzsche's "Genealogy of Morals". The various brochures of Joseph McCabe, published by the Haldeman-Julius Co. at Girard in your own state, are also enlightening. A good article on the vanishing of religious belief among modern thinkers will be found in *Harper's Magazine* for August, 1934—"Religious Beliefs of American Scientists", by James H. Leuba, Prof. of Psychology at Bryn Mawr.[3]

However—despite my disagreement with its philosophical assumptions, I appreciate none the less the grace and excellence of your essay "Intimations—The Hand in the Dark", which I return herewith plus a few very trifling changes of text. This sketch is extremely well-phrased and imaginatively developed, and certainly ought to quiet any apprehensions of yours regarding the equality of your writing. I hope it may eventually appear in print—either in the N.A.P.A. or elsewhere. My objections are solely against the logic of certain assumptions—for example, I see no reason why the ability of the human imagination to conceive certain aesthetically impressive and emotionally gratifying passages of literature (an ability fully explained by materialistic psychologists) should be regarded as "proof" that man has a 'divine spark' or that he cannot (as he certainly will) become 'drifting dust on a burned-out planet.' What this imaginative ability proves is merely that man is a very complexly organised form of matter—that he stands very high in the scale of development as measured by degree of removal from primitive unorganised substance. This, no one wishes to deny. Man is indeed by far the most advanced product of the cosmic flux of which we have any direct knowledge—*but what has this high status to do with the quality of permanence* (i.e., the mythical condition of "immortality") *or with the kind of relationship which the species has with the basic force-patterns of cosmic entity?* It is absurd to think that any being very highly developed must be essentially different *in principle* from beings of much lower development . . . . or, conversely, that it is a slur upon the greatness of a high species to declare that it is not the especial and eternal pet of a conscious and personified cosmos. Joseph McCabe[4] has aptly and truly said that there is no difference *in kind* (despite the enormous difference *in degree*) between the howl of a dog and a symphony of Beethoven. Still—all this doesn't make your concept any the less poetical, or your essay any the less graceful. Congratulations on a good piece of work!

Religion and Social Progress

[The following is an extract from a letter to Helen Sully (17 October 1933). Sully (1904–1997) was one of the relatively few women who corresponded with Lovecraft. She had evidently experienced a disappointment in a love affair, and Lovecraft's letter explains that modern "decadent" behavior is not a direct corollary of religious disbelief; his own system of morals is not religious, but he is in no way inclined to behave boorishly to women (or men) as a result of it.]

I did not realise how low the general educational level of Quebec province is, although of course I knew that the sectarian limitations must make the culture very one-sided. I fancy that scholastic standards vary locally. Montreal is very proud of its schools, and a municipal law makes it obligatory that French be taught in the English schools, and English in the church-managed French ones. Thus all the population is becoming bi-lingual—every young Anglo-Montrealer knowing some French, and every French youngster knowing some English. The almost unparallelled degree of ecclesiastical domination in French Canada is certainly a retarding influence, and seems to arouse resentment in most visitors despite its picturesqueness . . . . silver steeples, tonsured, sandalled, brown-robed friars, curiously coiffed nuns, etc. Peasants will

133

have their religion, just as workmen will have their whiskey—but the financial drain and intellectual stultification sometimes seem a disproportionately high price to pay for the emotional soothing and titillation. If simple people must grovel before mythical conceptions, they might at least have a less expensive, retarding, and politically bothersome set of idols than those of an arrogant Catholic orthodoxy. Ordinarily I am not at all hostile to any sort of Santa-Claus belief that anyone may wish to harbour, but of late years I feel that formal religions may cause very much trouble in the period of social and economic readjustment which lies ahead. All the powerful orthodoxies represent celestial projections of the now obsolescent political order, hence are pledged to defend it against all change. With a mechanised world of radically altered conditions, great changes will certainly be necessary from now on—yet all the official faiths recognise the extinct fabric as sacred, and blindly oppose any rational readjustment based on current needs. Of the various mythologies dominant in the Anglo-Saxon world one might form a scale based on relative absurdity. The least irrational is undoubtedly the very liberal theism represented by Dr. Fosdick and a few other actual thinkers among theologians. Next comes ordinary Unitarianism. Below this stand the loosely liberalised evangelical sects whose orthodox tenets are quietly dropped one by one— Congregationalists, Presbyterians, and the best grade of Baptists. Next— though much higher as an *aesthetic* proposition—comes the Anglican church with its ingeniously evaded 39 articles, and after that (though higher up *aesthetically*) the ancient Catholic hierarchy with its impossible assumptions and eel-like logic-twisting. Lowest of all are the literal and orthodox evangelical sects—the dense and wilfully brainless Presbyterians, Baptists, & Methodists with their hysterical 'kiver to kiver' hill-billy gospel. And the Mormons, Christian Scientists, Holy Rollers, etc. fit in *intellectually* near the bottom, though social prestige gives some of these freak sects a borrowed impressiveness in certain local areas. All of these systems of blindly inherited tradition mean well, and all have the common usefulness of giving people the illusion of significance, direction, and value in the meaningless welter of conscious biological existence. They are the natural conceptions of a primitive and ignorant race, and embody a vast amount of really useful precept—the massed experience of mankind worked out by trial and error and given a fictitious heavenly authority. Certainly, it would cause chaos and harm to strip the world of their influence before a more rational psychological and ethical regimen, based on aesthetics and the actual mental and physical needs of the group in its existing environment, can be worked out and given effective force. We can see already the somewhat squalid decadence in emotional sensitivity and ethical harmony which prevails amongst these "sophisticates" who have lost their traditional faith without replacing it with a suitable aesthetic and practical substitute. The trouble is that substitutes can't be devised over night. They have to grow by gradual accretion through long centuries of homogeneous and continuous experience before they can dominate the subconscious mind and provide that sense of direction and purpose which alone saves life from becoming a nightmare. Exceptions to this rule of gradual growth are very rare—coming only when some psychological accident raises up a new illusion so potently captivating that it sweeps all before it. Such an accident was the blazing up of Islam in the 7th century, and such, to a lesser and perhaps temporary degree, is the spread of communism (a religion despite its anti-theism) in modern Russia. Yes—I read George Moore in youth, and have always thought the Catholic system weak in its relation to individual character. Ironically, it is the least personally strengthening because it is the most purely *religious*. Theoretically—and as a matter of universal acceptance in pre-Reformation times—the function of religion is primarily to exalt and serve some mystical and intangible entity or group of entities outside mankind. It has relatively little to do with human conduct and character—hence in classical and pre-classical antiquity we find religion largely ritualistic and orgiastic, whilst conduct (based on reason) remained the province of the non-religious philosopher. Christianity—or rather, the Judaism on which it was based—was the first religion to take a primary interest in ethics and assume a responsibility for conduct and character. That was the unique contribution of the Semitic temperament to western civilisation—a very doubtful gift; since it removed ethics so completely from the aesthetic and logical field, transferring it to the jurisdiction of a mythical belief, that order and good taste threaten to vanish upon the ultimate and inevitable decline of the mythology. It would have been far better if we had kept our classical conception of ethics as a matter of beauty, good sense, and taste—the province of the non-supernatural philosopher—for its survival would not then have been so imperilled by the decline of religion. As Aryans, lacking the almost savage ethical sense of the desert-bred Semite, we are vastly better adapted to the conception of character as related to beauty, reason, and pride, than to the notion of "divine moral law". Meanwhile our dominant religion has always been torn betwixt two tendencies—one to return to the Aryan concept and become a system of *mystical adoration* letting morals more or less slide or putting them on a bargaining and excusing basis, and the other to live up to the specifically Christian ideal and mould better and more harmonious characters in the immediate world around us. The first tendency breeds the Catholic psychology, and the second the Protestant. As a result, Catholics are more purely *religious*—since Protestants, being after all Aryans to whom the feverish Semitic religio-moralism is impossible save for brief periods (such as that of intensive and literal Puritanism in England and New-England), tend to lay more and more stress on human character and good deeds as opposed to mystical adoration, and therefore to exercise the functions of the classically conceived philosopher rather than those of the classically conceived priest. Today religion is on the decline as an influence—necessarily so, on account of what we have learned about the workings of the cosmos and of our own minds and emotions. It is, then, our task to save existence from a sense of chaos and futility by rebuilding the purely aesthetic and philosophical concept of character and cosmic pseudo-purpose—reëstablishing a realisation of the necessity of *pattern* in any order of being complex enough to satisfy the mind and emotions of highly evolved human personalities. Obviously, the Protestant mind is the one best fitted to execute this important work—best fitted because it is the most philosophical and least religious. While Protestantism itself—as a supernatural faith—will decline because of the graduation of its thoughtful members to philosophic atheism or agnosticism (and of its thoughtless members to decadent and disorganised drifting), its actual work will continue as a sort of legacy. The framework it has bequeathed will serve a useful purpose—ensuring for the increasingly non-religious ethics of the future that force of *traditional continuity* which realists recognise as so essential to any really working system of action or emotion. The steeple, the Gothic tower, and the chromatic and magical twilight of painted windows can still have an effective psychological and social function long after their supernatural background is disowned. But, of course, only if decadence, speed-and-quantity worship, and other emotionally coarsening and impoverishing influences can be held in check. The issue—survival or decadence—is still in doubt. And meanwhile the Catholic religion, a ceremonial and mystical institution independent of the details of conduct, plugs along in its ancient, deeply-rooted way—hampering good social organisation now and then, yet at least giving a consoling emotional opium to millions incapable of an aesthetic or philosophic attitude. There is always room for a kindly narcotic of this sort—at least, until reason solves the perhaps insoluble problem of bringing decent comfort and contentment of a material kind to the totality of the population.

But pardon senile prolixity on abstractions—Grandpa's favourite pastime! That's the way things get going when the invincible and indivisible triad of Belknap, James Ferdinand Morton, and E'ch-Pi-El sit down for a little light persiflage. Regarding The Modern Young Man and his wandering emotions—a detached observer must simultaneously sympathise with the transitional perplexity which drives him to his ugly, feverish, ruthless, and ultimately futile course, and deplore and oppose the pursuance of that course itself. One must, to twist the sense of a line which Mr. Pope writ in my 18th century, "love th' Offender, yet detest th' Offence."[1] Without doubt, the brutally primitive, experimental, socially irresponsible, animally capricious, aesthetically low-grade, callously anti-traditional, and really personally insulting amative attitudes of modern youth are primarily products of reaction against a system of interpreting human relationships which was fully as ridiculous and unrealistic—even if not so emotionally low-grade, anti-social, and insulting to human nature—as the existing opposite. Family organisation was an artificial fetish, and the nature of the emotional ties betwixt individuals was so wholly falsified and reduced to pompous sentimental fiction that no person of sense could survey the popular pretences—either in literature or in speech and manners—without a surge of hilarity, anger, or disgust, according to his temperament. Any "serious" romance of 50 years ago makes comic reading today—values, assigned motivations, human reactions, and so on. Hypocrisy was loathsomely encouraged and exercised, and people in practice had to keep two sets of data in their heads—life and motives as outwardly represented, and life and motives as actually existing. Since the latter phase was not officially recognised, there was no unanimity of knowledge or attitude regarding it. Under religion and the self-deluding psychology it bred, such a mental muddle might well remain permanent. The ethical code enjoined by religion was near enough to the optimum of common sense to prevent acute social friction, and the absurdity of the assigned motivations was suffered to remain unnoticed. When, however, religion began to crack, acute thinkers began to pause and ask themselves how real the commonly assigned values and motives might be; and thence, how much actual validity the existing emotional attitudes and social institutions might possess. That was the age of Ibsen, Wilde, Nietzsche, Shaw, and Wells . . . . and presently of Freud, Adler, and Jung. After the analysis and shakeup it became pretty clear that the moving impulses of mankind, their relation to the basic structure of the universe, and their manner of operation under various given sets of conditions, are far—infinitely far—from what orthodox religion and conventional sentimentality had assumed. Human instincts were boiled down to about a dozen, the relative strength of these in different individual types and races and under different environmental conditions was estimated, and the multifarious phenomena of human emotional life were traced to the interaction and mutual checking of these instincts, plus the infinite wealth of associational combinations which the memory, the symbolic imagination, and the pattern-sense superimpose upon the primitive substratum. Men's feelings and moods and aspirations were seen to be neither "divine" nor universal, neither eternal nor simple and basic, neither consciously ordained nor related to any larger end—but rather to be the net chance results of a complex array of originally mechanical forces peculiar to the organisms bred in this part of the universe; having no larger connexions in time or space, and conditioned by their environment. What the oxidation of iron and the crystallisation of salt and the sensitivity of a sunfish and the anger of

138

a fighting dog are on lower rungs of the organisational ladder, so are the dreams of a poet and the vision of a seer and the devotion of a lover amongst the complex types of organisation called advanced mammal primates, or human beings. Obviously, the flatulent old sentimentalities were pretty thin stuff!

And right here is where the difference between rational balance and hysterical decadence is illustrated. What has been shewn us? Simply that certain phenomena and conditions have *causes* and some *details of operation* other than what was formerly supposed. Has anything suggested that any of the phenomena or conditions ought to be changed or abolished? Obviously not. What we have found out means nothing one way or the other so far as recommending or condemning various courses goes. All it signifies is that supernatural constraint to one arbitrary course does not exist. It sends us back to nature—and any full-witted person realises that this means *our whole complex nature, including the most delicate associational sensitivities* rather than the merely instinctive or simian part of our nature—for guidance, and bids us reconsider our accustomed ways *only so far as is necessary to bring them into harmony with the one reasonable purpose of making the most of our opportunities for symmetrical development and permanent, heightened enjoyment under such environmental conditions as we have or can make.* To assume that the discovery of the mechanical and fortuitous nature of our complex higher emotions at once reduces those emotions to hypocritical ignominiousness, or even to mere equality with the dozen or so primitive dog-and-ape instincts and emotions, is a breach of logic so utterly childish, unjustified, and hilariously ridiculous that I honestly cannot see how any adult person of normal intelligence and grammar-school education can make it. It is to me one of those inscrutable mysteries beyond solution—like the sudden blight which caused the collapse of architectural taste in the Victorian age. I give it up! What is this "young intelligentsia" driving at, anyhow? Don't they realise that the essence of all quality is *fineness of organisation?* What if the *basic substance* of a finely-wrought thing *is* the same as that of other coarsely wrought things. Is a delicate watch or micrometer no better than a horseshoe or flatiron merely because its chemical substance is similar?

We know from observation, record, and analysis how infinitely keener and finer-evolved human life is, than primitive lower-animal life. We can recognise our superior grasp of the universe, and can feel the increased pleasure accruing from the exercise of many emotional and imaginative faculties instead of a pitiful few. This is intrinsic and basic—if we keep our heads clear we don't need any "divine" nonsense to justify the more complex, delicate, and human aspects of life as opposed to the primitive and brutish aspects. The bottom hasn't dropped out of anything merely because we've made a discovery about the mechanism. Nothing of the "dignity and value of human life" has been lost in the change of perspective. And yet what nonsense certain poor devils (both on the theological and on the decadent side, as a matter of fact!) spout! Without a shadow of justification, the decadent "sophisticate" leaps to two *perfectly irrelevant* assumptions—first, that human nature, not being divine and cosmic, must necessarily be bestial; and second, that all highly evolved emotions must necessarily be valueless, non-existent, or reprehensible, *merely because they were formerly mis-explained.* As a complete and puerile violation of all logic, this modernistic philosophy furnishes a classic and immortal example! And yet, as I said at the outset, I can sympathetically understand the feelings of the decadent. He is so exasperated at the outrageous bull and crap of theology-dictated sentimentalism that he feels impelled to fly to the remotest possible extreme. The trouble is that this other extreme is just as silly and even more harmful and violative of richness in life than the first one! He doesn't realise this because he allows his first exasperation to cut off his mind and put blind emotion in the saddle. He feels so much that he doesn't think—hence peters out in futility and brutish degradation.

It is needless to say to persons of good sense and reflectiveness that the one rational object of life is—for all the absence of a deity or of a high-flown cosmic basis of thoughts and feelings—the harmonious utilisation and satisfaction of our existing equipment to the greatest possible extent; a pursuit which, in view of the well-known conflicts between different tendencies and groups of tendencies within us, postulates an intelligent choice of keener, more permanent, and more rewarding faculties over duller, more transient, and less profoundly rewarding faculties for favouring and cultivation. This is not a theological or moral dictum—it is merely materialistic common sense. If it offends the "younger advanced intelligentsia" by sounding excessively like what ancient philosophers used to say, that's just too bad . . . . . . although the youngsters could realise if they'd stop to think that much of ancient philosophy and ethics comes primarily from plain observation and common sense. The trimmings of pomp and poetry are tacked on later. It is true that cosmic "good" and "evil" do not exist—but it is also true that in human conduct and emotional guiding there are certain courses which (environment being confined within given limits) tend to give profound and lasting satisfaction and expansion to a maximum of our faculties, and certain courses which yield a net return (whatever the momentary effect) of dissatisfaction and frustration. We don't have to call such courses "good" and "evil"—it is never wise to become slaves to nomenclature—but it would be unscientific not to recognise them and differentiate betwixt their properties. So after all, the triumphant and blatant immoralist is in a pretty bad fix philosophically and scientifically. He hasn't much ground to stand on. Unfortunately his voice isn't impaired—so he still makes a great noise.

As for *details*—rational, materialistic ethics will of course have certain points of difference from theistic, traditional ethics; though the hidden rational factor in ancient morals, plus the present psychological value of continuity, will combine to make the future's code much more like the past's than the thoroughgoing materialist will relish. The decent citizen of the machine age will have a disconcerting number of points in common with the decent citizen of the Greek, Roman, mediaeval, and modern Western civilisations. So far as the element of human affection is concerned, there is not nearly enough change to please the young Casanovas who aspire to the carefree refinements of the canine or feline worlds. In spite of their fine talk, and in spite of the mythical nature of that cosmically derived and mysteriously unalterable passion postulated by bygone sentimentality, it remains a rather obvious fact that of the many perfectly separate elements which enter into any typical human tie (for there is no *one* thing which may be called love or affection; each

141

individual emotion-group classified as such being a complex fuxion of various dissimilar factors acting accidentally toward the production of a given resultant expression), those which make for sudden, violent, and transient infatuation are the very lowest in the biological-psychological scale, whilst those which endure over long periods (and it is simply childish—a denial of obvious evidence—to ignore the thousands of well-defined and unmistakable cases of virtually permanent affection on record) belong to that higher, more complex, and more associative order which involve the recognition of finely evolved faculties in their object and afford deeper, maturer, and more poignantly developed psychological satisfactions in their possessor. In other words, when a "young modern" says that a temporary or at least limited affair of intense emotion is the only sort of romance really satisfying to him, he is merely confessing that his emotional development has remained at a rather simian level; that he is not seeking a companion to honour as a fellow human-being, but is looking for a fellow-ape with whom he may amuse his transient and superficial emotions after the casual fashion of the ape species. Without knowing it—for one must give him credit for his naive ignorance if possible—he is giving the momentary object of his doubtful affections the gravest possible insult; that of placing her on a level essentially sub-human, as one who does not possess the qualities which, in really equal and sincerely beloved human beings, elicit so varied and general an array of emotional bonds that the passing of the crude temporary factors is virtually unnoticed in comparison to the tremendous residue of really human affection (recognition of mental kinship, harmony of highly-developed emotions, piling up of tender symbolic and associative factors, etc.) which permanently remains. His is the essentially crippled, cheapened emotional nature which cannot envisage or experience fine shades and subtleties of feeling. He gets on finely with Ovid's Ars Amatoria, but doesn't understand what the tale of Baucis & Philemon in the same author's Metamorphoses is about.[2] In this naive blindness he falls below even the callous gallants of antiquity; insomuch as they recognised standards but did not live up to them, whilst he recognises no standards at all. In defence of his position he points to the certainly large-enough number of persons who find permanent and congenial ties impossible of achievement. Here, again, he is exercising that childish lapse of logic which marks his estimate of human emotion as a whole. Merely because the world is haphazard and imperfect, with certain satisfactory adjustments attainable by only a part of the population, he jumps to the erroneous and irrelevant conclusion that *nobody* can attain such adjustments; that those who say they do merely pretend it, and that it is a waste of time to seek such a type of felicity. In other words, because *some* people can't appreciate music, it is foolish for *anybody* to seek the pleasures of harmony. Because *some* are colour-blind, it is foolish for *anybody* to seek any art other than black and white. What crap! And yet these smart-alec Lotharios call *themselves* acute and sophisticated, and brand the rational conservative as an outmoded fogy! As a matter of fact, the very growth of rationalism from which they draw their silly conclusions does much to emphasise the hollowness of their position—for with the decline of the crazy "one-great-love-in-a-lifetime" hallucination of Victorian days, and the disappearance of the savage anti-divorce prejudices of darker times, the number of permanently unadjustable individuals is bound to be vastly cut down through opportunities for the rectification of mistakes and the formation of new and sounder alliances with better prospects of dignified permanence. There is *less and less* excuse, rather than more and more, for abandoning the quest for that full and permanent union of psychological lives which is obviously the only real fulfilment of human affection on equal human terms.

It seems to me, then, clear that in spite of all his stale, misquoted Freud, his cleverly juggled divorce statistics, and his pompous anthropological extracts from Briffault and Calverton[3] and other flashy conclusion-jumpers, the fickle young modern is holding and defending a false (and if he knew it, insulting) position when he rants in favour of canine romantic ethics. In view of what is known regarding the constituents of human affection, we cannot but conclude that he is upholding cheapness and inferiority against emotional richness and all that we truly respect. Whatever be the possibilities of error, delusion, and disappointment—and in what human venture are they absent?—it seems certain that any person possessing for another the equal and honourable affection which involves respect, congeniality, understanding, and recognition as a fellow human-being of intelligence, as well as the more glamourous temporary factors, will not wish or propose any union other than an open and socially acceptable one intended (whatever melancholy revision the future may perchance dictate) for permanent duration. I may be a crabbed bigot, but any other sort of romantic sighing to a daughter of mine, if I had one, would earn a modernistic gallant an extremely decided momentum down those selfsame stairs which tripped my aunt,[4] transmitted through a hard-soled #8 Regal! In dealing with "advanced and emancipated" youths of this sort, no one need feel impelled to exercise undue tact or harbour undue scruples. Good sense and good taste—proximate principles based on the real fulness of human nature—furnish solidly workable and wholly non-theological standards to which no soberly reflective person will be ashamed to be true. And no excuse is ever needed for acting according to such standards, or upholding them against any of the fly-by-night bolshevisms of fad, fashion, fever, and foolishness! Restoration ethics had their day—but the fame of "unfashionable" Milton has lived longer than that of

". . . the sons
Of Belial, flown with insolence & wine."[5]

Protestants and Catholics

[The following is an extract from a letter to Frank Belknap Long (April 1931). In an earlier letter, Long had proclaimed himself a devotee of "splendid traditionalism," but Lovecraft here maintains that, in spite of his shedding of the religious beliefs of his ancestors, he is the more traditionalist of the two because he instinctively retains many of the social and moral inclinations formerly inclulcated by religious belief. Lovecraft goes on to engage in a discussion of the fundamental difference between Catholicism and Protestantism.]

Now as to our rivalry about which is the more truly traditional—I still insist that Grandpa belongs more to the past despite a lack of belief in any of the old illusions. The reason I do insist is that I deny the ability of any modern *really* to duplicate the sensations of the past, no matter how much he may *want* to duplicate them or *think* he duplicates them. If you *really* felt about the universe as your grandfather did, or as Louis XI did, or as St. Augustine did, I would gladly concede your greater traditionalism despite a tendency to take motors and typewriters as a matter of course. But you and I both know damn well that you don't and can't—that no living peson of maturity and cultivation can at this date. Chesterton doesn't—he is merely a frantic old man trying to cover up confusion with a joke and a chuckle. You only *try* to believe in cosmic purpose and values. Every educated man over twenty-one and under fifty knows today in his *subconscious* mind that the ultimates of the universe are unplumbed and without evidence to suggest any save an automatic and impersonal organisation. To declare that the feverish and strained efforts of moderns to believe in old values are in any way equivalent to the actual beliefs of the ancestors they are trying to copy, is to commit an error of the most glaring and misleading sort. There is a whole element of profound significance—the element of dual attitude and half-insincerity—which distinguishes the pseudo-belief of the neo-traditionalist from the actual attitude of the past. This element, to my mind, creates such a gulf between the past and the pseudo-traditional modern, that I truly think the disillusioned and nihilistic modern, with his sincerity and integration, comes closer to repeating the ancestral pattern of single-mindedness than does his artificially pious or humanistic contemporary. Even the humanist or traditionalist unconsciously recognises this when he applies the old tag of "dogmatism" to the nihilist because of the latter's single-minded (and therefore traditional) facing of the "is-or-isn't" question. In the sophistical pretence at suspended judgment which characterises the self-styled "traditional sceptic" there is something more profoundly alien to the traditional facing of the universe than there is in the most ruthless negation of the honest impersonal mechanist. At this moment I believe that my own attitude toward the whole question of external reality is far closer to Cotton Mather's or Duns Scotus's or Aristotle's or Leucippus's than yours is. Those old boys, amidst all their subtleties, did not have actual knowledge of any powerful body of evidence overthrowing their claims, and therefore approached externality with no problem but the honest one of distinguishing truth from error. They were to their day what honest materialists are to this day—men who are not afraid to construct an elaborate system with two sets of circumstances in mind—(a) the universe as one would like it to be, and (b) the universe as one is rather afraid it may be. I don't give a god damn what the universe is, but merely want to know what is and what isn't. And by that token I believe myself to be more of a traditionalist than you. You are all at sea if you fancy that there is any identity between a traditional credo as held by our ancestors and the same thing as pretendedly held by ourselves. The only element in common is empty language. Words . . . words . . . words . . . I am constantly advising you to get away from mere words and down to actual things. What honest materialists like me cast away is not the credo of our fathers. That was gone long ago, whether we like the loss or not. The thing cast away is simply the pretence of adhering to an old and devitalised credo. I believe I am firmly sound in holding the *forms* of antiquity to be more truly capable of preservation than the *beliefs*. The beliefs *cannot* survive today—hence the greatest traditionalist is he who clings to the residue which *can* conceivably (though not certainly) survive. Yesterday's beliefs are nothing—they do not and cannot exist. But the forms are at least forms—tangible rhythms, which do not need to pretend to be anything other than they are. There is nothing else of the past to keep. We must keep either those or nothing. Those who pretend to keep the spirit only are really keeping nothing, for what they retain is not truly the old spirit after all. As to fondness for ancient objects as opposed to fondness for ancient credos—I claim that the object-lover is the greater traditionalist, because the objects can emotionally represent for him something nearer what the credos once represented for his ancestors, than the emptied verbiage of those selfsame credos now can. Don't fool yourself . . . . nobody can believe in the ancient credos now, no matter what they try to kid themselves into thinking. Do you suppose for a moment that the elder world could shew any figures with the peculiar type of sheepish obscurantism represented by T. S. Eliot, Chesterton, Fulton J. Sheen, or the late Harvey Wickham?[1] There used to be obscurantism, but never before did the obscurantists have so much trouble in keeping up their own surface convictions. I dislike traditional credos because they are no longer valid—because they symbolise contraction and falsity and smallness and limitations of the rational faculty which is man's chief claim to preëminence. They have lost their own favourable symbolism because their relation to ourselves and to our actual subconscious conceptions of reality is changed. They now represent an element of pusillanimous deception and limitation which they did not formerly represent, since their claims and real essence no longer coincide. Traditional *objects,* on the other hand, have lost nothing which they once had; because they

147

never made any demands on the reason. They did not *argue* or *compel*—
they were content simply to *be*. They can now serve as very valid
symbols of that mastery over time and change which we all desire,
because their appeal is *only* that of simply association re-visualisation. It
is, of course, all a matter of symbolism. Surely you realise that the actual
objects are at bottom only hieroglyphics representing the general
emotional experience of expansion, continuity, and the defeat of time,
space, and natural law. Keys, that is, to unlock the doors of eternity and
infinity to the expansion-craving ego.

But this isn't all. In another way I am undeniably more traditional
than you—and that pertains to every-day, unintellectual instincts and
sympathies and predilections. As you are well aware, I retain, apart from
all conscious philosophy, an enormous amount of hangover material
from my immediate blood-ancestry and personal milieu—habit-
patterns, spontaneous likes and dislikes, standards and associations,
geographical points of view, and all that—things which are perfectly
meaningless in my conception of the universe, but which are
undoubtedly a greater part of the sum total of my personality (the
general conglomerate of irrational patterns and scraps which forms
anyone's personality) than their intellectual insignificance would
indicate. These things are physical phenomena—gland functionings and
nerve-patterns—and therefore greater realities than mere ideas or beliefs.
Well, I get these in unbroken tradition from the past. They are what lies
behind me, inherited with unbroken continuity. Emotionally, I have
had no cleavage with the early-American scene, no matter what I may
believe intellectually . . . . . . and it hardly takes a moment's reflection
to see that this kind of traditionalism is a thousand times more genuine
than any sort which one may gain by reading romantic books of the past
and forming a sentimental attachment for `good old faiths' that sound
nice and exotic and glamourous until one tries to think too deeply and
minutely about them. One drop of blind emotion inherited in direct
succession from one's real blood and geographical background is a far
more potent factor in the real personality than reams of half-digested
romantic allegiances picked up from books. The test, in a way, of any
man's professed traditionalism is its degree of identity with the actual

body of tradition which lies personally behind him. The *genuine* traditionalism of an American is the early-American Protestant tradition. That is what we all come by honestly, in the blood-and-cradle-song line of legitimate descent. When a modern American has the general emotional cast of the old American-Protestant type, we may say that his personality is a really conservative one which has held to ancestral function-patterns no matter what his free mind has decided about the is-or-isn't question. But when such a one announces his loyalty to the Italian Pope or the Gallic decadents, or goes over to the Japanese like Lafcadio Hearn,[2] we are justified in believing that he is not inherently conservative or traditional at all; but that he is simply a restless unrealist seeking escape somewhere in some jumble of foreign images which may blur for him the sharp outlines of unwelcome truth. There is nothing reprehensible about all this, but it must not be called traditionalism. It is not traditionalism because its acquisition involves a mode of thought and feeling alien to that of traditional inheritance. The possessor regards his harbourage of the alien tradition as a sort of gleeful adventure—the possession of a new toy—while the real holder of an inherited tradition takes this natural attribute as a matter of course, as he takes the colour of his eyes or shape of his nose. He does not get consciously excited about it except in the blind way whereby we all have spasmodic nerve-reactions in favour of whatever is our own, good or bad—and he may often despise it intellectually, and wish that he were free from its inhibiting or imagination-dulling influence if it happens to be that kind of a tradition. No person is a real traditionalist if he holds a tradition simply because he wants to hold it. Indeed, any tradition with which the possessor too glibly agrees in a conscious way is open to investigation. But of course the real test is as to whether one gets the tradition through direct and genuine inheritance or not. If an American professes a tradition other than that of early-America, it must be a spurious acquisition . . . . . . spurious, that is, *as personal traditionalism.* That's nothing against it as an artistic attitude—but it is not a genuine personal characteristic on which a body of creative art can be erected. I like to be a Roman, or an Abdul Alhazred . . . . but I would not try to base a serious work on such foundations. What I really am, is a growth of the soil. My instincts were formed by the functioning of a certain line of germ-plasm through a certain set of geographical and social environing conditions. They are genuine, not literary or aesthetic or conscious or voluntary in any way. Most of them seem supremely ridiculous to me. But they are *me* . . . . and so I continue to react spontaneously and unconsciously in the manner of my forefathers, liking the same superficial forms and types and attitudes they liked, except when such things conflict with the fundamental laws of truth or beauty. The emancipation of my consciousness has left my emotions all the freer to follow the ancient patterns without supervision. Without question, my deepest, instinctive, personality belongs to early America in unbroken continuity. And that, young man, is tradition! I might add that I also believe my conscious untraditionalism to be really a traditional feature in the deepest sense. As I pointed out before, the single-minded facing of the universe adhered to by the modern materialist is really far more like the honest truth-seeking of the past than is the doubtful, muddled abyss-straddling of the professed neo-traditionalist. The pose of the neo-traditionalist involves a whole added element of duplicity which the old traditionalist never had, and which gives to neo-traditionalism a basic psychological core far more alien to the old universe-facing than is the core of the mechanist's straightforward is-or-isn'tness. Part of the old Protestant tradition (the only tradition an American can genuinely hold by inheritance) involved a ruthess sweeping aside of shams and a rigid quest for truth at any cost—no natter whether it overthrew everything in church and state that went before it. Our forefathers kicked out the rotten carcass of Popery first, and then, in the New World, began kicking out the simple-minded dogmatick bigotry which was left. The Massachusetts Puritans—honest fools—were the first stage. The anti-Puritan revolt which founded Rhode Island, and which lies directly behind me, represents another stage. Roger Williams called himself simply a "seeker", and would be bound by no creed. He left the Baptists six months after he established the First Baptist Church whose later steeple is our glory. The Unitarians are another stage. The living and respect-deserving Dr. Harry Emerson Fosdick is another. Harry Elmer Barnes, Charles Francis Potter,[3] and the ethical humanists form another. *They are all far more perfect traditionalists than your snivelling little neo-papists and Chesterbellocs,*[4] because they are functioning absolutely in line with their original ancestral impetus. They are doing what the Rev. John White and William Bradford and John Winthrop and William Blackstone and Roger Williams did before them. They are cutting out the pose and acting simply and naturally on lines of blood impulse. American Anglo-Saxons perpetuating the habit-patterns inherited from the past. If they pretended to switch over to popery or Continental Europeanism or anything else outside their direct line of inheritance they would be departing from the traditional pattern of thought. Blood and experience have put sincerity and truth-seeking in the forefront of the racial emotions—and not unless the American continues to feel this emotional pull is he truly a traditionalist. The next stage of racial thought-development after the Humanists is that of complete materialistic scepticism—the inevitable product of cosmos-confrontation by the honest, straightforward, and uncompromising mind. It is a Protestant, Puritan zeal—an Anglo-Saxon and early-American scorn for falsehood and evasion—which makes the modern American nihilist face openly the evident lack of purpose, values, goal, or central consciousness in the space-time continuum. We are still Protestants though no longer Christians. It is the same old leaven at work—the feudal loyalty-instinct having been transferred from a non-existent deity to the one fundamental cosmic element of truth. Who can declare that the ape-like ritualism and prehensile imitativeness of your little T. S. Eliots and such-like is in any sense real traditionalism as compared with this genuine article? What comes in the blood is a damn sight more basic and important than what one picks up from historical novels. Well, young man, I'm not saying that you don't hold over any of the old American traditionalism from your genuine blood and geographical background. The amusing thing is that you do hold over a vast amount more than you are yourself willing to admit. Unconsciously, and over your own protest, you are really tremendously American; with instinctive, automatic American reactions to various images and ideas that seem delectably familiar in contrast with the fundamental alienage of Greenwich-Village types whose emotional cleavage from the past has become actual. To that extent I freely admit your traditionalism, and shake hands with you on it! But you have lost more of this kind of thing than I have, because novel-reading and aesthetic theory have put alien European ideas into your head and caused you to despise, consciously, the real American stream of traditions and folkways behind you. You ought to be a growth of the old New York soil—with deep roots in its slowly fused historic antecedents, and an intimate knowledge of its past and its constituent streams—just as others may be growths of the New England or Southern or Quebec soil. Look at young Talman[5]—that kid has the right idea in never losing touch with his Rockland County provenance. He is a New Netherland Dutchman first, and other things later on. One speck of one's own inheritance is worth a bushel basket full of borrowed traditions from some distant and not really half-understood milieu. Whatever is genuine in you is the old American Protestant stuff that has come down from Longs and Belknaps and Mansfields and Dotys. Stand on your own feet, boy—don't borrow some damn Dago's stilts! The only "great tradition" which comes in direct line to *you* is the American Protestant tradition. Anything else you may try to put on will always be a far poorer fit than your own natural garments. Take an old man's advice and don't try *not* to be what you *are*. If you stop being a growth of the American soil you'll merely succeed in not being a growth of anything. You'll be like the Aesopic dog who reached for a new bone-reflection in the water and lost the real bone he had in his mouth before. But you aren't as bad as that yet. You have a lot of the old stuff left. All Grandpa urges is that you keep hold of it and stop fancying that somebody else's "great tradition" can be as real to you as your own "great tradition" of American straightforwardness and fact-facing. Meanwhile Grandpa must claim to be the greater traditionalist for the moment—not because flaming youth needs to be less so, but because flaming youth insists on putting the old heritage aside and picking up book romanticism under the impression that it can form a continuous traditional background for him. Of course, I hardly need say that the early-American tradition has absolutely nothing in common with the mechanised Babbitt-America of the present and future. That cursed hybrid mess is more alien than Timbuctoo. God Save the King!

[. . .]

As for the relative hypocrisy of true Christianity and Popery—why, Sir, I see nothing at all in your sophistical, second-hand, and herd-minded modernistick arguments! If, Sir, there be any substance at all to the precepts of the Christian religion, that substance is a wish to mould men to a certain pattern, to clear their hearts of deception, and to exalt a certain group of instincts at the expense of certain other groups. There is no intention, in a real faith, of having persons believe one thing and do another. That, Sir, is a spurious afterthought bas'd upon those subtle and alien incrustations which the Semitick faith of the Ieshua-cultus receiv'd upon being fus'd with our normal paganism. In our own hereditary religions, ethical elements were indeed subordinate to mystical adoration; but that is paganism pure and simple. I agree with you most unreservedly that our Aryan paganism is infinitely superior to the Semitick farce of Christianity. It is the only rational type of religion; and if revived *frankly* and *honestly,* with Zeus, Jupiter, Odin, or some other real god as the head, wou'd be deserving of the respect of adults. But for bastard hypocrisy, only contempt is due. The declining Roman world had a chance to stick to the honest Aryan religion of the fathers, but feebly relinquish'd it in favour of the Syrian slum-cult which had sprung up in the gutters. That cult had nothing to do with our kind of religion, except for what it had picked up through stupid fusion with Dionysiac mysteries, Pythagoreanism, and other odds and ends of Aryan feeling. In its stark, true outlines it was a typical Semitick ethics-cult, differing only in minor details from the various Jewish sects of which it was originally one. It represented a whole world of thought and feeling regarding cosmick relationship which no man of our blood ever has felt or ever could feel except through unconscious hypocrisy or irrational imitation. It is meaningless to us, and only through pretence—through engrafting our own hereditary forms upon it—celebrating Saturnalia as Christmas or Floralia as Easter, and so on—have we ever whipped it into any sort of semi-acceptable shape. But when we so distorted it we did not change the objective fact of what real Christian faith meant and must always mean in its pure form. The real thing remains a conduct-regulating pattern of the normal Semitick type, with no genuine core other than the moulding of human ways—in fact, not in sham or symbol—to a given ideal pattern. No Christian who does not try his best to conform in literal fact to the Christian pattern of conduct, and to induce others to do so so far as he can, is any real Christian at all. Nor is any faith truly Christian, which does not attempt to the best of its physical and psychological power to make all its adherents obey literally the Christian precepts—yea, and to spread those precepts by force through as much of mankind as possible. The existence of ideals of conduct without the insistence that everyone approach them as closely as possible is absolutely irrelevant, meaningless, hypocritical, contemptible, and undeserving of adult notice. Paganism is not ridiculous because it did not specialise in such ideals. It is the distinguishing feature of Christianity, among the faiths professed by Aryans, that it does so. And unless such ideals of conduct are enforced, no religion can pretend to call itself Christian. It may be more sensible than Christianity—in fact, it cannot help being so—but it will always be an hypocritical imposture until it unmasks and openly calls itself the good old Aryan ancestral paganism...until it drops the pretence of idealism which lack of enforcement makes useless, meaningless, and patently infantile. Christianity is a Syrian ethicks-cultus whose crucial essence is the moulding of mankind to a specific artificial pattern. Unless it tries to effect this moulding of mankind in a literal and not a merely poetick sense, it is not Christianity but a puerile fake. It can be religion, but not Christianity; and the use of the Christian designation becomes a breach of taste and an insult to the mythical or semi-mythical Christus-images which underlay the original delusion. Real Christianity was dead long before the close of the Middle Ages. It was genuine amongst the martyrs and ascetics of the dying Empire, but was merely parodied and blasphemed by the drunken syphilitick monks and murderous, illiterate barons of Gil Chesterton's beloved 12th century. The middle ages is enough to make a gentleman puke—or turn to coarse language through contagion. Of all curst hypocrisy, squalor, sham, ignorance, mock-heroicks...god! Now I hold no abstract brief against dirt and crudity—but I do hate sham like poison. The damn trouble with this bastard thing call'd popery was that it try'd to combine the ordinary coarseness of healthy barbarick living with an aesthetick image of supernal delicacy and beauty which was insulted by the combination. Popery is the nadir of vile taste because it depends upon

154

an immoral, inexcusable incongruity. The middle ages under frank paganism wou'd have been as crudely interesting as the age of our remote Teutonick forbears under Arminius or Ariovistus. It is the degradation and mockery of an incongruous and irrelevant profest faith which makes them so intellectually and aesthetically squalid. It is so rawly ridiculous to think of adults as pretending to uphold ideals which have no counterparts in reality. As a matter of fact, there is no adult justification for any ideal without counterparts in reality. Oh, shit! I get contaminated even thinking about the middle ages and popery. Long live William and Mary! Three cheers for Endicott who cut the red cross out of the flag at Salem!

Well, Protestantism is simply the tragick attempt of honest Teutons to restore the unity between human belief and human reality. We know now how tragick and ugly it was—but we respect the tragedy, and venerate the ugliness as we venerate the ugliness of some twisted, aged saint whose malformations were gain'd gloriously in battles fought for us and for truth. For centuries of darkness man's intellect had been paralysed and hypnotised by the shock of antiquity's fall and the lusts of sheer barbaric living; aggravated by the mass-insanity promulgated by mystics who fed upon human ignorance. The only civilised people in the middle ages were our Saracen foes. Then came light, as the sheer pressure of resurrected Greek reason, largely exhumed by the Saracens, broke through the murk of stupidity, barbarism, and faith. All modern attempts to deny this—to revalue the Middle Ages and belittle the Renaissance—are such feeble products of faddism as to need no notice beyond the simple act of record. As regarded religion, man had two choices. His revived reason saw the absurdity of upholding a serious faith impossible of reconciliation with any habitual, agreeable, or even possible way of life; and reacted to the situation in various ways according to the cultural heritage of the various nations involved. The Latins, most direct heirs of paganism, deliberately cast the practical programme of their faith into antique pagan form except for certain verbal quibbles and certain inconsistent flarebacks of irrational ethicism. They discarded the Christian idea of religion as an ethical force, and even let their ethicks slide down below that aesthetick point insisted on by the virile antique Romans. Priests who had been simply gluttons, wenchers, wine-sops, thieves, and beggars before, now became murderers, paederasts, sadists, and corrupters on a truly Heliogabalan scale. Among these people the Christian element in religion became so submerged that it ceased to be expected. Hypocrisy itself virtually disappeared, since the departure was so great as to make the religion a wholly new one, retaining the name of Christianity merely as one uses a word which is new to the present and which has had some alien, forgotten, and utterly antipodal meaning in the past. Thus, for Mediterraneans, Popery was perhaps neither inconsistent nor hypocritical. They had forgotten what Christianity ever was and what it had ever demanded. They were neo-pagans, and inferior to the ancients only because they had not the intellectual balance of classical antiquity. If anybody cares for this integrated people and religion with the archaic borrowed name, all very well. I cannot justly criticise their method of solving the inconsistency-dilemma—though it does exasperate me to see their paganism cluttered up with so many vestigial verbal hypocrisies and intellectual absurdities. I suspend judgment because I am not a Latin and have no power to fathom the real workings of the Latin mind.

But our Northern people, confronted by the same choices in getting rid of the conduct-belief dilemma, took an opposite route. They had the realistick temper of men accustom'd to responsible action, and could not see any significance in the altering of faiths or misusing of names. They were, in truth, more really like the classical ancients in their singleness of outlook. They were not so close to the outward classick heritage, but had more of the real classick psychology in them. It would have been ideal if they could have shaken off the deity-delusion at once and proceeded to use their recovered reason and single-mindedness in the working out of a new rational way of life—an openly pagan, materialistick, and nature-following way—but unfortunately the hypnosis of theism was too strong for them, and the hold of the word "Christianity" too firm to permit them to shift to something less absurd. They were saddled by a herd-fetish—and being honest and single-minded, could not proceed to forget what their fetish had originally meant. Filled with a new sense of obligation to fulfil the precepts of

Christianity which their books and legends enjoin'd upon them, they scorn'd any lying distortion of the meaning of those precepts. Instead of running away from consistency and honesty as those coprophagous little sewer-rats of papists did, they faced courageously—like white men and Romans, by god!—the blank wall of absurd and impossible myth which their limited vision led them to regard as reality. They were men—men in the antique sense—and I thank god there is no heritage but theirs in my past! Unbroken before the cosmos! No evasion for them—they were after the core of the is-or-isn't business. They turned on the rotten carcass of religion that stank around them, and try'd to find out what kind of an animal it had been before it began to putrefy. Men, by god! Out of the shards of the alien, incongruous gibberish they rescued the original exotic growth that lay at the base of the gibberish. Rescued not only the form, but the inner spirit to an inconceivable degree. For the first time since vermin-riddled Jews peddled their new cult around the gutters of Tiberian Rome the actual Christian religion existed in fact and not in pretence. Gone was the Dionysiac and Pythagorean and Neoplatonick hokum—gone the ignorant Gothick incrustations. Gone the pretence and the mockery and the evasion. The alien, unworkable importation from Syria stood on its own feet at last—no longer serving merely as a mask for the perpetuation of our normal ancestral paganism. Well, you know the rest, Son. Protestantism went back to what it thought were realities and tried like blue hell to live up honestly to the cosmick obligations which it honestly believed to be pressing upon men. Of course it was silly and ugly and grotesque, and of course it bred added hypocrisies amongst its bewildered lesser devotees. But for the first time since antique Rome, the world saw a religion of real men trying to fulfil honestly what they thought the personified cosmos had asked them to fulfil. We have to laugh at them today, because their system was so impossible of enforcement and survival, and because it did so relatively little to encourage the actual amenities of the farce called living. But while we laugh, we have to respect—which is more than we can do in the case of dirty little papists. These people, by god, were honest and sincere—the only religionists in the modern world who were willing to think like men and act to their poor, pathetick best on a straightforward and sham-free is-or-isn't principle. When they thought their Yahveh told them to do something, they didn't sneak out the back door and pretend that the Old Boy meant something else. They knew what they read in the silly Oriental hash which they and the papists equally revered, and they had the guts to stand by what they understood. They revived, more than any snivelling little mass-whiner, the antique boldness and honesty in approaching the universe; and would never have stooped to slobber empty words about "conceptions of the good life" which nobody but two or three freaks could live. Instead, they tried to obey the commands of the myth-cult which they acknowledged as their master, and moved heaven and earth to make the whole race do what they felt the whole race had been commanded to do. There is no Christianity in the post-Roman world except Protestantism, and of all Protestantism, the original Puritanism of the Massachusetts-Bay is probably the most honest form. It is the ugliest of modern religions because it is the most real. Religion itself is an absurdity and an anomaly, and paganism is acceptable only because it represents that purely orgiastic phase of religion farthest from reality. It is in the Semitick faiths, where religion is supposed to have something to do with human beings, that the silliness and impossibility and irrelevance of the whole thing is most flagrantly shewn up. But it is thus shewn up merely because it has achieved added contacts with reality. Protestantism is the reductio ad absurdum of all religion—but it is such only because it is more honest than Popery, and because it covers a larger ground. Popery is a child's tickling of itself—Protestantism is a man's honest facing of the unknown. Today we see as disgusting spectacles the stranded hulks of many backward caravels in the Protestant Armada—puerile orthodoxies which were once honest facings of the is-or-isn't question, but which are today infantile and irrelevant. We justly laugh at these—and yet there is something more inherently respectable in their atrophied decrepitude than there is in the brazenly mendacious and wily carcass of popery. Real Protestantism—the basic attitude of facing the universe honestly and trying to do what is most sensible in the light of what is real—is no more like its 17th century self today than your coat is like Edward Doty's doublet which he stripped off to fight the first duel in the new world. The same impulse, working with the augmenting body of data at its disposal, has supplanted Cotton Mather with

Jonathan Edwards, Edwards with William Ellery Channing and Theodore Parker, Channing and Parker with Fosdick and John Haynes Holmes,[6] Fosdick and Holmes with Charles Francis Potter and Harry Elmer Barnes, and Potter and Barnes with Joseph Wood Krutch, Mencken, and other moderns who keep to the principle of truth and reality in the face of the shifting phenomena of the external world. All this has nothing to do with art, beauty, or anything else except the question of honest observation and honest thought. If fervour and belief eclipsed beauty for a while, that is an inevitable result of the accident which foisted Christianity on a western world whose Teutonic inheritors were one day to take it seriously. But that phase is soon over. Religion as a vital issue is dead except on paper, and whatever beauty-baiting the future may witness will be the work of greed and trade, and not of honest cosmos-facing.

[. . .] The contributions of the New England type to the American stream will never be justly appraised until the confusions of nomenclature are smoothed out. Words . . . . words . . . . words . . . . . Just as bad as taking such words as "science" and "philosophy" and breaking down their fine meanings till they cease to mean anything at all. What New England bred in varying forms was a type of courageous fact-facer with a scorn of the irrelevant. In many cases the peculiar characteristics of the type reached such extremes as to produce absurdity and sterility, but I think the net contribution was favourable rather than adverse.

The Massachusetts-Bay bigot was only a link in a chain. He was a dismal sort of freak himself, but the stirring impulses at work within him were valuable, and capable of assuming superior forms in later generations and under modified milieus. You cannot separate the enlightened later generations from the dismal earlier ones—for they all belonged to the same line, as the butterfly and caterpillar do. Clear-spirited men of refinement like Thoreau, Channing, Williams, Holmes, and so on could never have existed if their forbears had not passed through an outwardly ugly period of revolt (all revolt is ugly) against the stinking putrescence of the popish culture as it worked in the north. And as for art—if you want to escape your own hated category of herd-myth-dupe, for god's sake forget the feeble lies of decadents who try to float the legend of New England aesthetick barrenness! All pioneer regions have to be barren for a while, but that is the curse of pioneering itself, and not of any particular religious or cultural twist. Before inquiring about New England art, ask what New Netherland or Pennsylvania or Virginia did in the same line—or Quebeck, where the little papists had their own sweet way. The plain truth is—and this is not any attempted paradox or epigram or "clever" confutation of the anti-Novanglians—that nine-tenths of all the art and learning that the colonies had came out of "Puritan" New England. I am not saying that N. E. could not have done better if it had not been "Puritan", and I am not belittling the amenities of life worked out in Virginia and Carolina—regions which I admire vastly and sincerely. I am simply stating the objective fact for what it is worth—that the best in American painting, architecture, literature (except Poe), scholarship, and so forth always proceeded until lately from the New England region. Probably the real reasons were social and biological and economic rather than religious or philosophic, though the austerity of Protestant philosophy may have helped to promote a classick simplicity conducive to true artistick restraint. New England was settled by a special class in a state of mental ferment, and largely of those middle orders of society which possess the most biologically vigorous brains. Also, it was settled more thickly and rapidly than any other region, so that it was soon a genuine duplicate of England with all the coördinated functions of an established community working without extreme pioneer handicaps. By 1750 it was a really mature region with schools, colleges, roads, good architecture, gracious living in the towns, easy communications, prosperity, and a local way of life already matured by over a century of continuity. In 1750 people could look back to a long history in the same place—there were houses and towns which even then had the mellow patina of relative age. The landscape had reacted typically on the people—a lovelier landscape than is to be found anywhere else, with the stone walls, village spires, and cottage roofs that we know so well today. It is futile to think what this or that change in the people's heritage might have effected. As it was, they did more than anybody else in the colonies—handicapped by creed or not—and perhaps set the record of all time for pioneer achievement. What their Puritan origin gave them was a certain restless truth-seeking cast of mind, an unbroken courage, and an uncompromising honesty—all good qualities from any point of view, pagan or otherwise. You ought to be proud to be descended from them—and as a matter of fact you have exactly as much of their blood as I have, if not more in the long run, since my paternal line is directly British and Anglican, whilst yours involves names as typically Novanglian as Belknap. Nor must you imagine that the comic-opera conception of early Massachusetts life is anything more than a caricature so far as New England as a whole is concerned. Whole regions were entirely outside the cultural and religious influence of the Bay, and in many cases actually hostile toward it. New Hampshire was a liberal American region—with Portsmouth as sanely civilised and unbigoted a town as the old world itself could shew. And as for Rhode Island—I don't need to tell you that this colony marks a direct revolt against all that Massachusetts signified, so that although we have the same blood, we have always followed a tradition nearly as antipodal as Virginia's. Phases of life existed in the Narragansett country—the west shore of the bay, where all the Phillipses, Caseys, Places, Hazards, etc. were settled after the first Newport generation—which approached the liberal South far more than anything in Massachusetts. We had large estates with great houses, plenty of niggers, Anglican or liberal Quaker background (which, however, began to yield to the dissenting sects after the Revolution), and in general all the appurtenances of the most civilised sort of colonial life. If you'd let Grandpa shew you around Newport some day, you'd get a new idea of this "sterile" New England which produced John Singleton Copley; Gilbert Stuart; Edward Greene Malbone; Benjamin Thompson; Count Rumford;[7] and so on, and so on. Was it a sterile uncivilised background which welcomed Dean Berkeley in 1732, and which founded libraries, philosophical societies, and so on, and had houses, family plate, coaches, dress, and social elegances equal to any in the western world? I verily believe that some of these half-baked Waldo Franks picture the cultivated Newport gentleman of 1740 or the corresponding type of Providence gentleman of 1770 (Joseph Brown, Stephen Hopkins, Benjamin West, Nathaniel Balch, John Merritt, Rev. John Checkley, etc.) as a sour-faced cartoon in the black doublet and conical hat whose very existence had been forgotten before 1700. The one zone where bigotry lingered longest was that peopled by the non-revolting element of the Endicott-Winthrop colonising enterprise—Salem 1628, Boston 1630. These people come nearest to the savage type caricatured as puritans—but you must not mix them with the mild Plymouth people who produced your Dotys, with the liberal Anglicans who settled Portsmouth and Exeter in New Hampshire, or with the Rhode Islanders who (though their nucleus came to America with the Winthrop-Endicott outfit) soon revolted in disgust and founded the anti-Puritan traditions of Providence, Newport, and Narragansett. You'll find the hard-shell'd Puritan mostly around Boston and north of there, in the centre of Massachuetts—Worcester and Springfield—and (pardon me if I get personal) in the Connecticut region where Hartford, Saybrook, and New Haven ultimately joined to form the Colony of Connecticut. I'm no doter on the Bostonian type myself—but I can't help recognising in fairness that the general movement which reached an extreme in this type was also responsible for the peerlessly high intellectual and aesthetic standing of early New England. Painters, miniaturists, historians, essayists, teachers, architects, versifiers—good god, what do you expect from a community before it has rounded out three centuries? The real troubles of New England came later, when the emigration of good old stock, the shifting of economic conditions, and the injudicious admittance of foreign scum produced the unfortunately vitiated condition visible today. But we aren't quite dead yet—there have been strange comebacks in history, and even now we lead almost undisputedly in education. And whatever we are, we can never forget that we've been something. We'd rather have these reminders than be utterly obliterated under the chaos of a new alien civilisation, as you in New York have been. Take your pick—a mouldering steeple on a New England hillside, or an old brownstone front in East Forty-somethingth street inhabited on the top floor by Jew-Wop hybrids, with a shady hotel on the ground floor and a speakeasy or night club in the basement. But no—this matter of Manhattan is an extreme and special case. I will concede that much of old New Netherland remains in the upper Hudson Valley, and that possibly the life of some of the Hudson valley cities—Albany,

Schenectady, Poughkeepsie—may harbour approximate survivals of the old urban culture which once flourished in New York City. But you have to get down to Richmond and Charleston for cases of widespread and untainted American survival. O tempora, O mores! The old man rambles. Well, anyway, I'm not ashamed to have a full half of New England blood in me. I don't think it's done a bit of harm in letting me face honestly the is-or-isn't question. Whether my repudiation of traditional shams as opposed to traditional realities is due to this side of me or the Anglican side of me, no analyst could have much success in deciphering. Both sides are Protestant, anyway—Old Tom Casey[8] the Mick was a Protestant of Dublin, and that's why the Papists murdered him and his wife and left little Tom an orphan at six to be carried to Gloucestershire and later migrate to the New World and breed counterfeiter-silversmith grandsons.

The Psychology of Puritanism

[The following is an extract from a letter to Robert E. Howard (4 October 1930). Howard, a Texan by birth, was fascinated with the exhibition of New England psychology—especially the seventeenth-century belief in and fear of witches—found in Lovecraft's horror tales. In this letter, Lovecraft expounds the psychological causes for such beliefs and maintains that there was a kernel of truth to them.]

[. . .] it is the night-black Massachusetts legendry which packs the really macabre "kick". Here is material for a really profound study in group-neuroticism; for certainly, no one can deny the existence of a profoundly morbid streak in the Puritan imagination. What you say of the dark Saxon-Scandinavian heritage as a possible source of the atavistic impulses brought out by emotional repression, isolation, climatic rigour, and the nearness of the vast unknown forest with its coppery savages, is of vast interest to me; insomuch as I have often both said and written exactly the same thing! Have you seen my old story "The Picture in the House"?[1] If not, I must send you a copy. The introductory paragraph virtually sums up the idea you advance.

There is genuine grisliness, all apart from the supernatural legends, in the inside chronicles of Massachusetts. It begins to appear as early as 1642, when the correspondence of Gov. Bellingham with Gov.

Bradford[2] of Plymouth reveals a genuine alarm on the part of both executives regarding the wave of utterly abhorrent and unnatural crime—very different from the ordinary offences common in England, and today classifiable as extreme forms of sadism and other pathological perversions—which had sprung up among the more ignorant orders of the people. "It may bee demanded how it came to pass," writes Bradford, "yt soe many wikked persons and prophane people shou'd soe quickly come over into this land, and mixe them selves amongst them? Seeing it was religious men yt began ye work, and they came for religions sake."[3]

Well—although he doesn't know it—Bradford really gives part of the answer in his own question. The very preponderance of passionately pious men in the colony was virtually an assurance of unnatural crime; insomuch as psychology now proves the religious instinct to be a form of transmuted eroticism precisely parallel to the transmutations in other directions which respectively produce such things as sadism, hallucination, melancholia, and other mental morbidities. Bunch together a group of people deliberately chosen for strong religious feelings, and you have a practical guarantee of dark morbidities expressed in crime, perversion, and insanity. This was aggravated, of course, by the Puritan policy of rigorously suppressing all the natural outlets of exuberant feeling—music, laughter, colour, pageantry, and so on. To observe Christmas Day was once a prison offence, and no one permitted himself a spontaneous mirthful thought without afterward imputing it a "sin" of his soul and working up a veritable hysteria of pathological self-analysis as regarded his possible chances of "salvation". To read of the experiences of the Rev. Cotton Mather, and of his precocious little brother Nathaniel (who virtually tormented himself to death with hysterical emotional "soul-questioning") is to witness genuine tragedy—the tragedy of ignorance and superstition. Poor little Nat died at 19—I have seen his gravestone in the old Charter St. Burying Ground at Salem. His fortunate escape from life came in 1688, and his epitaph (a tribute to his prodigious learning) reads with unconscious pathos—"An Aged Person who had seen but 19 Winters in the World". Bradford—a Plymouth Pilgrim outside the worst pest-zone of Massachusetts mania—is not without some appreciation of the situation in this respect; and remarks with unusual penetration for his age—"An other reason (for the wave of morbid crime) may be, yt it may be in this case as it is with waters when their streames are stopt or dam'd up, when they get passage they flow with more violence and make more noys and disturbance, than when they are suffered to rune quietly in their owne chanels. Soe wikedness being here more stopt by strict lawes, and ye same more nerly lookt unto, soe as it cannot rune in a commone road of liberty as it wou'd, and is inclined, it serches every wher, and at last breaks out wher it gettes vente". Good old Bradford! But the real Puritans couldn't see it his way; hence (since they were forced to recognise the extent and unprecedented morbidity of the increasing crimes around them) there gradually grew up the commonly-accepted doctrine that the devil was making a special war on Massachusetts because of the holy purpose to which that saintly colony was dedicated by the Lord's Brethren. The Bradford-Bellingham correspondence was in 1642. Exactly fifty years later the Salem witchcraft affair broke out. Can anyone doubt what prepared the masses of the people to regard the matter seriously? As a sidelight on the nearly-unendurable strain to which Massachusetts theocracy subjected the nerves of its victims, we may note the vast numbers who withdrew to Rhode Island soil. It is much less known that really considerable numbers *went over to the Indians*—"went native", as modern slang would put it. This condition was much more frequent in the Puritan zone than anywhere else in Anglo-Saxon America. Authorities say that 100 times more whites were Indianised, than Indians were Europeanised. One Massachusetts man— the Rev. William Blackstone,[4] who had been the first settler on the Boston peninsula—became a hermit; taking his books and family and building a home in the wilderness in 1635, on territory later part of R.I. He said, "I came to Mass. to escape the Lord's Bishops, and now I leave it to escape the Lord's Brethren".[5] Blackstone was really the first white settler in R.I., but because he did not found a colony he is not considered a rival of Roger Williams as the local pioneer. After Providence was founded, he used to ride in on a white bull and pay visits to Mr. Williams and other friends. It was he who introduced the apple-tree to this colony. He was a great friend of the Indians, and it is merciful that he died in 1674, before King Phillip's War convulsed the colony. His house and books were burnt by the Indians two years after his death.

But there was still another reason for Massachusetts crime and abnormality—a reason rather embarrassing to many upholders of the myth that Mass. blood is a kind of unofficial patent of nobility. This was the rapid importation, after 1635, of a vile class of degenerate London scum as indentured servants. We escaped this in R.I., since at first we were too poor to have many servants at all, and later used Indians and negroes (we imported the latter in small numbers from the West Indies before our own "triangular trade" began) instead of low-grade whites. But Mass. needed servants sooner, and did not have our penchant for exotics; hence (in addition to enslaving some local Indians, and importing a *few* negroes and Carib Indians from the West Indies) went in on a large scale for "bound" English labour—paupers, convicts, "floaters", and so on. They had not learned the lesson that more actually anti-social perversion occurs amongst the decadent scum of a high race, than amongst the mentally and physically sound types of an inferior race. We can picture the result of bringing this warped, inhibition-stunted, free and easy degenerate element under the domination of the ironclad Puritan theocracy and moral strait-jacket. Repression and explosion—just as intelligent old William Bradford of Plymouth saw. 'Wikedness more stopt up by strict lawes . . . . . breaks out wher it gettes vente.' It is interesting to see how this same custom of importing inferior Englishmen worked out in less repressive colonies. Virginia had tried it prior to the beginning of the African trade in 1619, and the wretched mass of scum resulting therefrom was gradually settled on small farms. There was never any violence or well-defined clash with authority, and not a trace of any epidemic of morbidity. The inferior whites gradually retreated toward the backwoods, becoming in the course of time that "mean white" or "white trash" element so well-known to sociologists. One may add that an analogous phenomenon ultimately occurred in New England, small colonies of inferior or decadent stock springing up on the fringe of settled regions and receiving such names as "Hardscrabble", "Hell's Half Acre",

"Dogtown", etc., etc. In N.Y. and New Jersey, too—where the mean whites mixed with negroes and Indians and still survive as wretched semi-barbarians in the Catskills and Ramapos. But this segregation did not occur in Massachusetts till after the decadents had made many complications in the general situation.

Another and highly important factor in accounting for Massachusetts witch-belief and daemonology is the fact, now widely emphasised by anthropologists, that the traditional features of witch-practice and Sabbat-orgies *were by no means mythical.* It was not from any empty system of antique legendry that Western Europeans of the 17th century and before got their *significantly consistent* idea of what witches were, how they made their incantations, and what they did at their hideous convocations on May-Eve and Hallowmass. *Something actual was going on under the surface,* so that people really stumbled on *concrete experiences* from time to time which confirmed all they had ever heard of the witch species. In brief, scholars now recognise that all through history a secret cult of degenerate orgiastic nature-worshippers, furtively recruited from the peasantry and sometimes from decadent characters of more select origin, has existed throughout northwestern Europe; practicing fixed rites of immemorial antiquity for malign objects, having a governing system and hierarchy as well-defined and elaborate as that of any established religion, and meeting secretly by night in deserted rustic places. It has no inclusive name recognised by its own adherents, but is customarily called simply "the witch-cult" by modern anthropologists. Evidences of its persistent existence and unvarying practices are revealed by multitudes or trials, legends, and historic incidents; and by piecing these together we have today a very fair idea of its nature and workings. Originally it seems almost conclusively to have been simply the normal religion of the prehistoric Mongoloids who preceded the Nordics and Mediterraneans in northwestern Europe. It is based on the idea of fertility, as worshipped by a stock-raising race of pre-agricultural nomads, and its salient features from the very first were semi-annual ritualistic gatherings at the breeding seasons of the flocks and herds, at which primitive erotic rites were practiced to encourage the fecundity of the stock—much as certain savages practice such rites to this day. This religion was once dominant throughout Western Europe; but was naturally pushed to the wall when the Aryans conquered the land and brought in their own infinitely more refined, evolved, and poetic polytheism. It could not stand up against Druidism or the Northern religion of Asgard and Valhalla, so sunk (like the Mongoloid "little people" to whom it belonged) to the position of a subordinate and despised cult. It was probably never persecuted under the supremacy of the Celts and Teutons, but on the other hand no doubt gained converts from among the degenerate elements of these conquering races. The coming of the Romans—who generally disliked furtive, orgiastic religions, and had suppressed certain Dionysiac and Cybele cults in Italy as early as the 3d century B.C.—somewhat changed the complexion of the matter, and tended to drive the vestigial religion to cover. Yet it seems to have obtained degenerate Roman converts, and was probably carried into the British Isles (where the Mongoloids never were) by the Romans rather than by either Mediterraneans or Celts. It is possible that Sylvanus Cocidius, whose worship the Britanno-Romans discouraged, was connected with this cult. The semi-annual orgies (April 30 and Nov. 30) were what came later to be known as *sabbats.* In the main, they consisted of dances and chants of worshippers—mostly female, but presided over by a male hierophant in shaggy animal disguise, called simply "The Black Man". The conclusion of the ceremony was obscene to an extent which makes even Juvenal's sixth satire seem milk.[6] The cult as a whole was subdivided into local units called *covens,* each with its "black man", and all joined by a common body of tradition and system of passwords and nomenclature. Every member was given a new mystic name for use within the cult. Originally, the distinctly *malign* features probably did not exist; the religion being merely emotional and sensual. When, however, the dominant races began to oppose and persecute it, it began to strike back and specialise in bringing evil to its enemies. This doubtless caused an emphasis to be laid upon the supernatural powers conferred on its devotees by their communion with the gods of Nature through the ritual of the sabbat. Little by little the idea grew up—accepted both by the half-crazed devotees and by the outside world—that the cult was a device for giving people a supernatural means of working evil. When

169

Christianity made its appearance, the persecution of the cult became infinitely strengthened; since this new faith had so fanatical a hatred of everything pertaining to eroticism. For the first time, in all likelihood, the cult became *wholly secret and subterranean*—and correspondingly, the general fear and hatred of it, and the tendency to regard it as a link with nameless powers of darkness, no doubt vastly increased. Once driven to cover, it seems to have stayed put fairly well, and it probably died out in many places—including Britain. Conquests by Gaels and Saxons finished any remnants of it which may have been left. From the late Roman period to late in the Middle Ages there are only glancing evidences of it, although it certainly maintained a steady existence on the continent of Europe, recruiting many degenerate and discontented people since it promised them so many more simple, understandable, and available boons than did Christianity. It was always waiting, ready to catch anybody who grew tired of the ethics and aesthetics of the ruling European civilisation—just as the Indians were always waiting to take in anybody who sickened of Puritan life in early Massachusetts. The big recruiting came in the 14th and 15th centuries, during that period of despair, degradation, and recklessness following the ravages of the Black Death. This is the period, you know, when the sardonic conception of the "Dance of Death", as exploited by Albrecht Dürer, gained form. Dissatisfied with all that civilised life gave and promised, thousands undoubtedly went over to the witch-cult (a gesture by this time identified with the conception of "selling oneself to Satan") and extracted from its mummeries and its Sabbats what pleasure and excitement they could get. Nor could this be kept wholly secret on so vast a scale. For the first time the cult began to be generally known and feared and identified with the worship of Satan. (Its connexion with the Black Mass would be a good subject for learned research.) Undoubtedly, it would have virtually wrecked European civilisation if left unopposed, for it fostered a spirit of seditious malignity aimed against all existing institutions. Let us appreciate, therefore, that the first mediaeval opposers of witchcraft were *not* mere fanatics fighting a shadow. They were deluded in that they thought themselves to be fighting something supernatural, but they were most certainly right in believing that they were fighting a genuine menace. Of course, *reports of* witchcraft far

170

exceeded the actual number of instances of its practice; so that many individual witch-condemnations were indeed unjust. Also, the legend of witch-ceremonies undoubtedly spread far beyond the actual areas in which the real cult had its activities. For some reason or other, *Germany* was the scene of the most actual cult-doings, though covens undoubtedly extended into France and Scandinavia and perhaps as far south as Italy. The cult does not seem to have crossed into Britain till late in the 15th or early in the 16th century; and it there found its chief seat in Scotland. It entered Wales, but never seems to have had any foothold in either England or Ireland. From the time of Pope John XXII's bull against witchcraft in the first half of the 14th century, the war of civilisation against the cult gained headway. In 1484 Pope Innocent VIII launched the most tremendous campaign of all—the one during which the Germans Sprenger and Kramer prepared their famous treatise on witchcraft and witch-finding: "Malleus Maleficarum".[7] Nor was it any phantom that Church and State alike were fighting. On the contrary, the degenerate cult gained strength, struck back, and increased in malignancy, until it seemed to be almost beyond control. In southern Germany it attained such magnitude that the wholesale collapse of civilisation seemed to be threatened; hence—amidst the impotence of all legal agencies—many fearless noblemen organised a wholly extra-legal society for detecting and punishing cult-adherents; a sort of mediaeval Ku Klux Klan called the "Holy Vehm", which seized miscreants, tried them at dead of night in lonely forests, and saw that they never appeared again if judged guilty. This very practical "malleus maleficarum" really worked, hence after 1500 cult witchcraft was never a real menace. The scare, however, continued; and prosecutions and executions by both Church and State were exceedingly numerous until far into the 18th century. In Britain the chief witch fright occurred during the reign of James I—early in the 17th century—and was undoubtedly based on actual cult activities in Scotland. The last witch-trial in England occurred in 1712, though such things lasted on the Continent till the beginning of the 19th century. The witch-cult itself is probably now extinct, but no one can say just when it perished—for of course the rumour and legend-form must have persisted long afterward. It is the opinion of most, that no actual coven-meetings or sabbats occurred after

171

the beginning of the 18th century—if indeed after the middle of the 17th. Interestingly enough, the existence of this cult was not suspected by moderns till late in the 19th century; the previous opinion of students being that all witchcraft scares were pure hallucinations. Arthur Machen made splendid fictional use of the discovery before it became widely known or universally accepted. Not until 1921, however, was the matter systematically presented—honour for this step being due to Prof. Margaret Alice Murray of London University, author of "The Witch-Cult in Western Europe".[8]

And now—getting back to the main topic—where does all this hitch on to the history of witch-belief in colonial New England? Well, we may see at once that all the colonists had minds well prepared by historic experience to believe in the possibility of diabolic manifestations. They knew all about incantations and sabbats, and had had enough glimpses of actual cult-practices to take such things pretty seriously. Naturally—since the cult was always concealed, and never fully admitted by everybody to exist—there were many sceptics about the whole matter; and of course, there were also many well-balanced people who, although admitting witchcraft to be possible, were nevertheless in no danger of imagining cases of it where no true ground for suspicion existed. This latter type probably predominated among the American colonists as a whole. Since they believed in orthodox religion, it was not extraordinary that they should believe in other forms of the supernatural; but they were hard-headed enough not to apply their theoretical speculations to the actual world around them. Not so, however, with the Puritans. The whole nature of their theology taught them to be on the watch for manifestations of the devil; whilst the epidemic of morbid crime and perversion in their midst was to them unmistakable evidence of a Satanic siege. Many believed the swart Indians of the black woods to be diabolic allies of a sort—and of course the customary life of cheerless repression, rustic solitude, wintry cold, and hysterical religious introspection and espionage, all tended to make the population jumpy, and eager to seize on any unusual symptom as an indication of unholy magic. Then, once witchcraft was indicated, there was no choice about a course to follow. Did not Jehovah thunder forth the inexorable command, "Thou shalt not suffer a witch to live"?[9]

To me, this background seems to explain all the New England witch trials (the first was in 1648) up to the time of the Salem scare. The witch-cult was not here, but its echoes and traditions were. Trials were by no means numerous, and executions very few. Then came Salem with its 50 trials and 19 executions, and with the strange parallelism of testimony in many cases, which profoundly impressed some of the most scholarly men in the Province. Cotton Mather—a learned man who was no fool for all his extravagant Puritanism—heard and sifted the evidence, and egged on the prosecutions with all his power and influence, believing some new and definite Satanic attack to have been made upon Massachusetts. What is behind all this? Merely a natural outburst and culmination of the mood which produced the early sporadic trials—or something new and systematic and tangible?

Well, we shall never know. Miss Murray, the anthropologist, believes that the witch-cult actually established a "coven" (its only one in the New World) in the Salem region about 1690, and that it included a large number of neurotic and degenerate whites, together with Indians, negroes, and West-Indian slaves. Of this coven, she maintains, the Rev. George Burroughs was probably the leader or "Black Man"; (detailed legend, testimony, and anecdote certainly prove him by no means saintly!) so that this hanging was perfectly well merited. Of the other victims, some were probably guilty of cult-participation whilst others were innocent and accused only through malice. Thus conjectures the learned author of "The Witch Cult in Western Europe"—though of course without definite proof. Others—Americans who have possibly examined the Salem records more closely than she—think it improbable that any formally organised cult-branch could have been concerned; though all agree that the answers to trial questions shew a vast familiarity with cult-institutions—more than could easily be accounted for by common legend, or by any sort of leading questions. For my part—I doubt if a compact coven existed, but certainly think that people had come to Salem who had a direct personal knowledge of the cult, and who were perhaps initiated members of it. I think that some of the rites and formulae of the cult must have been talked about secretly among certain elements, and perhaps furtively practiced by the few degenerates involved. I would not be surprised if Burroughs were concerned—and also the West-Indian slave woman Tituba, who started the scare in the first place by telling tales to neurotic children. Most of the people hanged were probably innocent, yet I do think there was a concrete, sordid background not present in any other New England witchcraft case.

Puritan witch-belief by no means ended with Salem, although there were no more executions. Rumours and whispers directed against eccentric characters were common all through the 18th and into the 19th century, and are hardly extinct today in decadent Western Massachusetts. I know an old lady in Wilbraham whose grandmother, about a century ago, was said to be able to raise a wind by muttering at the sky.[10] Nothing of all this, however, reached Rhode-Island. With our colonists witchcraft was always a remote thing—at most, a whimsical thing to joke about or scare children with. Whatever real belief existed here, was confined to Indians and negroes. No witchcraft trial ever took place within our boundaries.

On Spiritualism

[The following is an extract from a letter to August Derleth (12 November 1932). Derleth (1909–1971), a prolific writer and editor, became Lovecraft's publisher after the latter's death in 1937, forming the publishing firm of Arkham House for the sole purpose of issuing Lovecraft's work in hardcover. Derleth, raised as a Catholic, was inclined toward spiritualism, and in the following letter Lovecraft attempts to show the extreme unlikelihood of such a belief.]

Regarding persons who claim second-sight and ability to know distant and future events, you are completely wrong in attempting to evade the plain evidence of my reminder that none of these persons have ever availed themselves of their claimed powers. You are in this case guilty of that sophistical over-application of the letter rather than the spirit of logic which really obscures instead of clarifying an issue. Common sense, and a general perception of the relations of things and of the natural probabilities of cause and effect, are infinitely more important than academic quibbles. The plain fact is—as easily perceivable by the unbiassed and un-fad-ridden adult mind—that our entire status is very largely determined by our universal ignorance of the future and of surrounding conditions inaccessible to the senses. Any person endowed with a perception of future events, or of the thoughts of others, (and of course our whole knowledge of the nature and workings of the cosmos indicates such perceptions as absolutely impossible) would have at his disposal unique conditions which could not fail to give him a prodigious advantage in his struggle with environment. Counting out the persons in whom such gifts would be quiescent because of an initiative too feeble to put them to use, it is clear that the bulk of real prophets and seers—if such existed—would lead lives much freer from uncertainty than the lives of the ordinary run of man. They would be complete fools if they did not turn their gifts to the foreseeing of commercial and political movements in such a way as to give them immunity from the blunders of the majority, and to lead them to unassailable security, wealth, and power. Only a person notably deficient in constructive imagination could fail to appreciate the stupendous possibilities opened up to any individual with even a rudimentary prophetic or divinational gift—and only a person notably deficient in knowledge of human nature could fail to realise how any normal individual would utilise those possibilities if they were his to command! The fact that nearly all claimants to supernatural powers and prophetic endowments are seedy, illiterate, and rather disreputable offshoots of a semi-underworld, is in sober fact a perfectly effective answer to all their claims. If they had the powers they boast of, they would be able to make something of themselves—and would be masters instead of furtive slum-dwellers dodging police and post-office inspectors. There is in all history no instance of any person's having foreseen any event, important or unimportant. Whenever any unexpected event affects a portion of mankind, it is easy to make a survey of the antecedent acts of various persons, and estimate how many did exactly what they would have done if they had known of the imminence of the event. Not in any case can it be found that anyone— save by accident, and for other reasons—did just that which a foreknowledge of the event would inevitably have caused them to do. Those who claim most loudly to be able to divine the future are often shewn to be among those whose acts before a sudden event are widely different from what they would do if really gifted with a knowledge of what was coming. All their misleading talk—afterward—of having foreseen the event is belied by the real record when it is discoverable.

Now the point is, of course, that if prophecy really were a possible human attribute, it would almost undoubtedly have left a record of its past operation. No such record exists. And to say that prophecy is *possible* even if it has never yet existed, is frivolous and irrelevant for this reason: that the only cause for assuming the existence of prophecy in the first place is the claim of some that manifestations of it have occurred. Destroy that claim—as the evidence of observation does destroy it—and the very principle of prophecy becomes gratuitous and unrelated to any conception or experience of ours that its advancement as a possibility becomes in turn a freak of childish inanity. The great trouble with occult believers is that they don't think things through in detail—and especially, that they don't appreciate the complete meaninglessness and irrelevance of assumptions unsuggested and unsupported by any trace of reputable evidence. That their attitude is largely due to the emotionally crippling force of hereditary and environmental tradition is certain— forming a strong argument for drastic changes in our methods of juvenile education. It would be a good idea to appeal to superstitious folk with diagrams and pictures illustrating the relative probabilities involved—and of course to call attention to the microscopically small numbers of all the reputable thinkers of the world who believe in the claims of the miracle-mongers. A good diagram to use on those impervious to verbal logic would be the *weighing* of the evidence touching a popularly reported miracle on a depicted pair of scales. In one pan would be the reasons in favour of believing it truly miraculous; in the other, the reasons in favour of believing it an illusion in a materialistic cosmos. Something like this:

PRO-SUPERNATURAL

FACT THAT THIS ESPECIAL THING IS NOT YET EXPLAINED

ANTI-SUPERNATURAL

LIKELIHOOD OF ERRONEOUS REPORTING

FACT THAT MILLIONS OF SIMILAR THINGS *HAVE* BEEN EXPLAINED ON A MATERIALIST BASIS

FACT THAT A SUP. EXPLANATION WOULD CLASH WITH ALL THAT WE KNOW OF NATURE, WHEREAS A NATURAL EXP. WOULD NOT

FACT THAT WELL-KNOWN MYTH PATTERNS SUGGEST MIRACULOUS BELIEFS OF THIS SORT.

Notes

Introduction

1. Letter to Elizabeth Toldridge, 24 April 1930 (*SL* 3.146).

2. Letter to Rheinhart Kleiner, 7 March 1920 (*SL* 1.110–11).

3. Letter to J. Vernon Shea, 4 February 1934 (*SL* 4.358–59).

4. Letter to August Derleth, 4 March 1932 (*SL* 4.26).

5. See, for example, Robert M. Price, "H. P. Lovecraft: Prophet of Humanism," *Humanist* 61, No. 4 (July–August 2001): 26–29. See also Price's chapter on Lovecraft in *Icons of Unbelief,* ed. S. T. Joshi (Westport, CT: Greenwood Press, 2008), pp. 223–39.

6. Letter to Rheinhart Kleiner, 13 May 1921 (*SL* 1.132).

7. Letter to James F. Morton, 26 May 1923 (*SL* 1.231).

8. Letter to James F. Morton, 30 October 1929 (*SL* 3.53).

9. Ibid. (*SL* 3.47–48).

10. Letter to Natalie H. Wooley, 27 November 1933 (*SL* 4.324).

11. "The Call of Cthulhu" (1926; *F* 367).

12. *At the Mouintains of Madness* (1931; *F* 769).

13. See David E. Schultz, "From Microcosm to Macrocosm: The Growth of Lovecraft's Cosmic Vision," in *An Epicure in the Terrible: A Centennial Anthology of Essays in Honor of H. P. Lovecraft,* ed. David E. Schultz and S. T. Joshi (Rutherford, NJ: Fairleigh Dickinson University Press, 1991), p. 212.

A Confession of Unfaith

1. In his stories Lovecraft would make Alhazred the author of the *Necronomicon,* a fictitious book of spells and lore about the "gods" that rule the universe.

2. Actually, this episode appears to have occurred when HPL was twelve. See *SL* 1.110–11.

3. *The Wonder-Book* (1852) and *Tanglewood Tales* (1853) by Nathaniel Hawthorne (1804–1864) are retellings of Greek myths for children.

4. Thomas Bulfinch (1796–1867), *The Age of Fable; or, Beauties of Mythology* (1855), a popular account of Greek, Roman, and Egyptian myths for children.

5. Elsewhere Lovecraft elaborates upon the point: "At seven I sported the adopted name of L. VALERIUS MESSALA & tortured imaginary Christians in amphitheatres" (*SL* 3.313). An earlier letter, however, dates this pseudonym to Lovecraft's fourteenth year (HPL to Frank Belknap Long, 26 January 1921 [ms.]).

6. Both works survive, after a fashion. *The Poem of Ulysses; or, The Odyssey* (1897) exists in a "second edition" dated 8 November 1897 (*AT* 3–5). As for the chemistry treatise, four volumes survive at JHL: *Chemistry; Chemistry, Magic, & Electricity; Chemistry III;* and *Chemistry IV.* The titles of the other two volumes are unknown, but HPL notes in a catalogue of his "books" at the end of *Poemata Minora, Volume II* (1902) that the series was in six volumes.

7. *Poemata Minora* evidently extended to two volumes, only the latter of which survives (volume 1 dates to 1901, volume 2 to 1902). Lovecraft published several of them, under pseudonyms and with slightly altered titles, in the April 1919 issue of the *Tryout:* "To Pan" appeared as "Pan" (as by "Michael Ormonde O'Reilly"); "To the Old Pagan Religion" appeared as "The Last Pagan Speaks" (as by "Ames Dorrance Rowley"); "Ode to Selene or Diana" appeared as "To Selene" (as by "Edward Softly"). For the original text of volume 2, see *AT* 11–13.

8. Ernst Haeckel (1834–1919), German biologist and a leading advocate of Darwinian evolution. See his influential treatise, *Die Welträthsel* (1899; translated as *The Riddle of the Universe,* 1900).

9. HPL refers to Samuel Butler (1835–1902), author of the utopian fantasy *Erewhon* (1872) and the novel *The Way of All Flesh* (1903), a strong criticism of Victorian religious and moral attitudes.

The Insignificance of Man

1. Cf. the story "Celephaïs" (1920), where it is stated that the narrator, through drugs, entered "a part of space where form does not exist, but where glowing gases study the secrets of existence" (*F* 113).

2. Apparently Paul J. Campbell, amateur journalist and editor of the *Liberal*.

3. See Homer, *Iliad* 5.114–65.

4. Alexander Pope (1688–1744), *An Essay on Man* (1733–34), Epistle II, ll. 3–18.

What I Have against Religion

1. The following dream served as the basis of the story "Polaris" (1918; *F* 33–36).

2. By "Co" Lovecraft refers to Ira A. Cole, part of the round-robin correspondence group, the *Kleicomolo* (Rheinhart Kleiner, Cole, Maurice W. Moe, and Lovecraft), in which each syllable was taken from the first syllable of the correspondents' last names. Cole was attracted to Pentacostalism and claimed to have visions.

3. "Mr. Dooley" is a character (a Chicago Irishman who speaks in heavy Irish dialect) in the humorous pieces of Finley Peter Dunne (1867–1936), which first appeared in the *Chicago Post* in the last decade of the nineteenth century.

4. The *Truth Seeker* (1873ff.) is the world's oldest freethought journal, founded by D. M. Bennett in Paris, Illinois. When Lovecraft wrote his letter, it was edited by George E. Macdonald.

5. The *Outlook* (1870–1935), originally titled the *Christian Union,* was a long-running Christian periodical founded by Henry Ward Beecher and later edited by Lyman Abbott.

6. Thomas Hardy, "God's Funeral" (1912); rpt. in Gordon Stein, ed., *A Second Anthology of Atheism and Rationalism* (Buffalo: Prometheus Books, 1987), pp. 203–5.

The Nature of God

1. Lovecraft alludes to *The Brook Kerith* (1916) by Anglo-Irish novelist George Moore (1852–1933).

2. *An Essay on Man,* Epistle II, ll. 219–20 ("Yet" for "But" in Pope).

3. Sir Oliver Lodge (1851–1940), *Raymond, or Life and Death: With Examples of the Evidence for Survival of Memory and Affection after Death* (New York: George H. Doran, 1916), a book claiming that Lodge had established contact with his son Raymond's spirit after his death in World War I. Lodge had previously been a respected physicist, but destroyed much of his reputation with this book and others expressing credulous belief in spiritualism.

4. Sir William Crookes (1832–1919), British chemist and physicist. His most important work was in the investigation of the conduction of electricity in gases. He developed the Crookes tube (mentioned in Lovecraft's story "The Shunned House" [1924]) and in it produced cathode rays for the first time. He also wrote *Researches into the Phenomena of Modern Spiritualism* (Rochester, NY: Austin Publishing Co., [1904]).

5. Eusapia Palladino was a peasant woman from Naples who claimed miraculous powers as a medium. Although most investigators who examined her work dismissed her as a charlatan, Lodge and others maintained a belief in the reality of the spiritual manifestations she produced.

6. Lovecraft refers to the celebrated saying by the Roman playwright Terence, *Homo sum: humani nil a me alienum puto* (I am a man: nothing human is alien to me) (*Heauton Timoroumenos* 77).

7. Ferdinand Canning Scott Schiller (1864–1937), German-born British pragmatist philosopher and author of *Studies in Humanism* (1907). See Edwin E. Slosson, "A British Pragmatist: The Philosophy and Personality of F. C. S. Schiller," *Independent* 89 (12 February 1917): 265–68.

Religious Indoctrination

1. Unidentified. Apparently a deceased amateur journalist.

2. Henry S. Whitehead (1882–1932), an Anglican clergyman and author of many tales of horror and the supernatural, many of them set in the Caribbean.

Idealism and Materialism—A Reflection

1. Lovecraft may have been thinking of James F. Morton, who was at this time a militant atheist (he would later convert to Bahaism). In the satirical poem "The Isaacsonio-Mortoniad" (1915) HPL describes Morton as "The Dean of Darkness, wrecker of the church, / Crowing with scorn from his exalted perch!" (ll. 95–96; *AT* 210).

2. For Haeckel, see n. 8 to "A Confession of Unfaith." Haeckel describes God as a "gaseous vertebrate" in ch. 15 of *The Riddle of the Universe* to denote the paradoxical qualities attributed to God in many orthodox religions.

3. Phil. 4:7.

4. John Dryden, *Religio Laici; or, A Layman's Faith* (1682), ll. 8–11.

5. The anecdote is told again in "A Confession of Unfaith" (p. *3*) ~~000)~~.

6. For Lodge, see n. 3 to "The Nature of God."

Remarks on Materialism

1. British chemist and physicist John Dalton (1766–1844) pioneered the study of atomic compounds by devising the first table of atomic weights. Relying on the atomic theory of Leucippus and Democritus, Dalton assumed that atoms were indivisible. The word atom comes from the Greek *a-* (without) and *tomos* (a cut), i.e., indivisible.

2. "Eternal recurrence," Nietzsche's belief that the infinity and eternity of the universe imply the eternal recurrence of all events. The

idea was used largely as a refutation of teleology and the belief in an omnipotent deity.

3. It is possible (though by no means certain) that Lovecraft refers to Twain's utterance (in *What Is Man?* [1906]) that "In *all* cases without exception we are absolutely indifferent to another's pain until his sufferings make us uncomfortable." Lovecraft read *What Is Man?* no later than June 1920 (see *SL* 1.119).

4. G. K. Chesterton (1874–1936), British novelist, essayist, and Christian apologist. The article under discussion may be "The Fashion in Psychoanalysis" (*Illustrated London News,* 29 May 1920), which attacks both Darwin and Freud. It has now been reprinted in *The Collected Works of G. K. Chesterton,* Vol. 29 (San Francisco: Ignatius Press, 1989), pp. 27–30.

5. Chesterton was a vigorous opponent of the Darwin theory of evolution. See "Darwin and Morality" in *Orthodoxy* (1908) and *The Everlasting Man* (1925).

6. "The will to power," Nietzsche's alteration of Schopenhauer's "will to live."

7. Anonymous, "Whither?" *Atlantic Monthly* 95, no. 3 (March 1915): 300–315.

8. Samuel Loveman, "To Satan," *Conservative* no. 13 (July 1923): 1–2. Rpt. in *Out of the Immortal Night: Selected Works by Samuel Loveman,* ed. S. T. Joshi and David E. Schultz (New York: Hippocampus Press, 2004), pp. 108–9. The poem is dedicated to Lovecraft.

9. "Slave morality," a term devised by Nietzsche as a counterweight to the *Herrenmoral* ("master morality") of his supermen.

10. A possible allusion to James F. Morton. See n. 1 to "Idealism and Materialism—A Reflection."

11. Lovecraft refers to British victories over the French in 1415, 1346, 1356, and 1805. The first three were during the Hundred Years' War; the last was against Napoleon.

12. "I believe because it is impossible," a common misquotation of Tertullian's comment *Certum est quia impossibile est* ("It is certain because it is impossible"), in *De Carne Christi* 5.

13. See Ernst Haeckel, *The Riddle of the Universe,* ch. 8.

14. Haeckel, *The Evolution of Man: A Popular Exposition of the Principal Points of Human Ontogeny and Phylogeny* (Eng. tr. 1879; 5th rev. ed. 1905).

15. "Fear of the truth."

The Materialist Today

1. By Modernism Lovecraft refers to a tendency among some contemporary religious thinkers to reject such notions as the total inerrancy of the Bible and to urge an updating or modernising of some of the metaphysical and ethical teachings of Christianity.

2. Shakespeare, *Hamlet* 5.1.235–36.

Religion and Relativity

1. Lovecraft refers to the children's writer Everett McNeil (1862–1929), who lived in the Hell's Kitchen district of Manhattan. Frank Belknap Long lived on the Upper West Side.

2. Harlow Shapley (1885–1972), American astronomer and physicist; Arthur S. Eddington (1882–1944), British astrophysicist; James H. Jeans (1887–1946), British astrophysicist and mathematician.

3. Robert A. Millikan (1868–1953), American physicist who won the Nobel Prize for physics in 1923. In the 1920s he coined the term "cosmic rays" for what he believed to be high-energy photons created by God to counteract entropy; but later research established that these rays are merely charged particles deflected by the earth's magnetic field. Millikan wrote several books and articles attempting to reconcile religion and science, such as *Evolution in Science and Religion* (1927).

4. William H. P. Faunce (1859–1930), president of Brown University (1899–1930). He became known for his social and moral conservatism.

5. Lovecraft refers to British biologist and philosopher Thomas Henry Huxley (1825–1895), a strong proponent of Darwinian evolution and materialistic thought. In other portions of this letter (not included here), Lovecraft had discussed the work of Huxley's grandson, the novelist and essayist Aldous Huxley (1894–1963). See the later reference to "Aldine" (p. 000). 94

6. Sir Frederick William Herschel (1738–1822), German-born British astronomer who discovered the planet Uranus, among other achievements.

Religion and Indeterminacy

1. The Jeans article is unidentified. Possibly it is an article about Jeans. About the time this letter was written, Jeans had just published his treatise *The Mysterious Universe* (Cambridge: Cambridge University Press, 1930), in which he asserted that "the Great Architect of the Universe now begins to appear as a pure mathematician."

2. Harry Emerson Fosdick (1878–1969), American clergyman who, as a Baptist minister, adopted the Modernist position within the church (see n. 1 to "The Materialist Today"). Henry Fairfield Osborn (1857–1935), American geologist who was a professor at Columbia University and president of the American Museum of Natural History (1903–33). Like Robert A. Millikan, he attempted to reconcile religion and science.

3. Lovecraft refers to imaginary entities created by writers of fantastic fiction: Robert W. Chambers (1865–1933), American author of *The King in Yellow* (1895); Lord Dunsany (1878–1957), Irish author of *The Gods of Pegāna* (1905); Frank Belknap Long (1901–1994), author of "The Hounds of Tindalos" (1929); Clark Ashton Smith (1893–1961), author of several tales about the toad-god Tsathoggua; and Lovecraft himself, author of "The Call of Cthulhu" (1926).

4. The Yezidis or Yazidis are a Kurdish-speaking nation who worship, among other entities, an angel named Melek Tawus. They were mistakenly assumed to be devil-worshippers because an alternate name for Melek Tawus, Shaytan, is the name for Satan in the Koran.

5. "Grandpa Theobald" was Lovecraft's playful name for himself, derived in part from Lewis Theobald (1688–1744), the British poet and editor who was the object of Alexander Pope's satire *The Dunciad* (1728).

6. John Herman Randall, Jr. (1899–1980), American philosopher and educator. He was an acquaintance of Long.

7. Carcosa was invented by Ambrose Bierce (1842–1914?) in the story "An Inhabitant of Carcosa" (1886). Yian was invented by Robert W. Chambers in "The Maker of Moons" (1896). For Tindalos, see n. 3 above. Chaugnar Faugn was a god (roughly in the shape of an elephant) invented by Frank Belknap Long in the short novel *The Horror from the Hills* (1931). The Aklo and Voorish mysteries were invented by Welsh writer Arthur Machen (1863–1947) in the story "The White People" (1904).

8. For Sir Oliver Lodge, see n. 3 to "The Nature of God." British novelist Sir Arthur Conan Doyle (1859–1930), devastated by the death of his son in World War I, subscribed to a number of mystical and occultist theories in the 1920s, including spirit photography. Léon Chevreuil (1852–1939) was a French painter and spiritualist and author of the book *On ne meurt pas* (1916; There Is No Death). Camille Flammarion (1842–1925) was a French astronomer and spiritualist. Lovecraft owned his book *Haunted Houses* (1924).

9. For Tsathoggua, see n. 3 above. Yog-Sothoth was a "god" invented by Lovecraft in several tales, most notably "The Dunwich Horror" (1928). The Doels were cited by Long in "The Hounds of Tindalos."

10. The little-known British philosopher Hugh Elliot wrote *Modern Science and Materialism* (1919), a strong influence on Lovecraft.

Religion, Art, and Emotion

1. Al Smith (1873–1944), governor of New York and Democratic candidate for president in 1928.

2. Lovecraft had a little-understood malady or condition whereby he could not endure temperatures under 20° F.

Religion and Ethics

1. Lovecraft refers to French materialist philosopher Julien Offray de La Mettrie (1709–1751), author of *L'Homme machine* (1750; Man a Machine).

2. H. L. Mencken (1880–1956), *Treatise on the Gods* (1930), an exhaustive account of the growth of religious belief and its present (Christian) state.

3. James H. Leuba, "Religious Beliefs of American Scientists," *Harper's Monthly Magazine* 169, no. 3 (August 1934): 291–300.

4. Joseph McCabe (1867–1955), prolific British atheist philosopher and historian.

Religion and Social Progress

1. Alexander Pope, *Eloisa to Abelard* (1717), l. 192.

2. Ovid's *Ars Amatoria* (The Art of Love) is a sexually explicit manual of seduction. The story of Baucis and Philemon in Ovid's *Metamorphoses* (8.611–724) is a sentimental tale of an old married couple in Phrygia who are the only ones to offer hospitality to Jupiter and Mercury (who arrive there disguised as peasants); as a reward, the gods transform them into an intertwining pair of trees, an oak and a linden.

3. Robert Briffault (1876–1948), French novelist and anthropologist and author of *The Mothers* (1927), a study of matriarchy; V. F. Calverton (1900–1940), American anthropologist and author of *The Bankruptcy of Marriage* (1928).

4. Shortly after Lovecraft and his aunt Annie E. P. Gamwell (1866–1941) moved into 66 College Street in Providence in May 1933, Annie fell down the stairs and broke her ankle.

5. Milton, *Paradise Lost* 1.501–2.

Protestants and Catholics

1. Fulton J. Sheen (1895–1979) was an American theologian and Roman Catholic archbishop. He became popular with a radio show, "The Catholic Hour," in the 1930s, and in 1951 he began a weekly television program, "Life Is Worth Living." Harvey Wickham (d. 1931) was an American literary critic and author of *The Impuritans* (1929), a condemnation of the increasingly explicit discussions of sex in modern literature.

2. Author Lafcadio Hearn (1850–1904) was born in an island off the coast of Greece and grew up in Ireland before coming to the United States in 1869. In 1890 he emigrated to Japan and remained there for the rest of his life.

3. Harry Elmer Barnes (1889–1968), American historian and author of *The Twilight of Christianity* (1929); Charles Francis Potter (1885–1962), American Unitarian minister and a vigorous advocate of humanism.

4. "Chesterbelloc" was the derisive name devised by George Bernard Shaw for the Anglo-Catholic polemicists G. K. Chesterton and Hilaire Belloc (1870–1953).

5. Wilfred B. Talman (1904–1986), a friend of Lovecraft and Long. He was of Dutch ancestry.

6. John Haynes Holmes (1879–1964), American Unitarian minister who helped to establish the NAACP and the ACLU.

7. John Singleton Copley (1738–1815), Gilbert Stuart (1755–1828), and Edward Greene Malbone (1777–1807), painters; Benjamin Thompson, Count Rumford (1753–1814), designer of the Rumford fireplace.

8. Thomas Casey (1636?–1719?), an Irish ancestor of Lovecraft's.

The Psychology of Puritanism

1. "The Picture in the House" (1920), set in the imaginary New England backwoods, begins with a disquisition on the psychological versions of Puritanism (*F* 124–30).

2. Richard Bellingham (1851–1672), deputy governor of the Massachusetts Bay Colony; William Bradford (1590–1657), a framer of the Mayflower Compact and governor of the Plymouth Colony for 30 years.

3. Presumably quoted from Bradford's *History of Plymouth Plantation* (1856).

4. Rev. William Blaxton (also Blackstone) (1595–1675) was the first European to settle in what is now Boston and lived in what is now Rhode Island. Ordained in the Church of England, he conducted the first Anglican services of record in Rhode Island, and his collection of books was probably the largest private library in the British colonies at the time.

5. Actually, he said he "'left England to escape the arbitrary conduct of the lord bishops; and Massachusetts, to be free of the rigid discipline of the lord brethren.'" In Alden Bradford, *History of Massachusetts, for Two Hundred Years: From the Year 1620 to 1820* (Boston: Hilliard, Gray & Co., 1835.), p. 20.

6. Juvenal (D. Junius Juvenalis, 60?–140? C.E.), author of fourteen *Saturae* (satires), the sixth (and longest) of which is a vicious satire on women.

7. Jacobus Sprenger and Henricus Institor [Heinrich Kramer], *Malleus Maleficarum* [Hammer of Witches], published in Germany c. 1486 as a guide to inquisitors in detecting, examining, and punishing witches.

8. HPL alludes to Machen's tales of the "little people," which Lovecraft (but not Machen) believed to have anticipated the ideas in Margaret A. Murray's *Witch-Cult in Western Europe* (1921).

9. Exod. 22:18.

10. I.e., the grandmother of Edith Miniter (1869–1934). HPL had visited Wilbraham in 1928, incorporating various scraps of legends encountered there in "The Dunwich Horror."

CPSIA information can be obtained at www.ICGtesting.com
Printed in the USA
239489LV00002B/145/P